Komi Can't Communicate

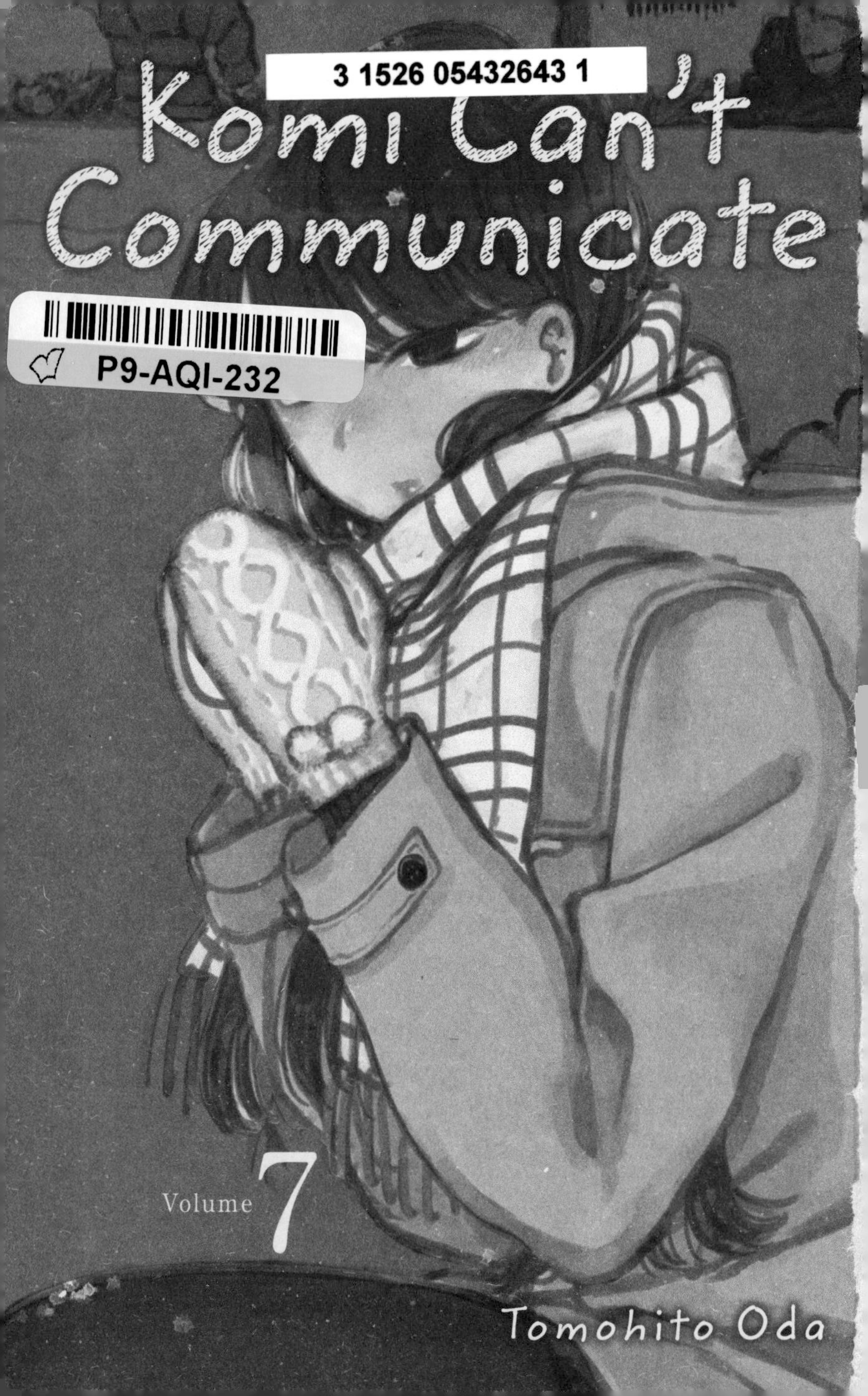

Volume 7

Tomohito Oda

C o n t e n t s

Komi Can't Communicate

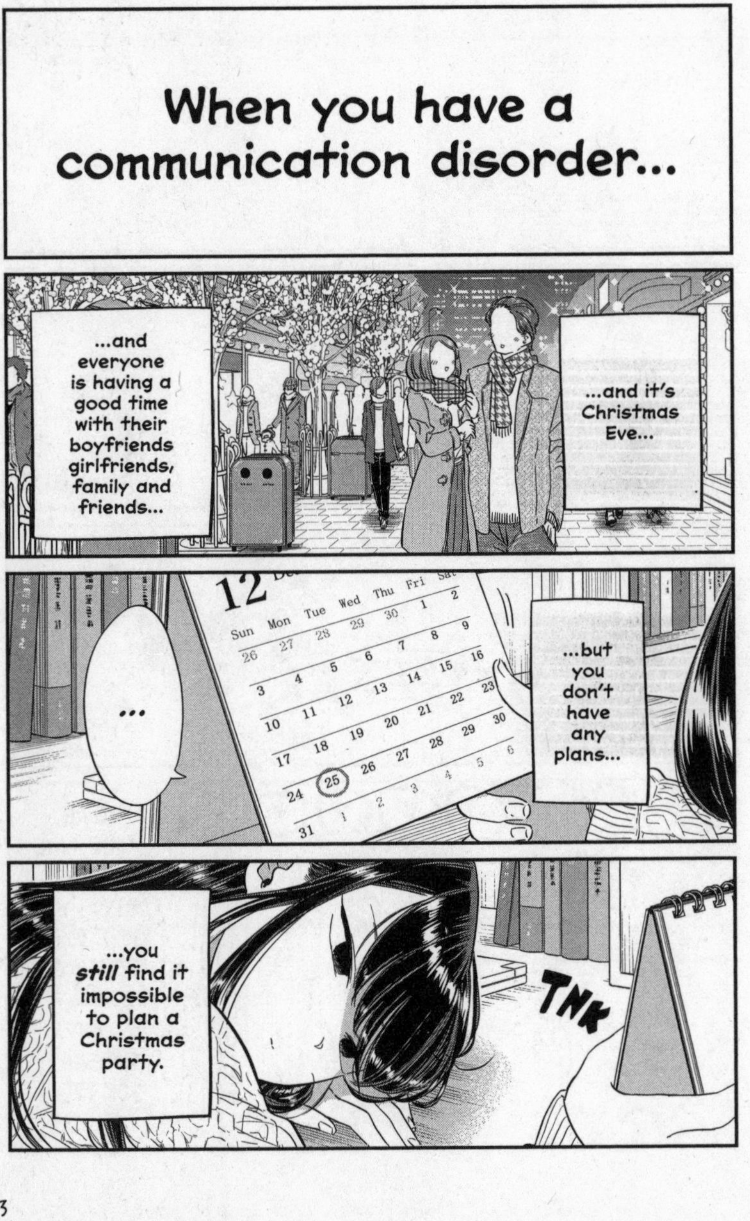
When you have a communication disorder...
...and it's Christmas Eve...
...and everyone is having a good time with their boyfriends girlfriends, family and friends...
...but you don't have any plans...
...
...you *still* find it impossible to plan a Christmas party.
TNK

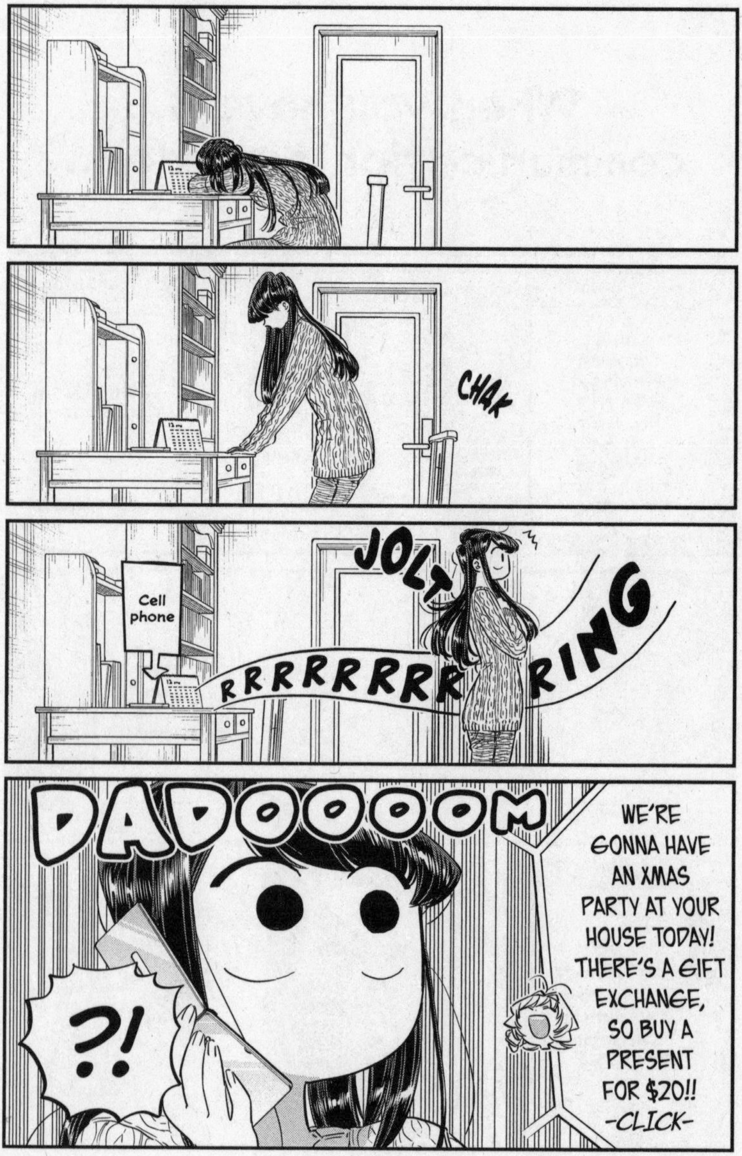
CHAK
JOLT
RRRRRRRRRRING
Cell phone
DADOOOOM
WE'RE GONNA HAVE AN XMAS PARTY AT YOUR HOUSE TODAY! THERE'S A GIFT EXCHANGE, SO BUY A PRESENT FOR $20!!
-CLICK-
?!

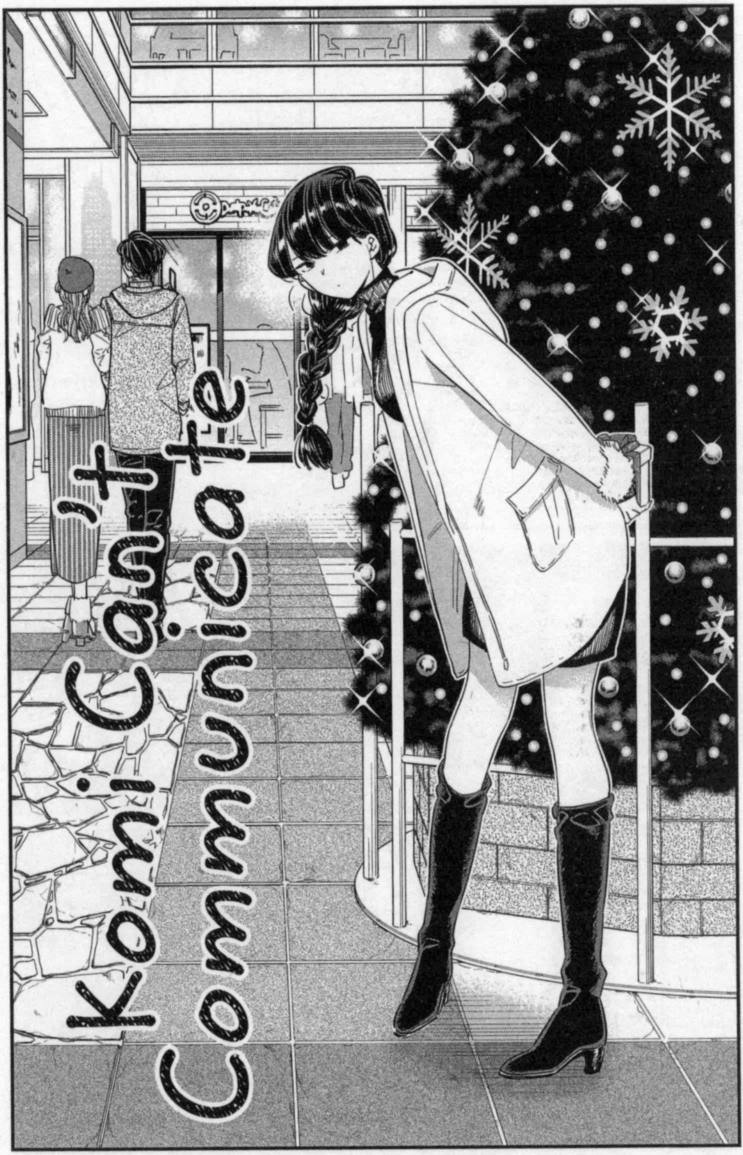
Komi Can't Communicate

Communication 86: Choosing a Present

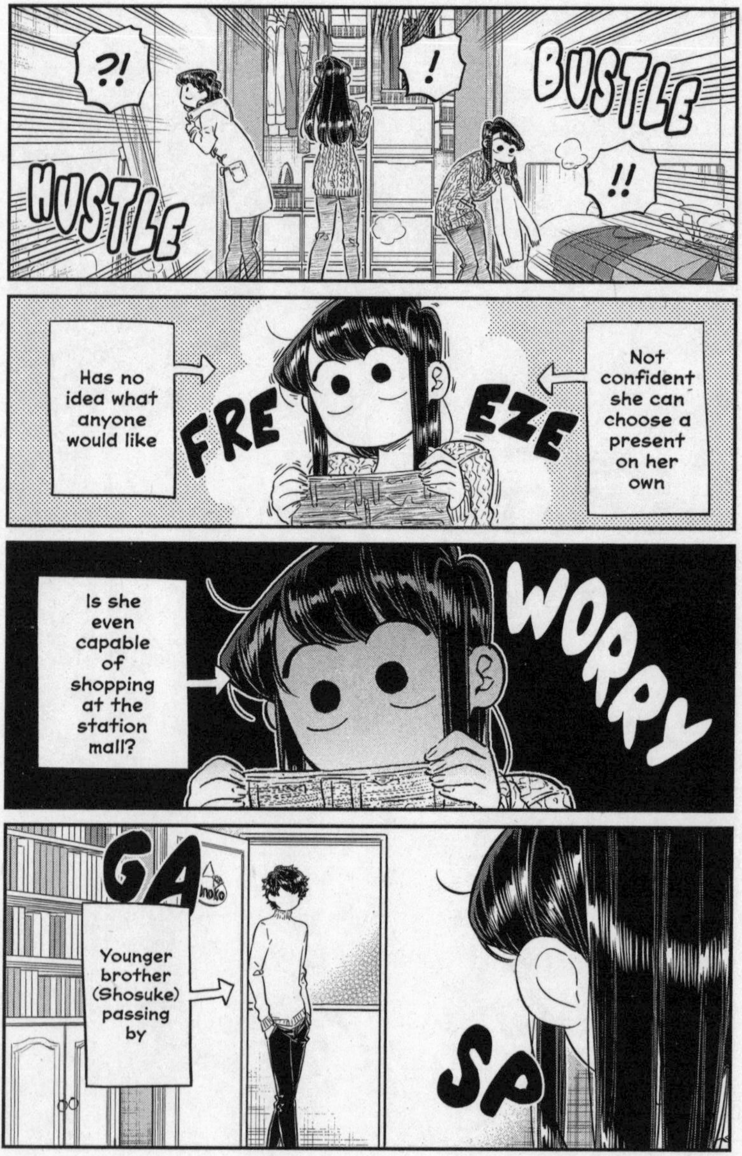
BUSTLE
!!
!
?!
HUSTLE
Not confident she can choose a present on her own
FRE
EZE
Has no idea what anyone would like
WORRY
Is she even capable of shopping at the station mall?
SP
GA
Younger brother (Shosuke) passing by

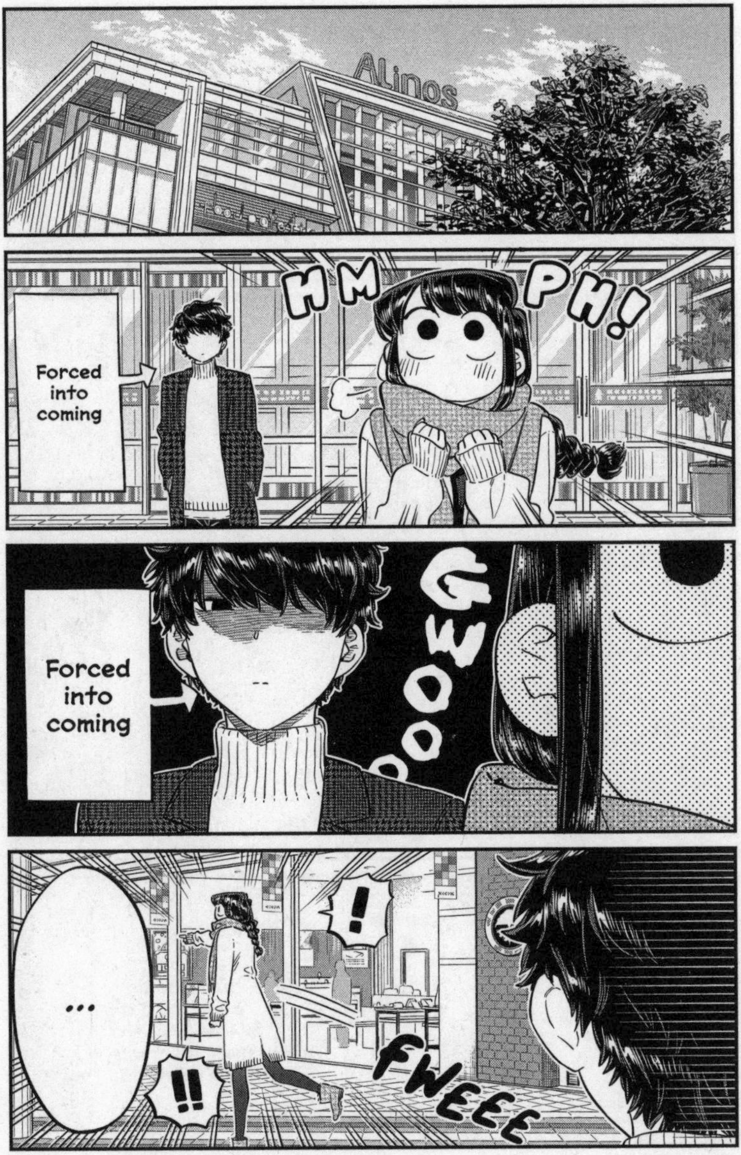
ALinos
HMPH!
Forced into coming
GWOOOO
Forced into coming
!
FWEEE
...
!!

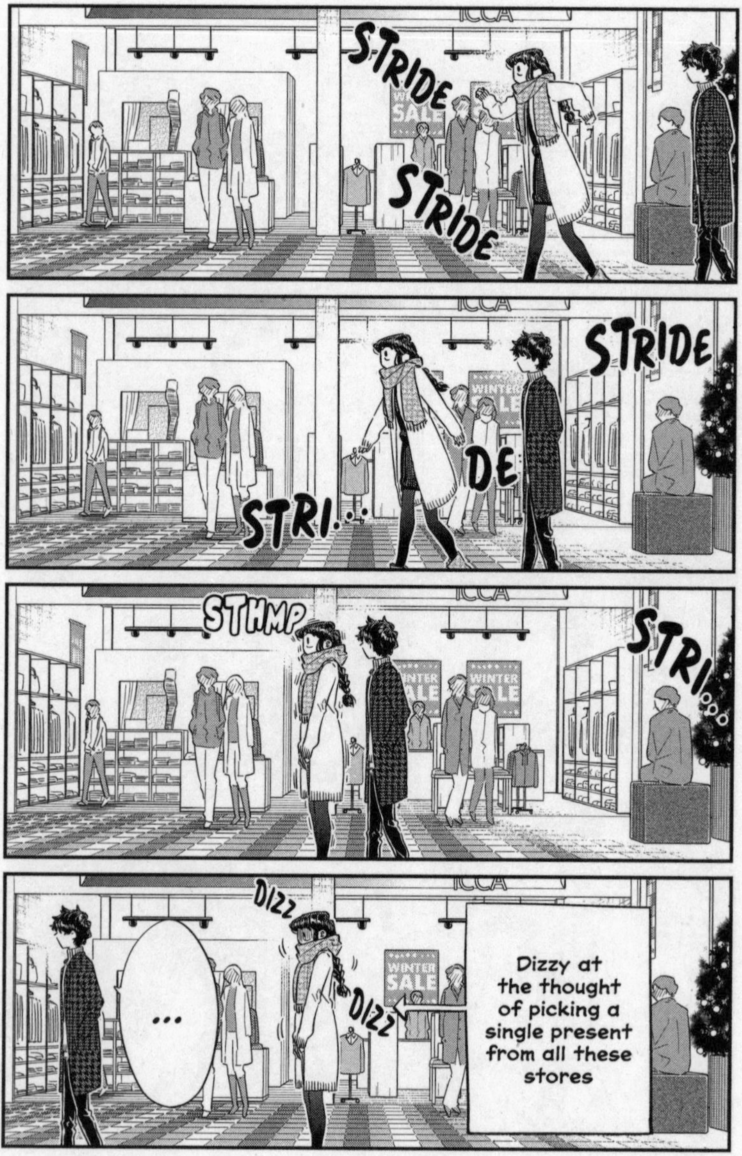
STRIDE
STRIDE
STRIDE
DE
STRI...
STRI...
STHMP
WINTER SALE
Dizzy at the thought of picking a single present from all these stores
DIZZ
DIZZ
...

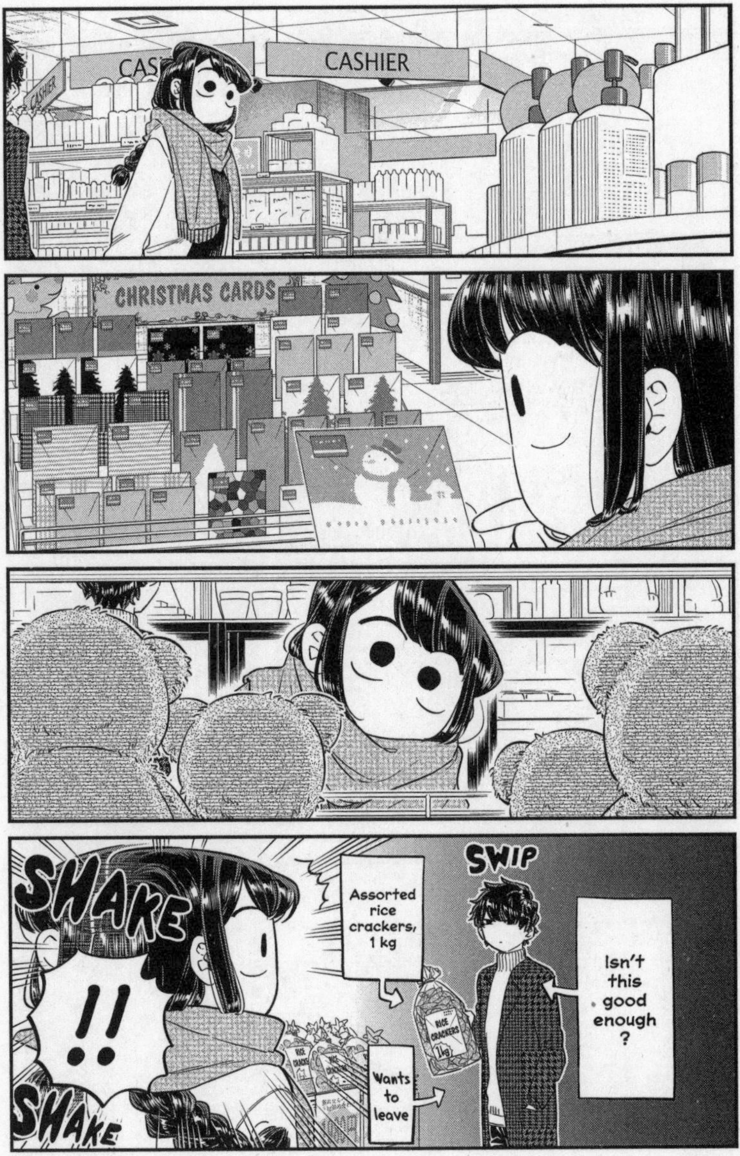
CASHIER
CHRISTMAS CARDS
Isn't this good enough?
SWIP
Assorted rice crackers, 1 kg
RICE CRACKERS 1kg
SHAKE
Wants to leave
!!
SHAKE

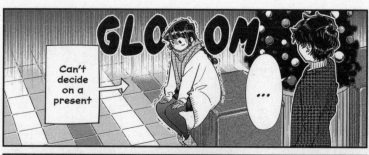

...
GLOOM
Can't decide on a present
What would be pleasing?
Something nonperishable would be a burden.
SPIN SPIN SPIN
But would something perishable be a decent present?
Something to wear depends on personal taste.
SPIN SPIN
STRIDE STRIDE STRIDE
?!
Oh dear... A lover's quarrel?
Three! I'll narrow it to three!
!!
SHUV
SHUV
!!
Even nice-looking couples fight at Christmas...

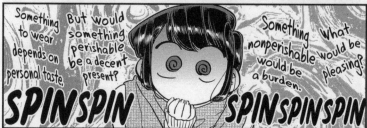

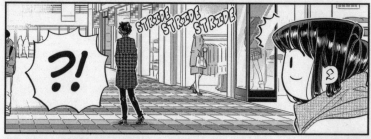

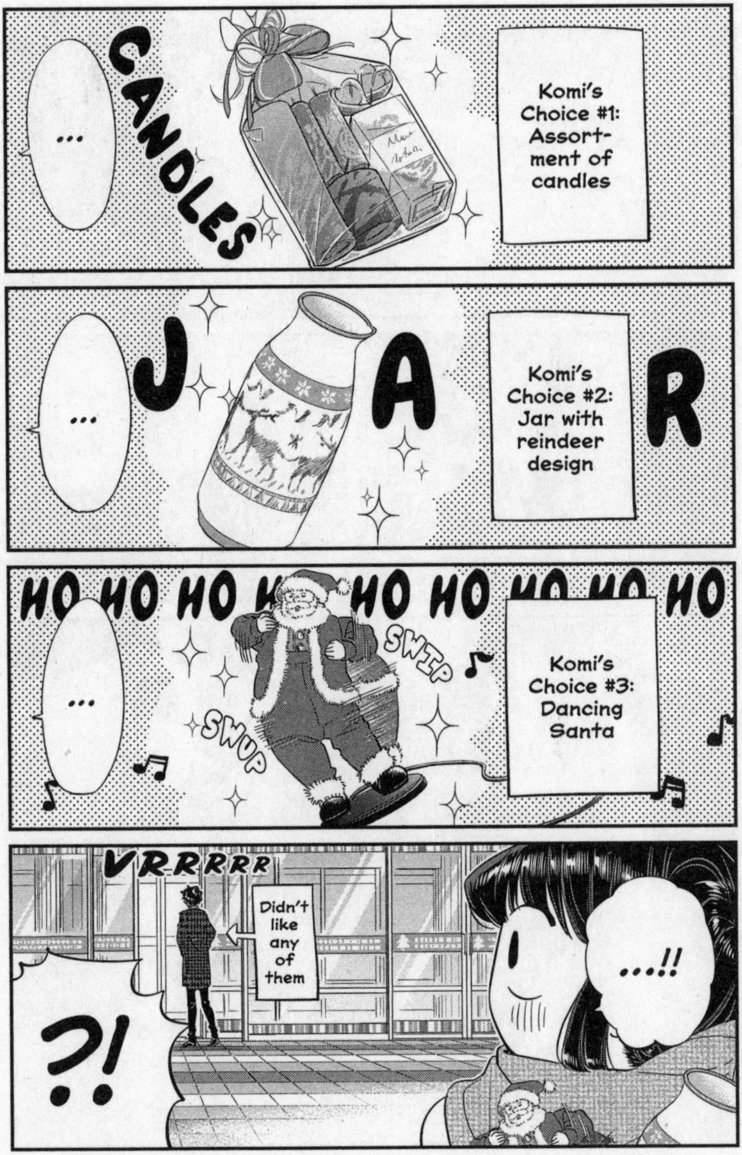
Komi's Choice #1: Assortment of candles
CANDLES
...
Komi's Choice #2: Jar with reindeer design
JAR
...
HO HO HO HO HO HO HO HO HO
Komi's Choice #3: Dancing Santa
SWIP
SWUP
...
...!!
Didn't like any of them
VRRRRR
?!

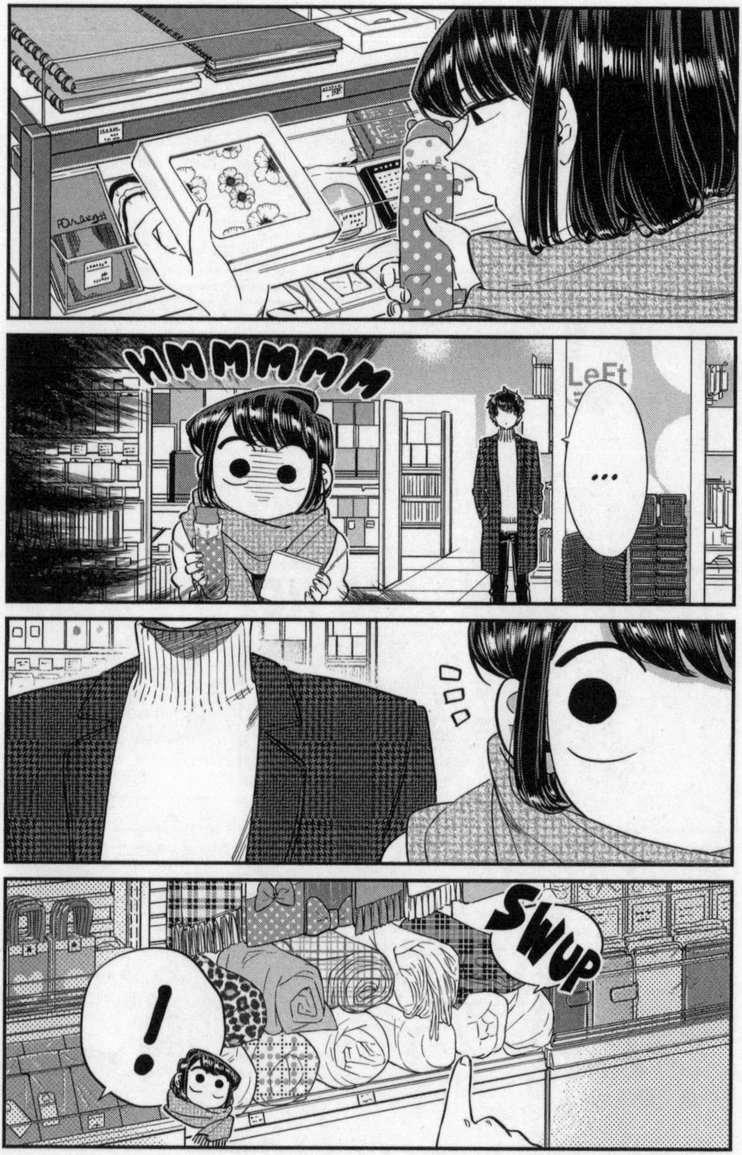
...
HMMMMMM
LeFt
SWUP
!

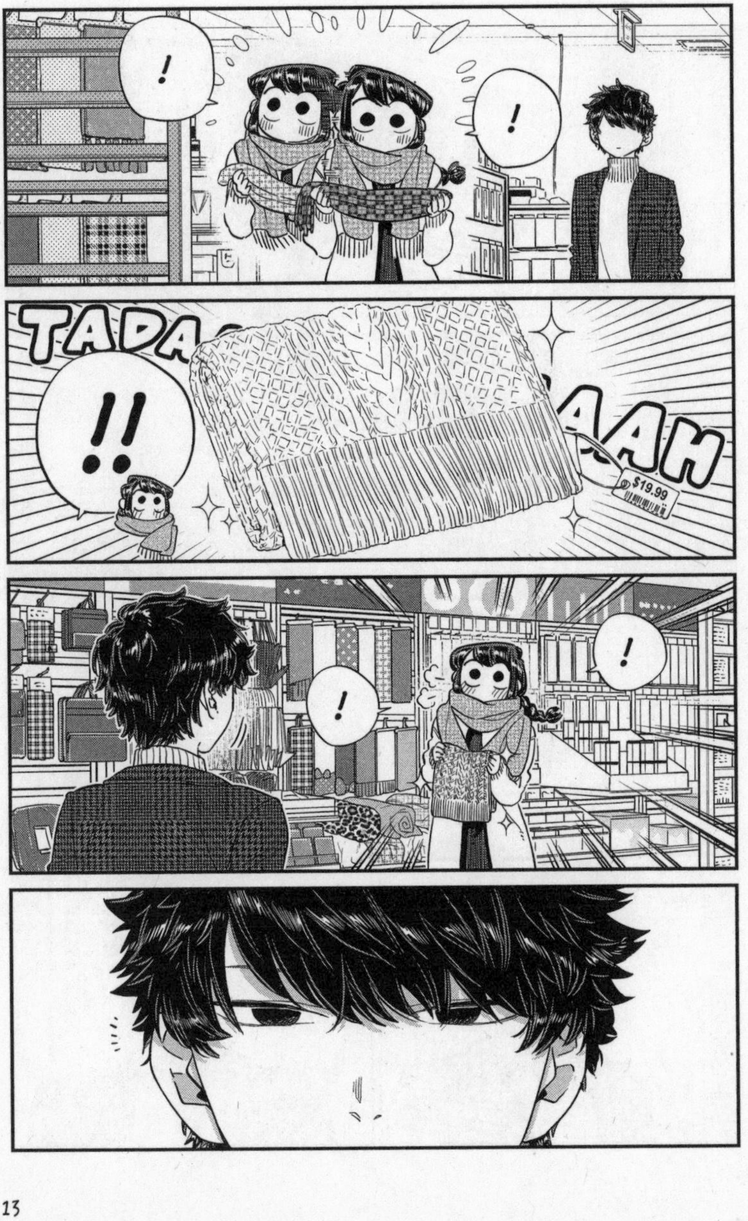
!
!
TADA
AAH
$19.99
!!
!
!

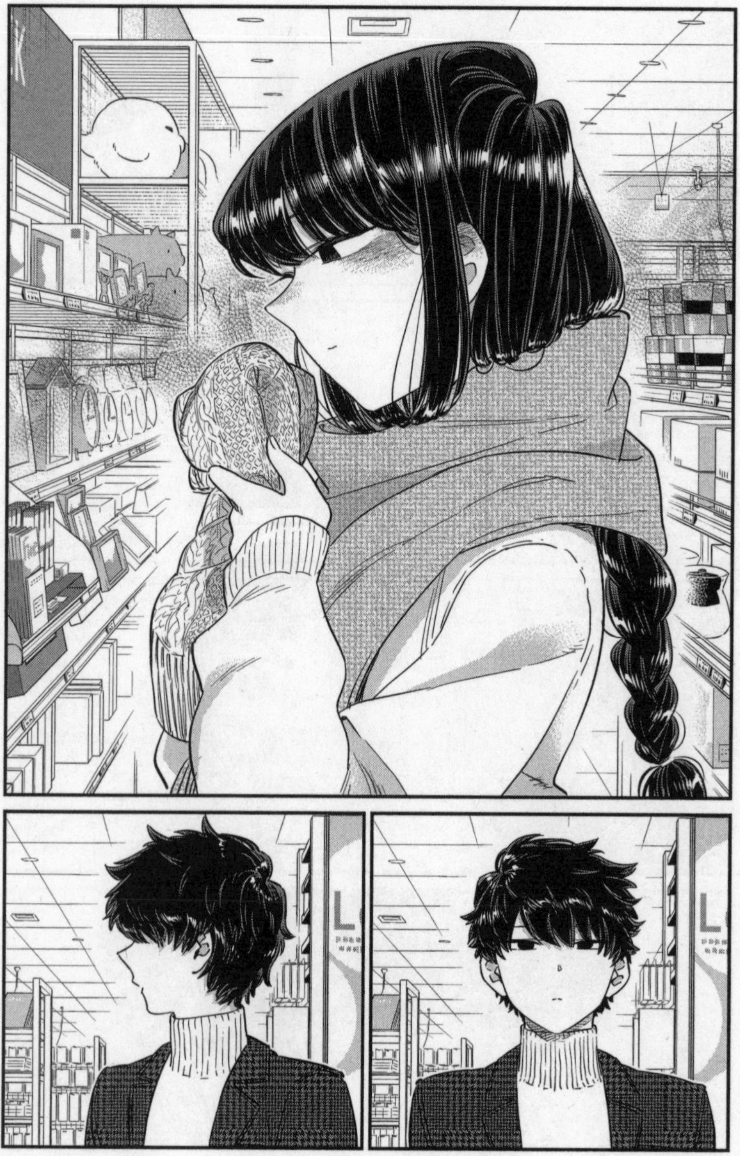

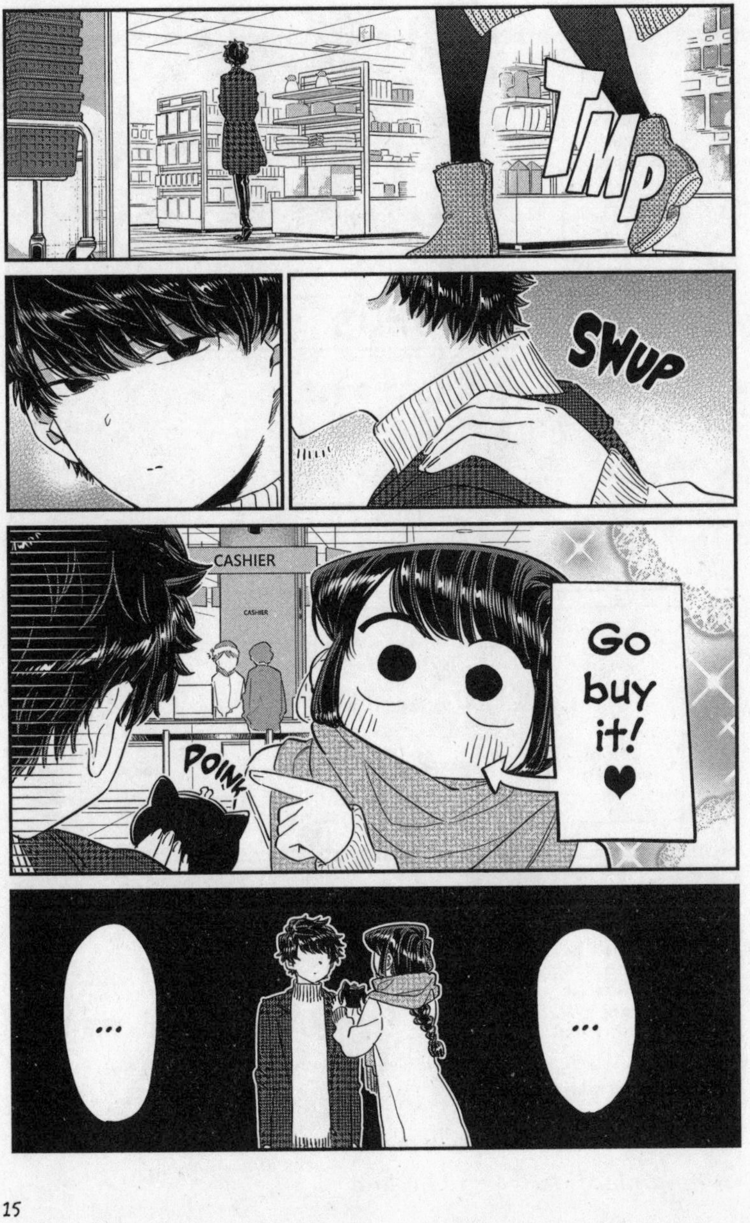
TMP
SWUP
Go buy it! ♥
CASHIER
CASHIER
POINK
...
...

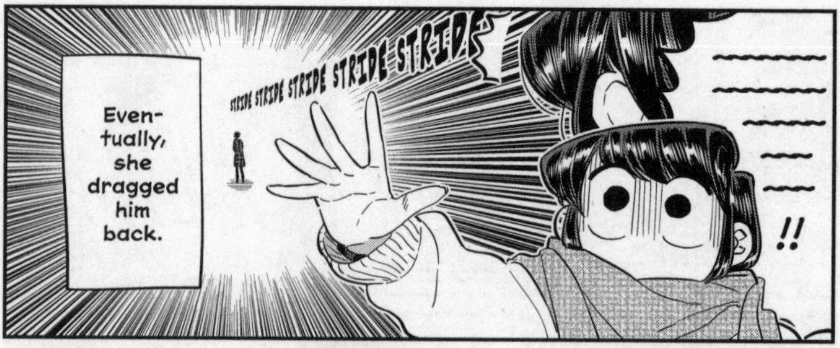
!!
STRIDE STRIDE STRIDE STRIDE STRIDE
Eventually, she dragged him back.

BONUS

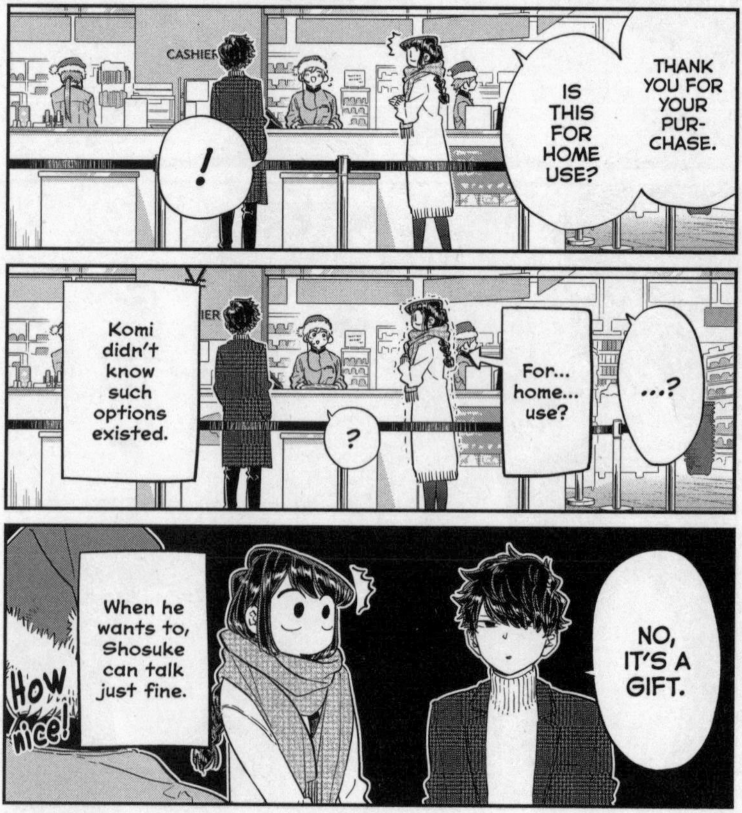
THANK YOU FOR YOUR PURCHASE.
IS THIS FOR HOME USE?
!
CASHIER
...?
For... home... use?
?
Komi didn't know such options existed.
NO, IT'S A GIFT.
When he wants to, Shosuke can talk just fine.
How nice!

Communication 86 — The End

Komi Can't Communicate

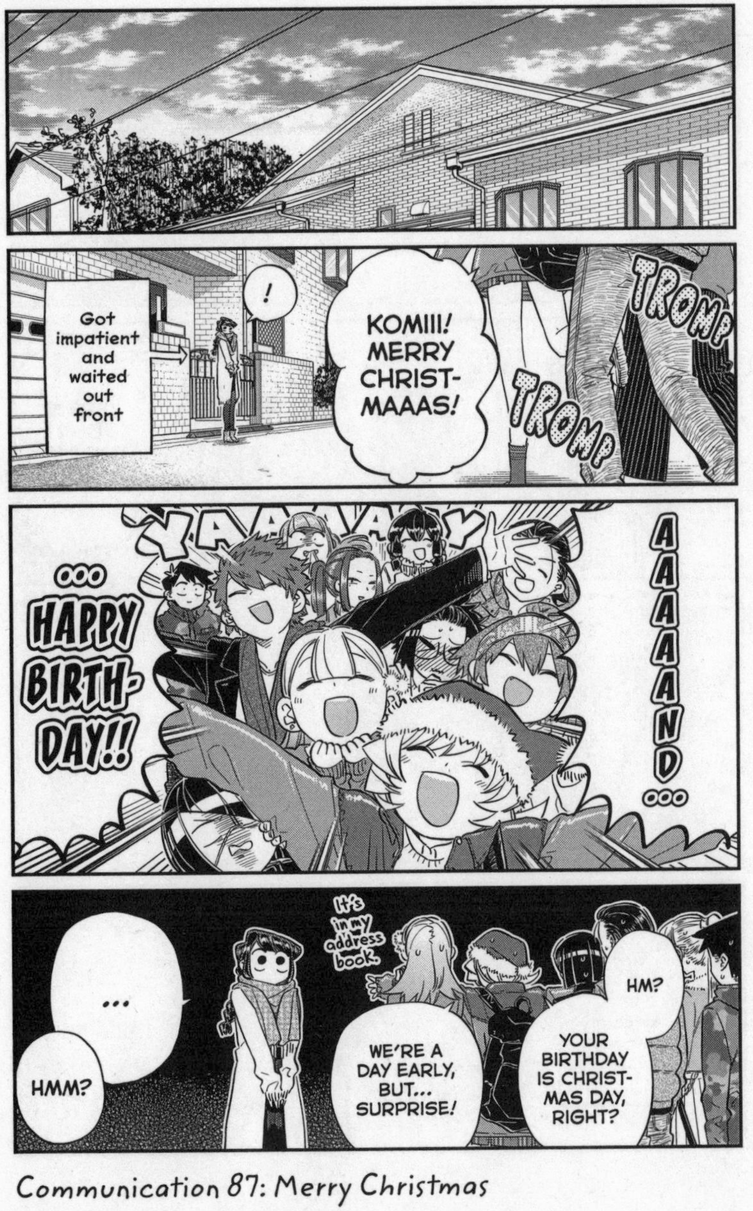
TROMP
TROMP
KOMIII! MERRY CHRIST-MAAAS!
!
Got impatient and waited out front
AAAAAAAND...
YAAAAY
...HAPPY BIRTH-DAY!!
HM?
YOUR BIRTHDAY IS CHRIST-MAS DAY, RIGHT?
WE'RE A DAY EARLY, BUT... SURPRISE!
It's in my address book.
...
HMM?

Communication 87: Merry Christmas

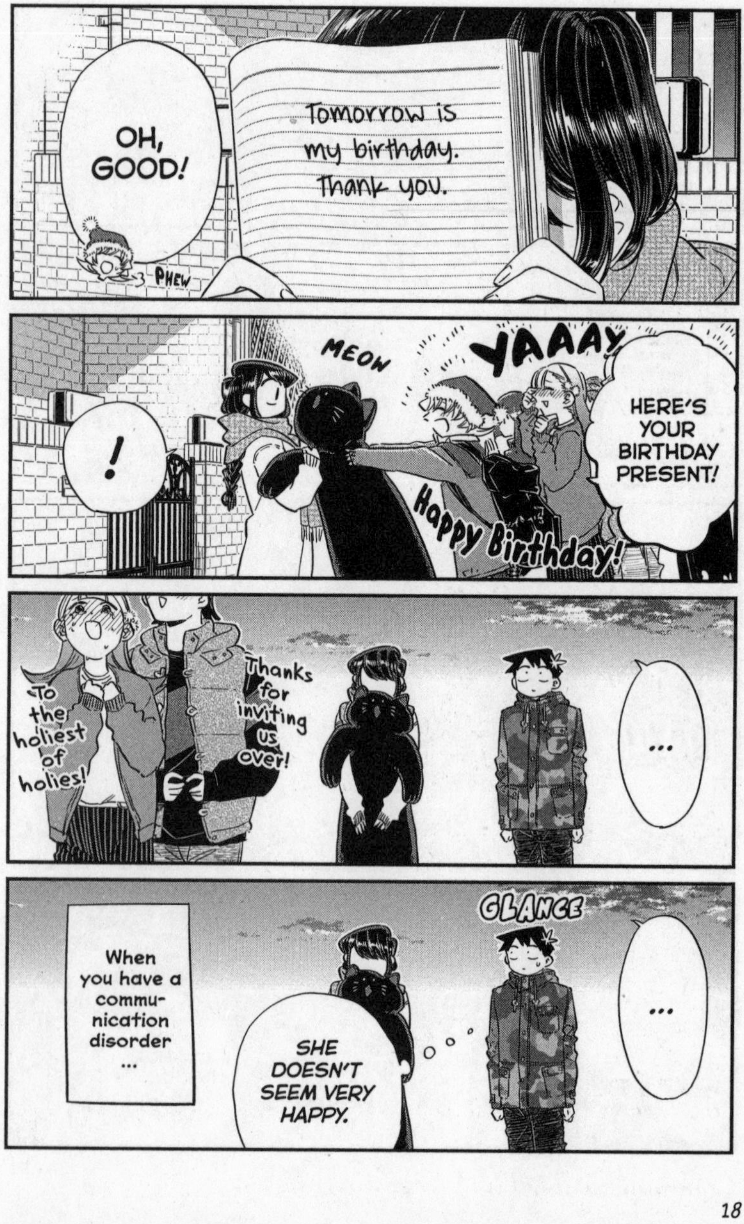
Tomorrow is my birthday. Thank you.
OH, GOOD!
PHEW
YAAAY
HERE'S YOUR BIRTHDAY PRESENT!
Happy Birthday!
MEOW
!
...
Thanks for inviting us over!
To the holiest of holies!
GLANCE
...
SHE DOESN'T SEEM VERY HAPPY.
When you have a communication disorder ...

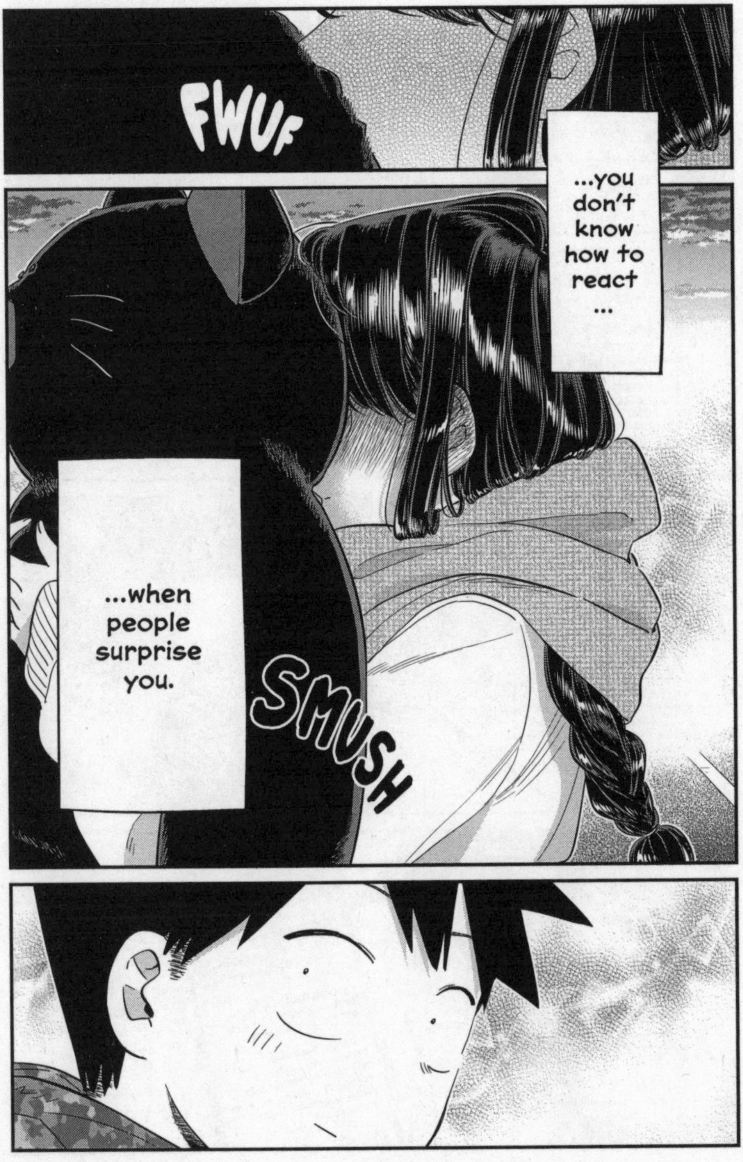
FWUF
...you don't know how to react ...
...when people surprise you.
SMUSH

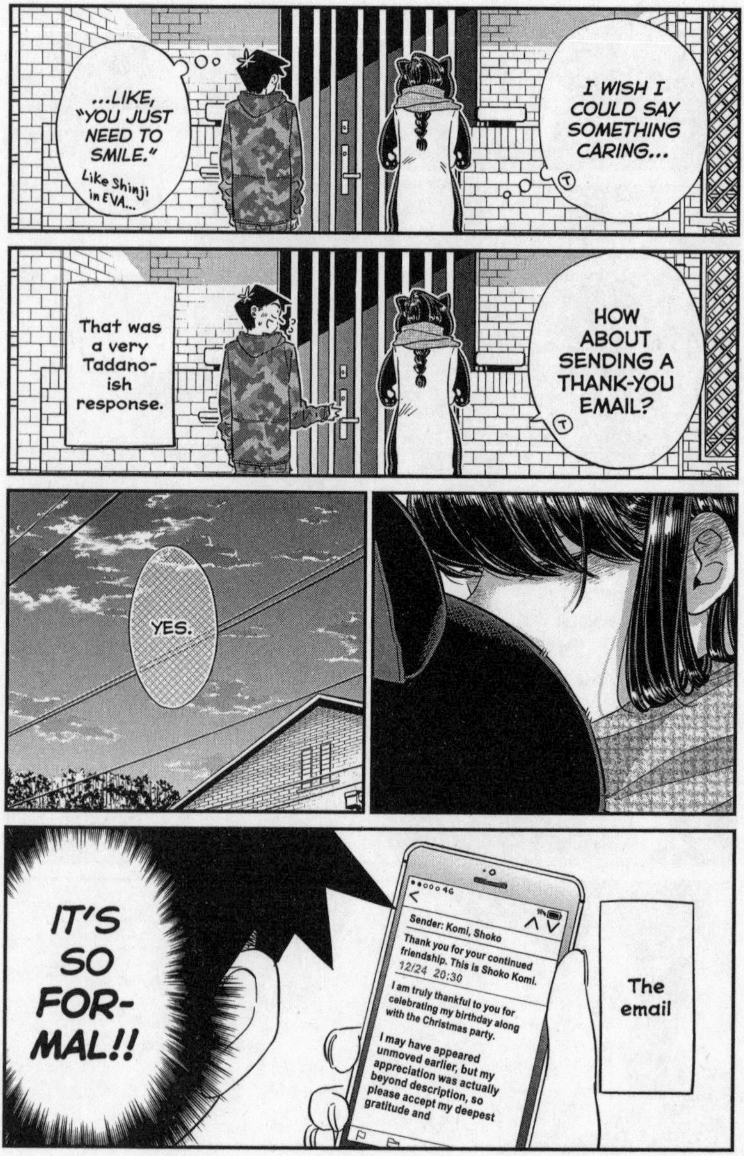
I WISH I COULD SAY SOMETHING CARING...
...LIKE, "YOU JUST NEED TO SMILE."
Like Shinji in EVA...
HOW ABOUT SENDING A THANK-YOU EMAIL?
That was a very Tadano-ish response.
YES.
The email
Sender: Komi, Shoko
Thank you for your continued friendship. This is Shoko Komi.
12/24 20:30
I am truly thankful to you for celebrating my birthday along with the Christmas party.
I may have appeared unmoved earlier, but my appreciation was actually beyond description, so please accept my deepest gratitude and
IT'S SO FOR-MAL!!

Komi Can't Communicate

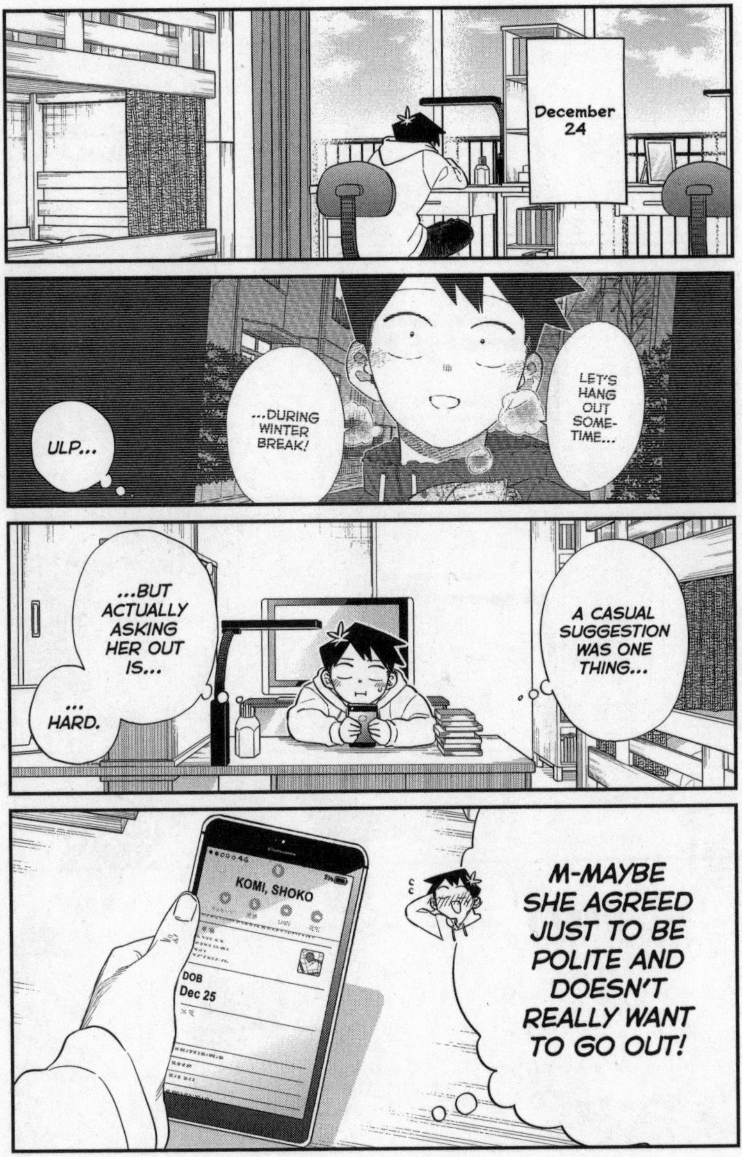
December 24
LET'S HANG OUT SOMETIME...
...DURING WINTER BREAK!
ULP...
A CASUAL SUGGESTION WAS ONE THING...
...BUT ACTUALLY ASKING HER OUT IS...
... HARD.
M-MAYBE SHE AGREED JUST TO BE POLITE AND DOESN'T REALLY WANT TO GO OUT!
KOMI, SHOKO
DOB
Dec 25

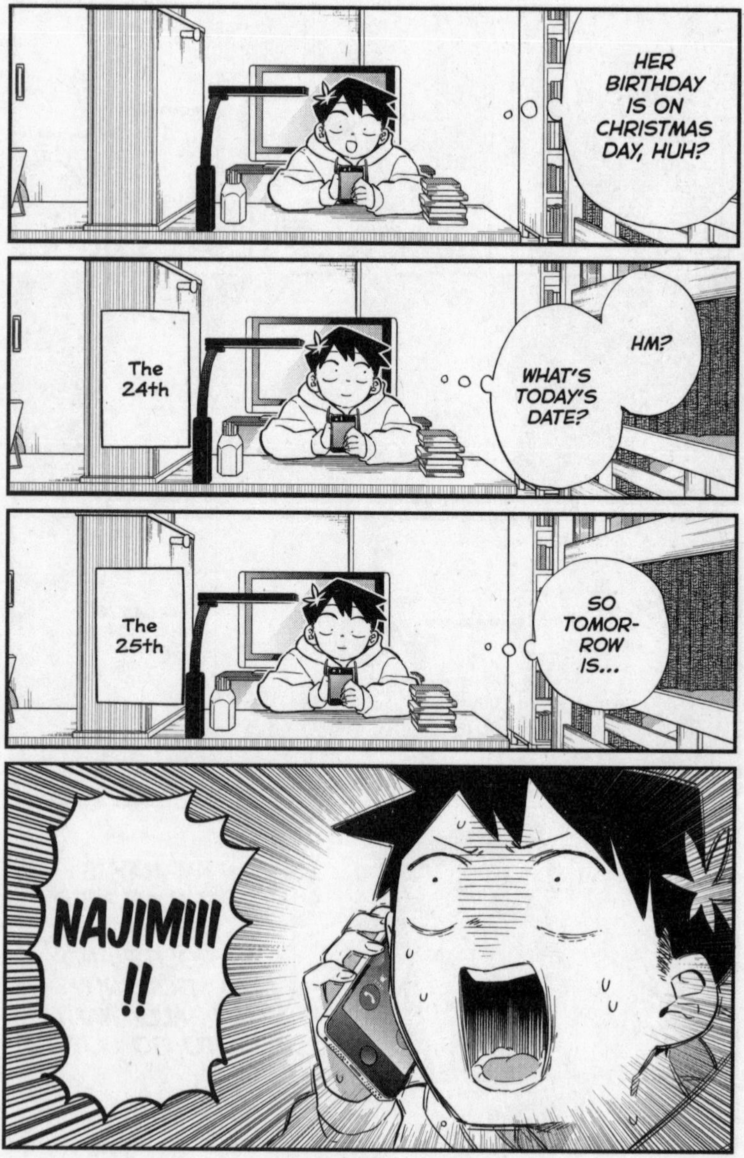
HER BIRTHDAY IS ON CHRISTMAS DAY, HUH?
HM?
WHAT'S TODAY'S DATE?
The 24th
SO TOMOR-ROW IS...
The 25th
NAJIMIII !!

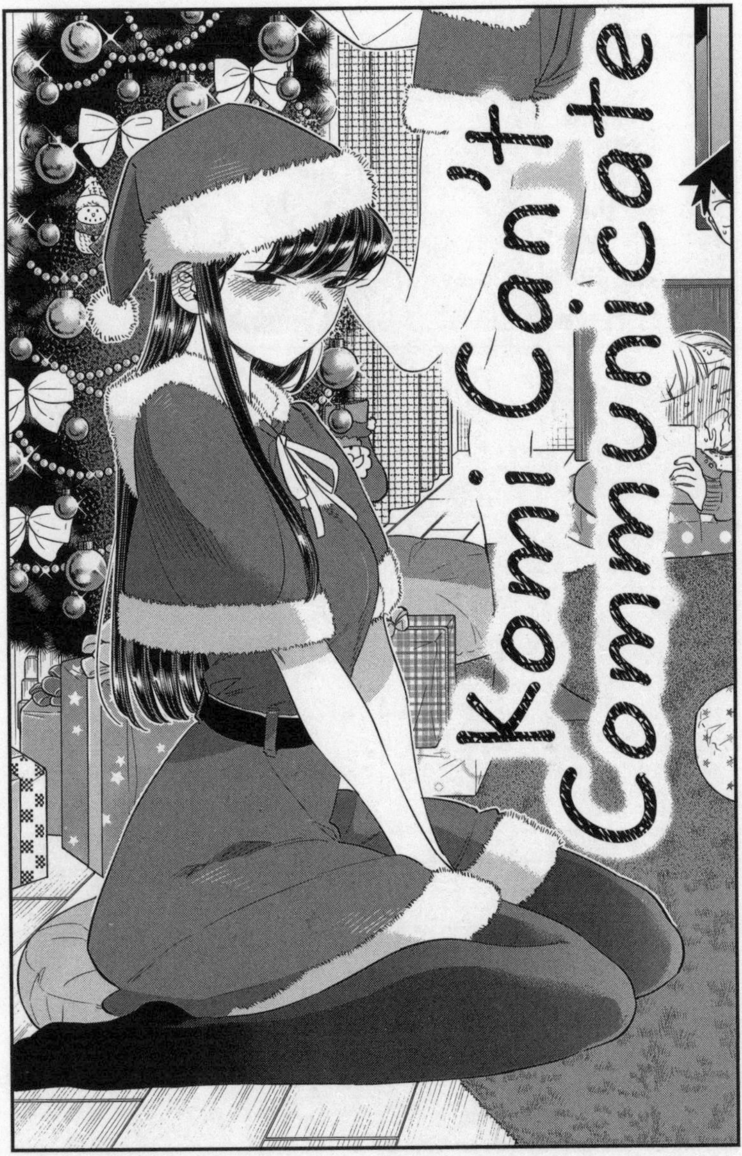
Komi Can't Communicate

Communication 88: Choosing One More Present

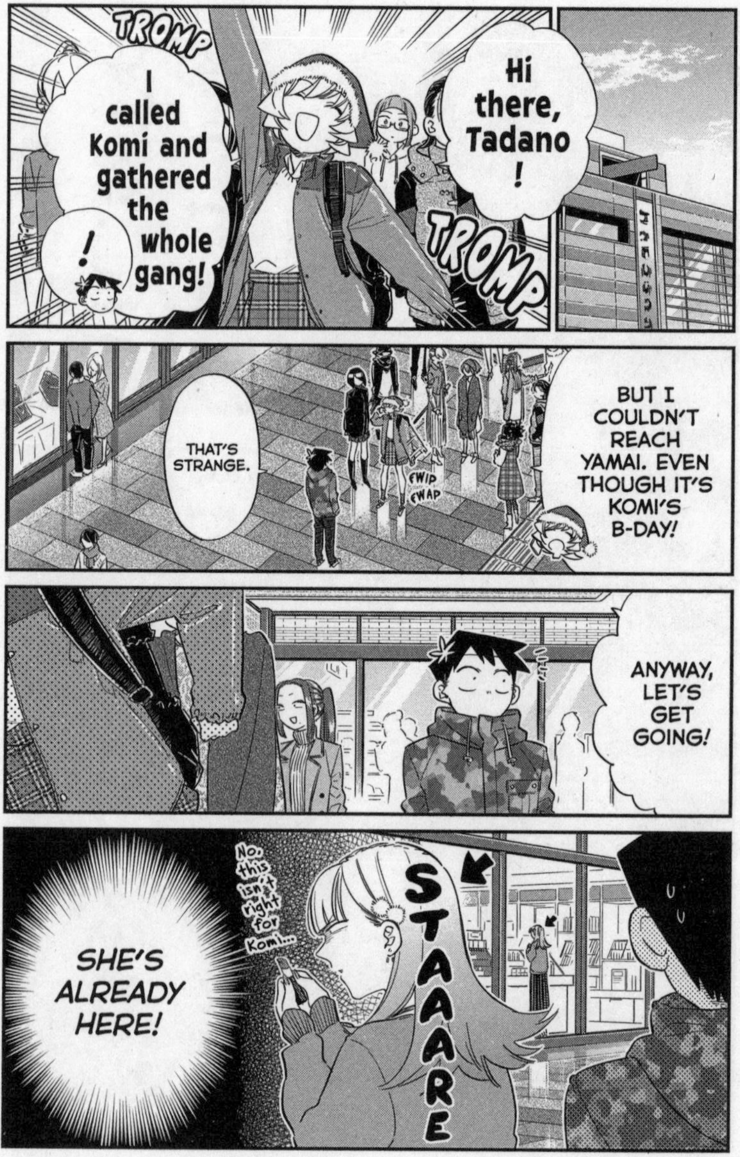
Hi there, Tadano!
TROMP
I called Komi and gathered the whole gang!
TROMP
!
BUT I COULDN'T REACH YAMAI. EVEN THOUGH IT'S KOMI'S B-DAY!
FWIP FWAP
THAT'S STRANGE.
ANYWAY, LET'S GET GOING!
STAAARE
No, this isn't right for Komi...
SHE'S ALREADY HERE!

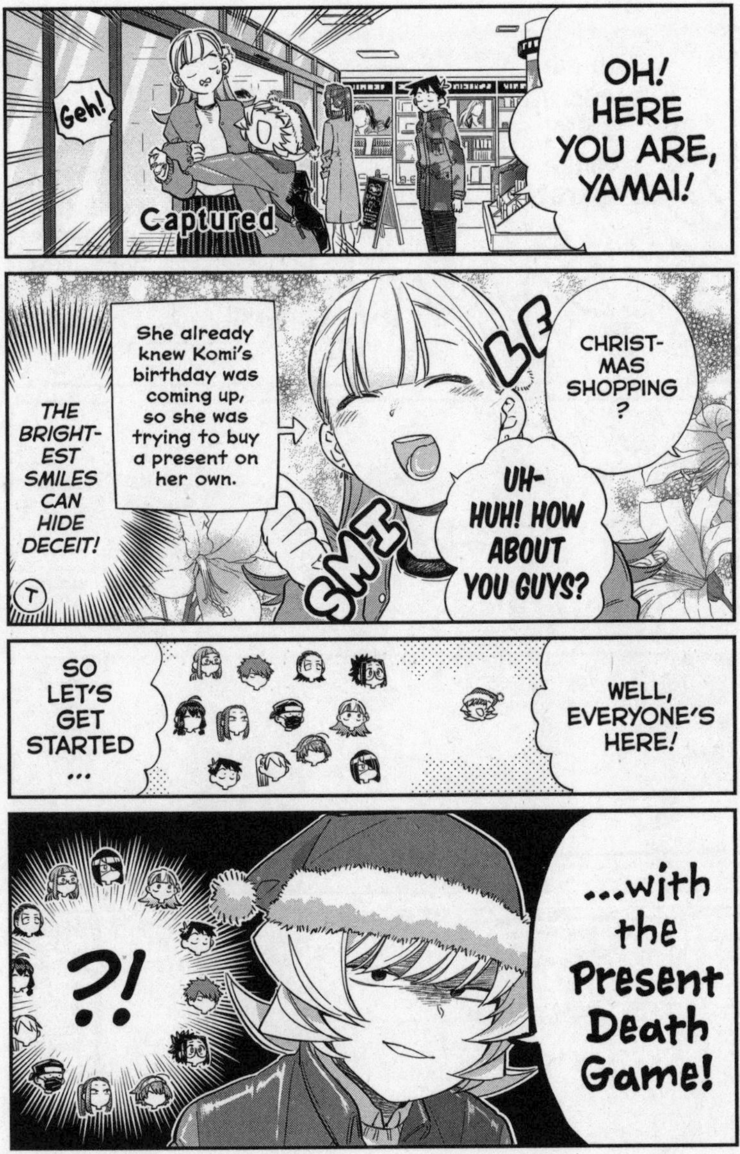
OH! HERE YOU ARE, YAMAI!
Geh!
Captured
CHRISTMAS SHOPPING?
SMILE
UH-HUH! HOW ABOUT YOU GUYS?
She already knew Komi's birthday was coming up, so she was trying to buy a present on her own.
THE BRIGHTEST SMILES CAN HIDE DECEIT!
WELL, EVERYONE'S HERE!
SO LET'S GET STARTED...
...with the Present Death Game!
?!

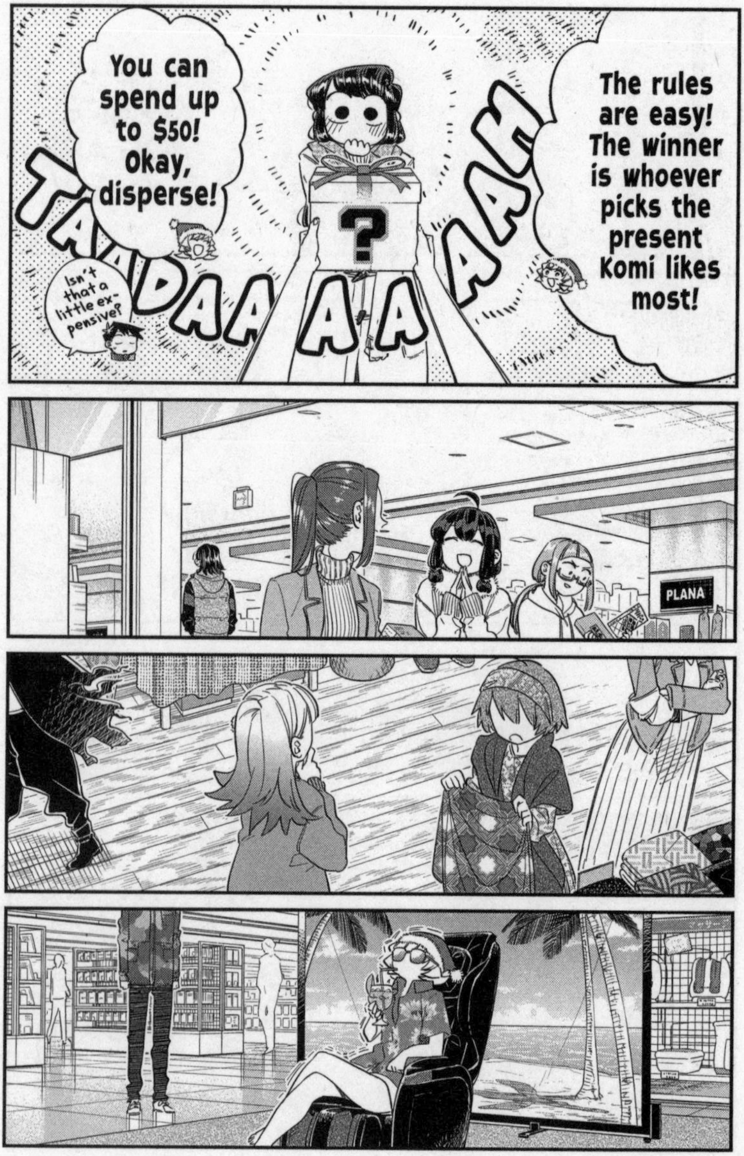
The rules are easy! The winner is whoever picks the present Komi likes most!
TADAAAAAAAH
You can spend up to $50! Okay, disperse!
Isn't that a little ex-pensive?
?
PLANA

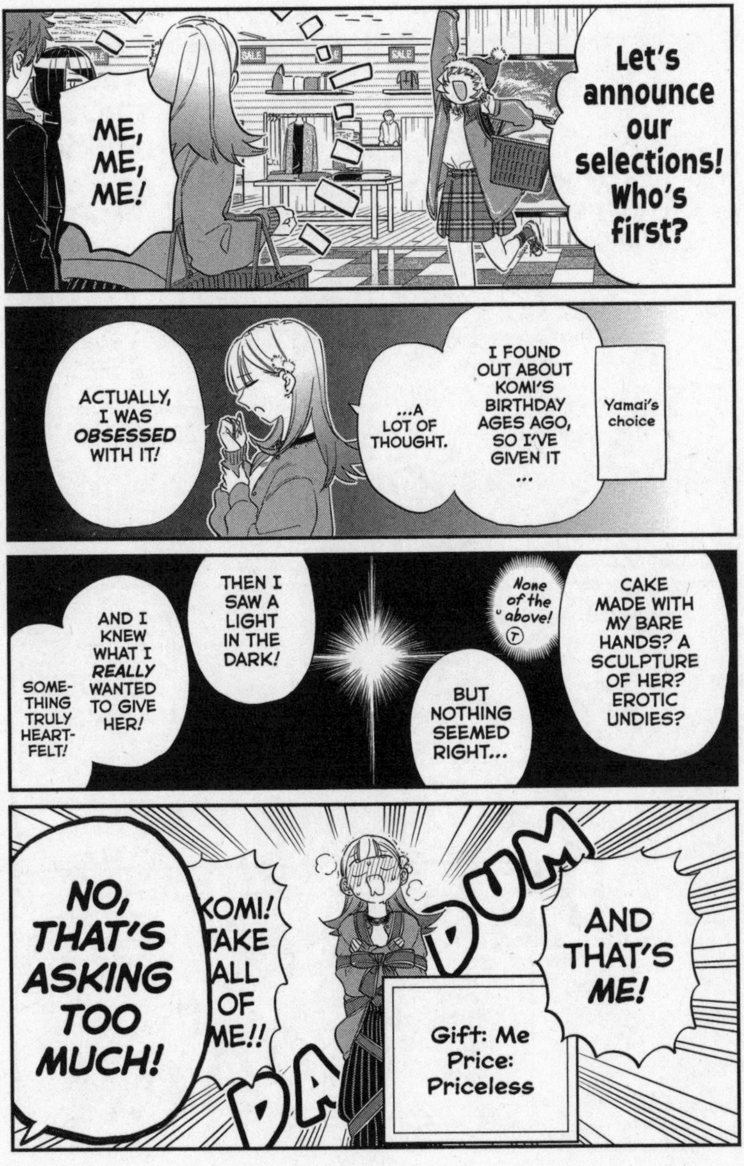
Let's announce our selections! Who's first?
ME, ME, ME!
Yamai's choice
I FOUND OUT ABOUT KOMI'S BIRTHDAY AGES AGO, SO I'VE GIVEN IT ...
...A LOT OF THOUGHT.
ACTUALLY, I WAS *OBSESSED* WITH IT!
CAKE MADE WITH MY BARE HANDS? A SCULPTURE OF HER? EROTIC UNDIES?
None of the above!
BUT NOTHING SEEMED RIGHT...
THEN I SAW A LIGHT IN THE DARK!
AND I KNEW WHAT I *REALLY* WANTED TO GIVE HER!
SOMETHING TRULY HEARTFELT!
AND THAT'S *ME*!
DA DUM
Gift: Me
Price: Priceless
KOMI! TAKE ALL OF ME!!
NO, THAT'S ASKING TOO MUCH!

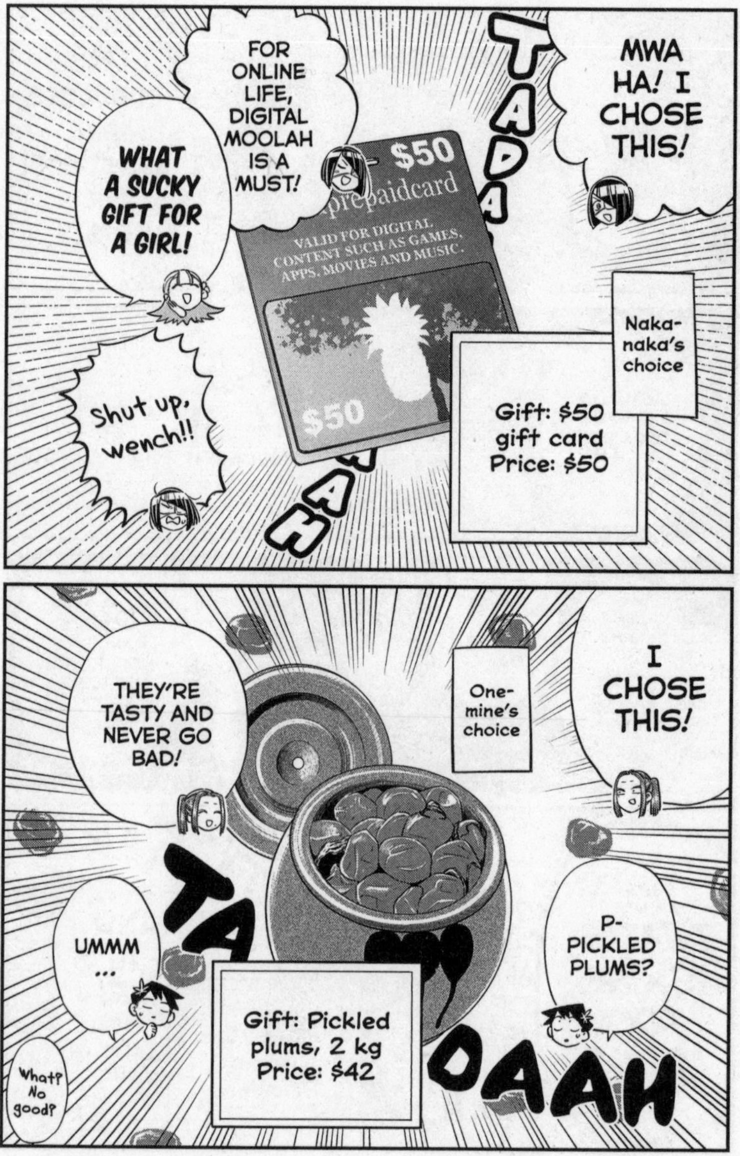
MWA HA! I CHOSE THIS!
TADA
Naka-naka's choice
FOR ONLINE LIFE, DIGITAL MOOLAH IS A MUST!
$50
prepaidcard
VALID FOR DIGITAL CONTENT SUCH AS GAMES, APPS, MOVIES AND MUSIC.
$50
AAH
Gift: $50 gift card Price: $50
WHAT A SUCKY GIFT FOR A GIRL!
Shut up, wench!!
I CHOSE THIS!
One-mine's choice
THEY'RE TASTY AND NEVER GO BAD!
TA
P-PICKLED PLUMS?
DAAH
Gift: Pickled plums, 2 kg Price: $42
UMMM ...
What? No good?

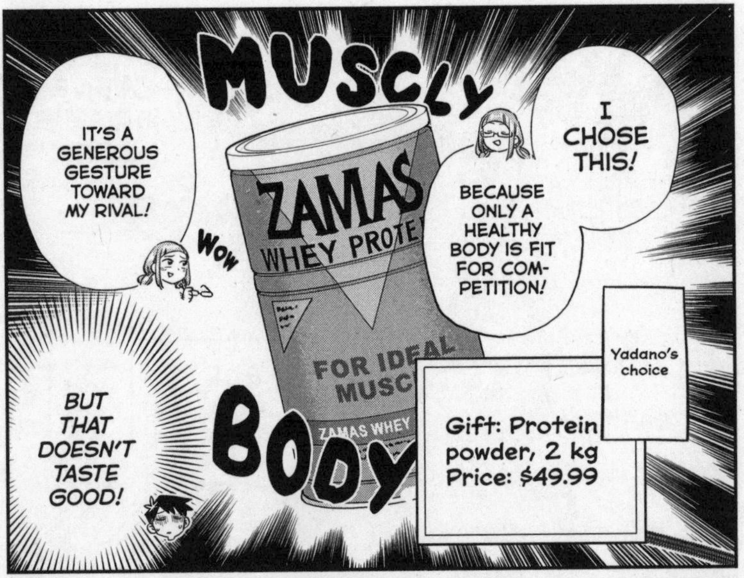
MUSCLY
I CHOSE THIS!
BECAUSE ONLY A HEALTHY BODY IS FIT FOR COM-PETITION!
Yadano's choice
ZAMAS
WHEY PROTE
FOR IDEAL MUSC
ZAMAS WHEY
IT'S A GENEROUS GESTURE TOWARD MY RIVAL!
WOW
Gift: Protein powder, 2 kg
Price: $49.99
BODY
BUT THAT DOESN'T TASTE GOOD!

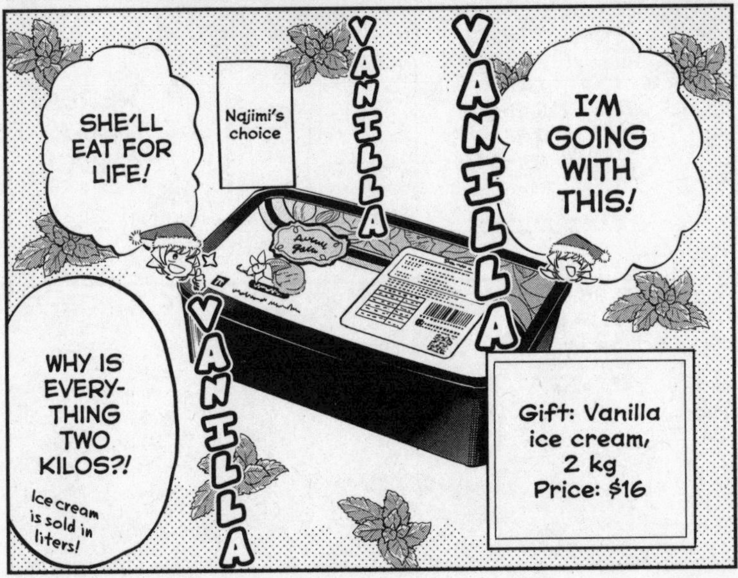
VANILLA
I'M GOING WITH THIS!
VANILLA
Najimi's choice
SHE'LL EAT FOR LIFE!
Gift: Vanilla ice cream, 2 kg
Price: $16
VANILLA
WHY IS EVERY-THING TWO KILOS?!
Ice cream is sold in liters!

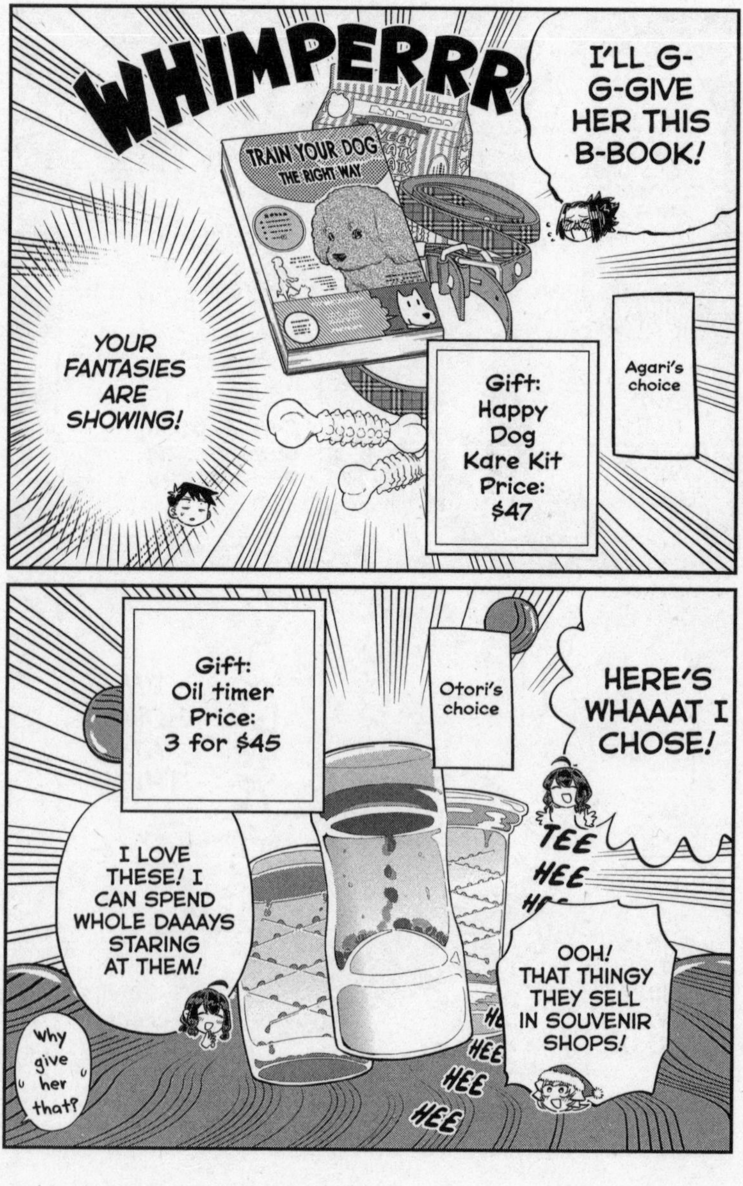
I'LL G-G-GIVE HER THIS B-BOOK!
WHIMPERRR
TRAIN YOUR DOG THE RIGHT WAY
Agari's choice
Gift: Happy Dog Kare Kit Price: $47
YOUR FANTASIES ARE SHOWING!
HERE'S WHAAAT I CHOSE!
Otori's choice
Gift: Oil timer Price: 3 for $45
TEE HEE
I LOVE THESE! I CAN SPEND WHOLE DAAAYS STARING AT THEM!
OOH! THAT THINGY THEY SELL IN SOUVENIR SHOPS!
HEE HEE HEE
Why give her that?

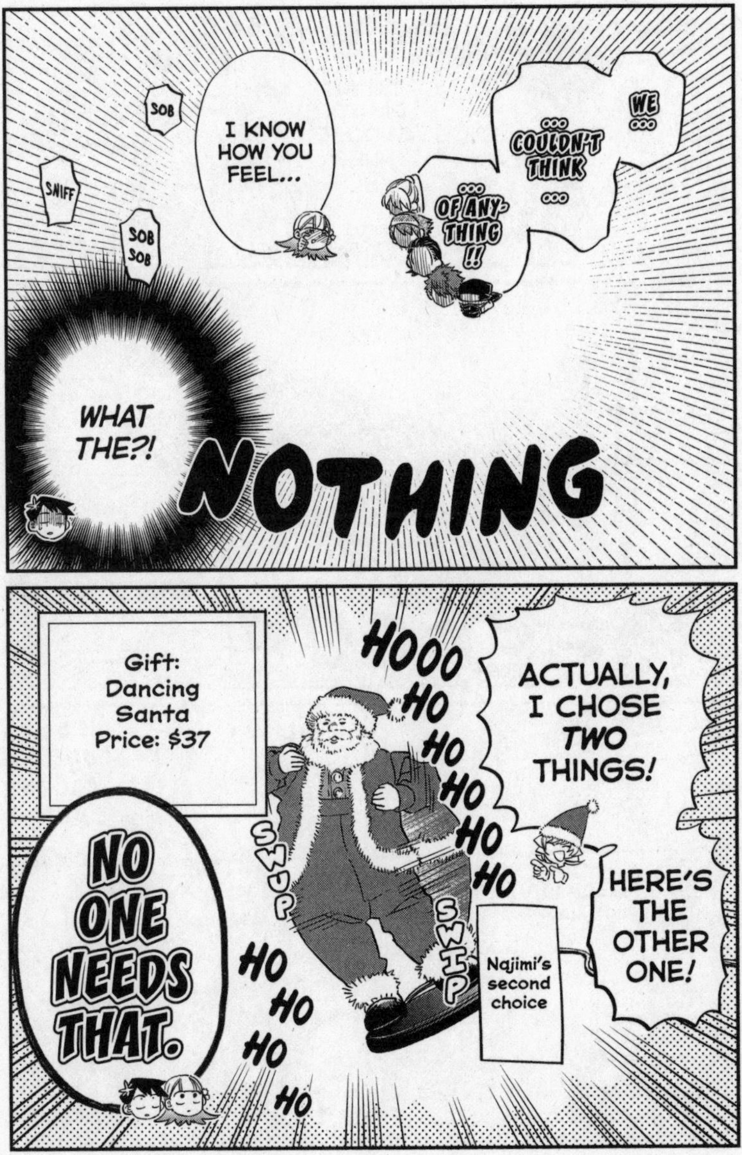
WE... ...COULDN'T THINK... ...OF ANY-THING!!
I KNOW HOW YOU FEEL...
SOB
SNIFF
SOB SOB
WHAT THE?!
NOTHING
ACTUALLY, I CHOSE *TWO* THINGS!
HERE'S THE OTHER ONE!
Najimi's second choice
HOOO HO HO HO HO HO HO
SWIP
SWUP
Gift: Dancing Santa Price: $37
HO HO HO HO
NO ONE NEEDS THAT.

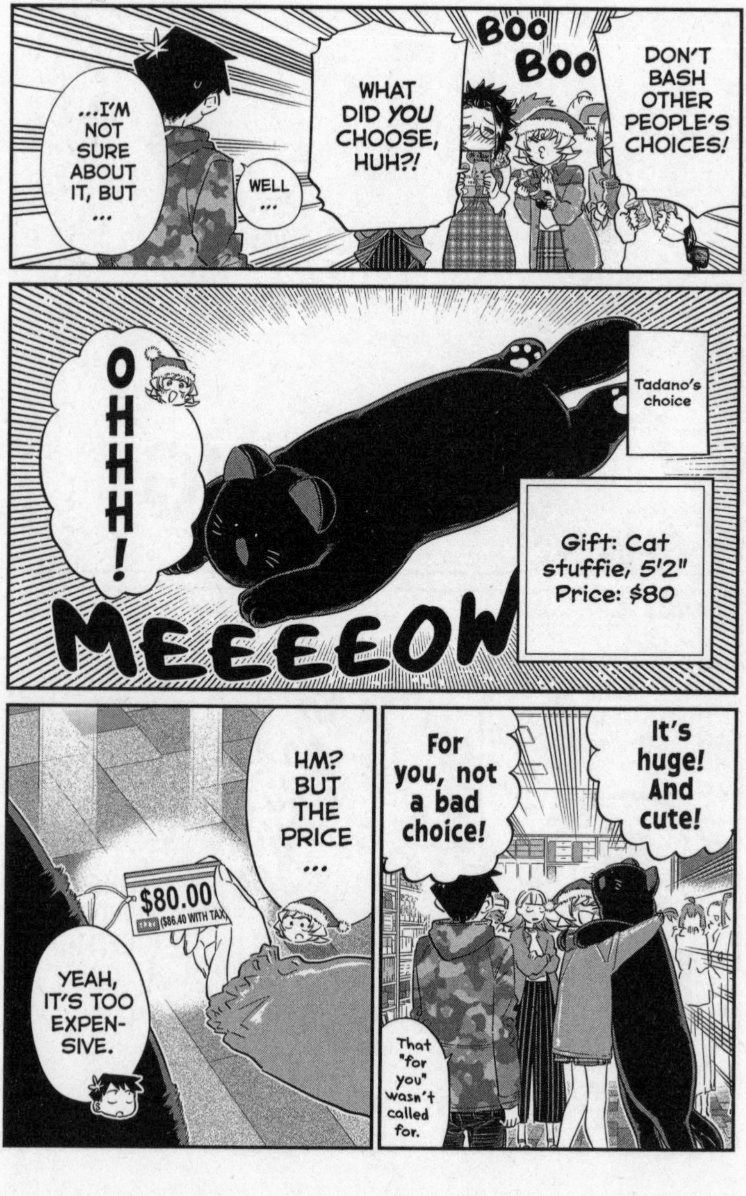
DON'T BASH OTHER PEOPLE'S CHOICES!
BOO BOO
WHAT DID *YOU* CHOOSE, HUH?!
WELL ...
...I'M NOT SURE ABOUT IT, BUT ...
Tadano's choice
Gift: Cat stuffie, 5'2" Price: $80
OHHH!
MEEEEOW
It's huge! And cute!
For you, not a bad choice!
That "for you" wasn't called for.
HM? BUT THE PRICE ...
$80.00
($86.40 WITH TAX)
YEAH, IT'S TOO EXPEN-SIVE.

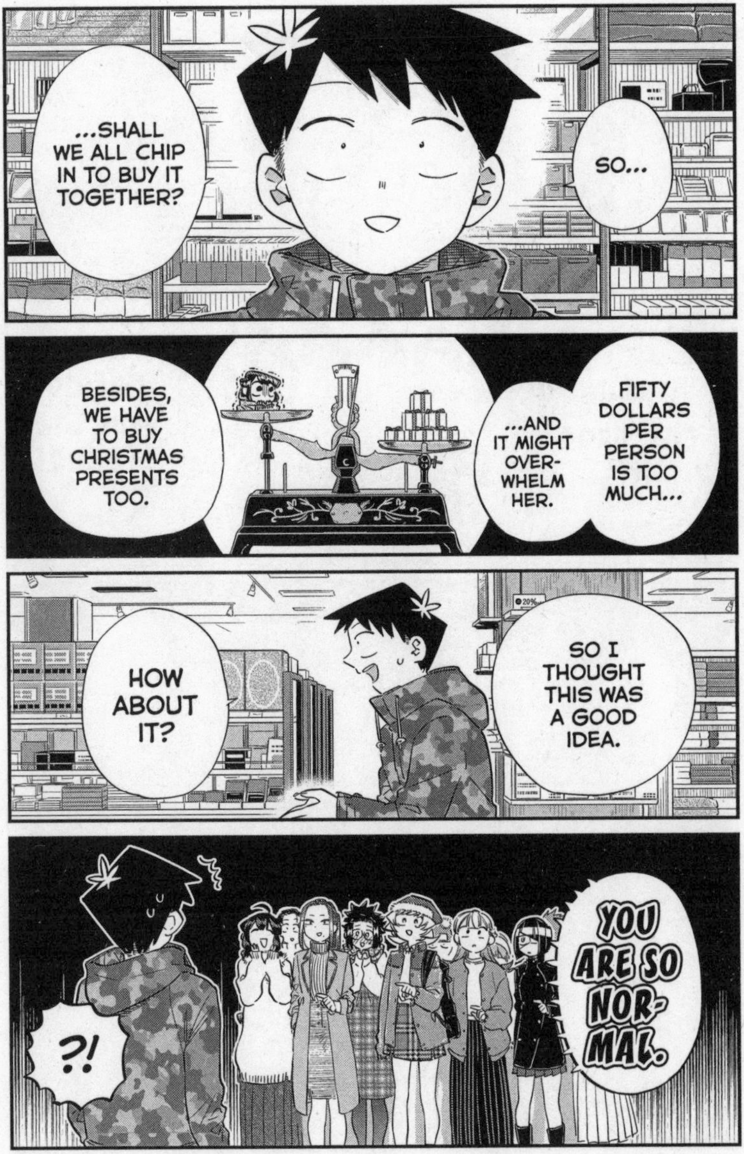
SO...
...SHALL WE ALL CHIP IN TO BUY IT TOGETHER?
FIFTY DOLLARS PER PERSON IS TOO MUCH...
...AND IT MIGHT OVER-WHELM HER.
BESIDES, WE HAVE TO BUY CHRISTMAS PRESENTS TOO.
SO I THOUGHT THIS WAS A GOOD IDEA.
HOW ABOUT IT?
YOU ARE SO NOR-MAL.
?!

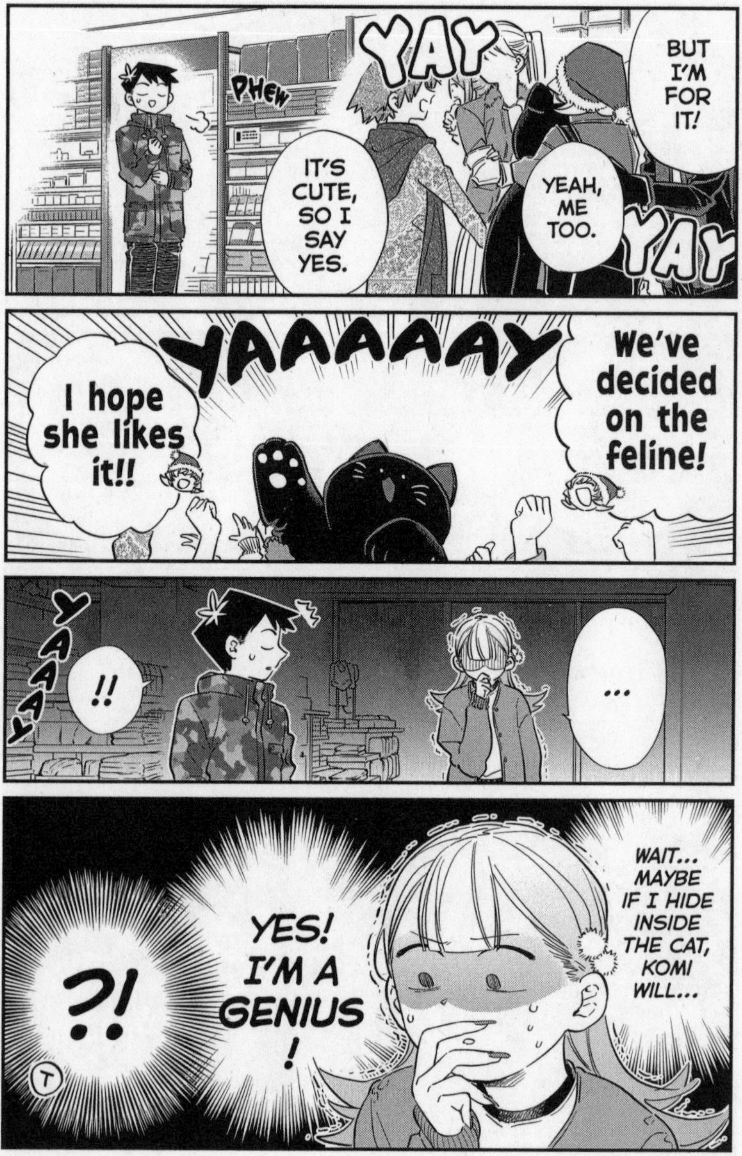
BUT I'M FOR IT!
YAY
YAY
YEAH, ME TOO.
IT'S CUTE, SO I SAY YES.
PHEW
We've decided on the feline!
YAAAAAY
I hope she likes it!!
...
!!
YAAAAY
WAIT... MAYBE IF I HIDE INSIDE THE CAT, KOMI WILL...
YES! I'M A GENIUS!
?!

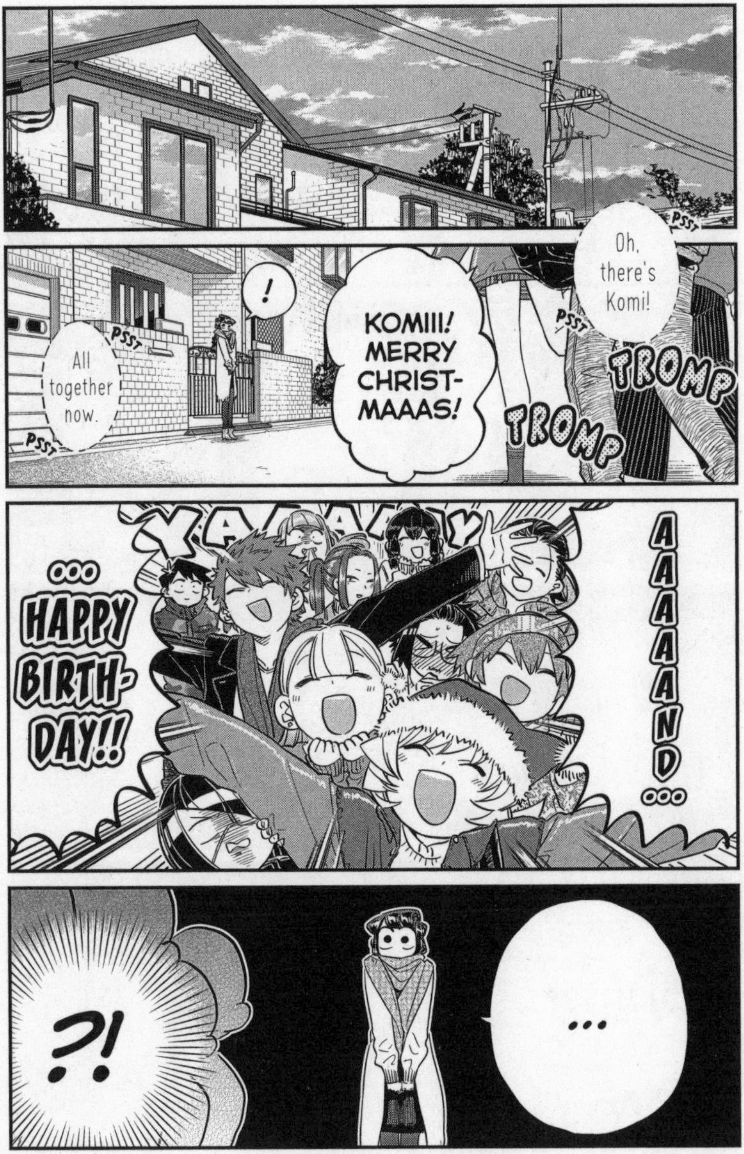
PSST
Oh, there's Komi!
PSST
TROMP
TROMP
KOMIII! MERRY CHRIST-MAAAS!
!
PSST
All together now.
PSST
AAAAAAAND...
...HAPPY BIRTH-DAY!!
...
?!

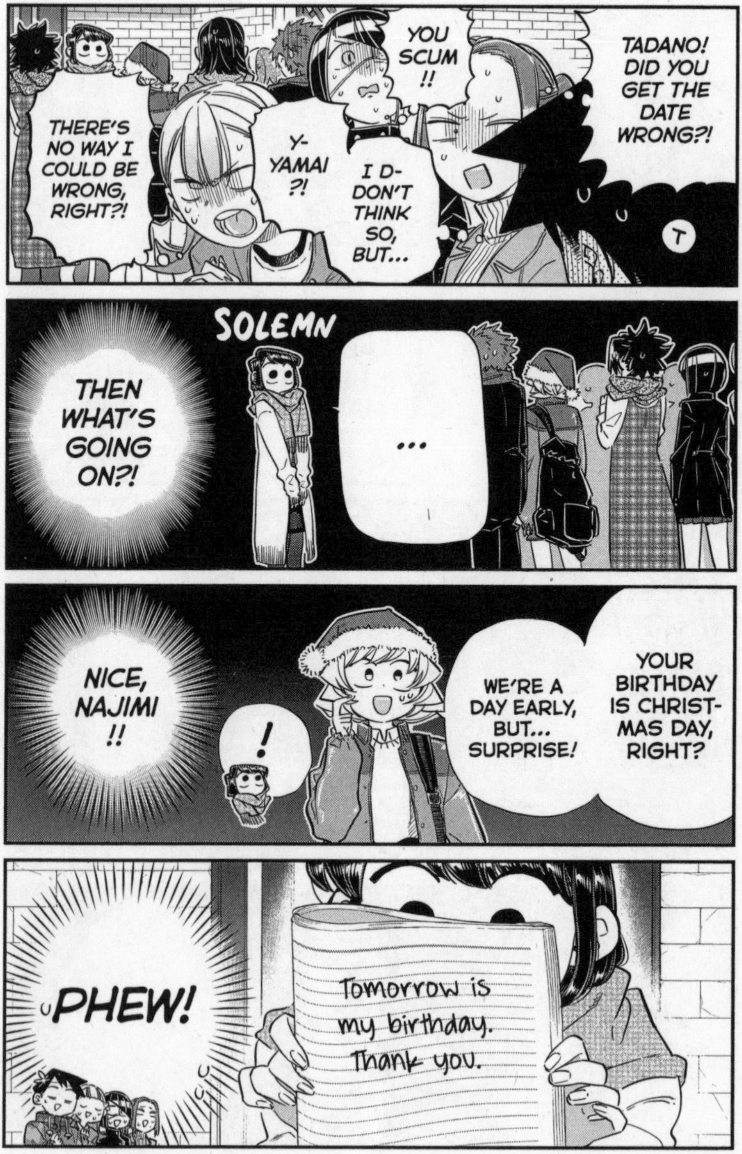
TADANO! DID YOU GET THE DATE WRONG?!
T
YOU SCUM !!
I D-DON'T THINK SO, BUT...
Y-YAMAI ?!
THERE'S NO WAY I COULD BE WRONG, RIGHT?!
...
SOLEMN
THEN WHAT'S GOING ON?!
YOUR BIRTHDAY IS CHRISTMAS DAY, RIGHT?
WE'RE A DAY EARLY, BUT... SURPRISE!
!
NICE, NAJIMI !!
Tomorrow is my birthday. Thank you.
PHEW!

HERE'S YOUR BIRTHDAY PRES- ENT!
N
YAY!
Con- grats !!
...
Happy birth- day!
SHE'S BARELY RE- SPONDING, TADANO!
THIS IS ALL YOUR FAULT, TADANO!
S-SORRY!
T
CLAP CLAP CLAP CLAP CLAP CLAP CLAP CLAP
AH HA HA
YAY
YAY
Thanks for inviting us!
SHLUF
SHLUF
Bye!
Bye- bye!
See ya later!
CHAK
GLOOM
IS THIS A WAKE ?!

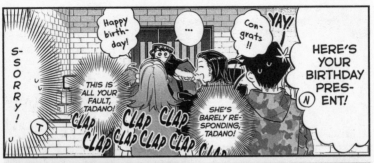

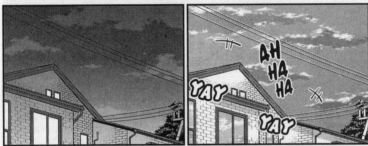

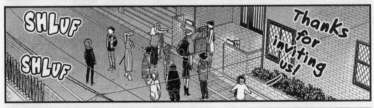

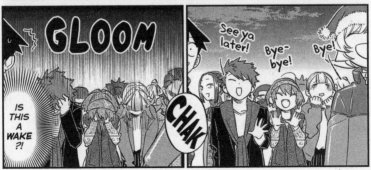

PAPING♪
HM? WHOSE PHONE IS THAT?
I THINK IT'S MINE.
OH, SORRY. IT'S ME.
MINE'S RINGING TOO.
EVERY-ONE?!
I got an email.
From Komi?
Thank you very much.
I wish for continued congenial relations between us and I am acutely desirous of conferring something
in return.
Here's to the days ahead.
Shoko Komi
Class 1-1
Itan Private High School
AH HA HA! SHE'S SO FORMAL!
What's this word mean?
HOW LIKE HER!
SOB
SOB
Are you crying?
Every-one saved that email.

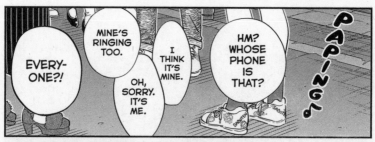

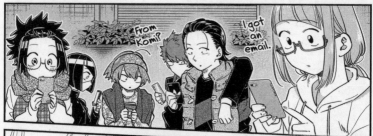

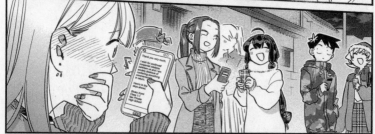

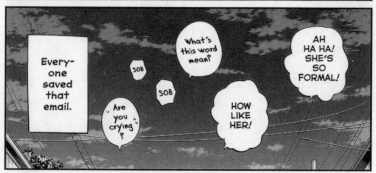

Communication 88 — The End

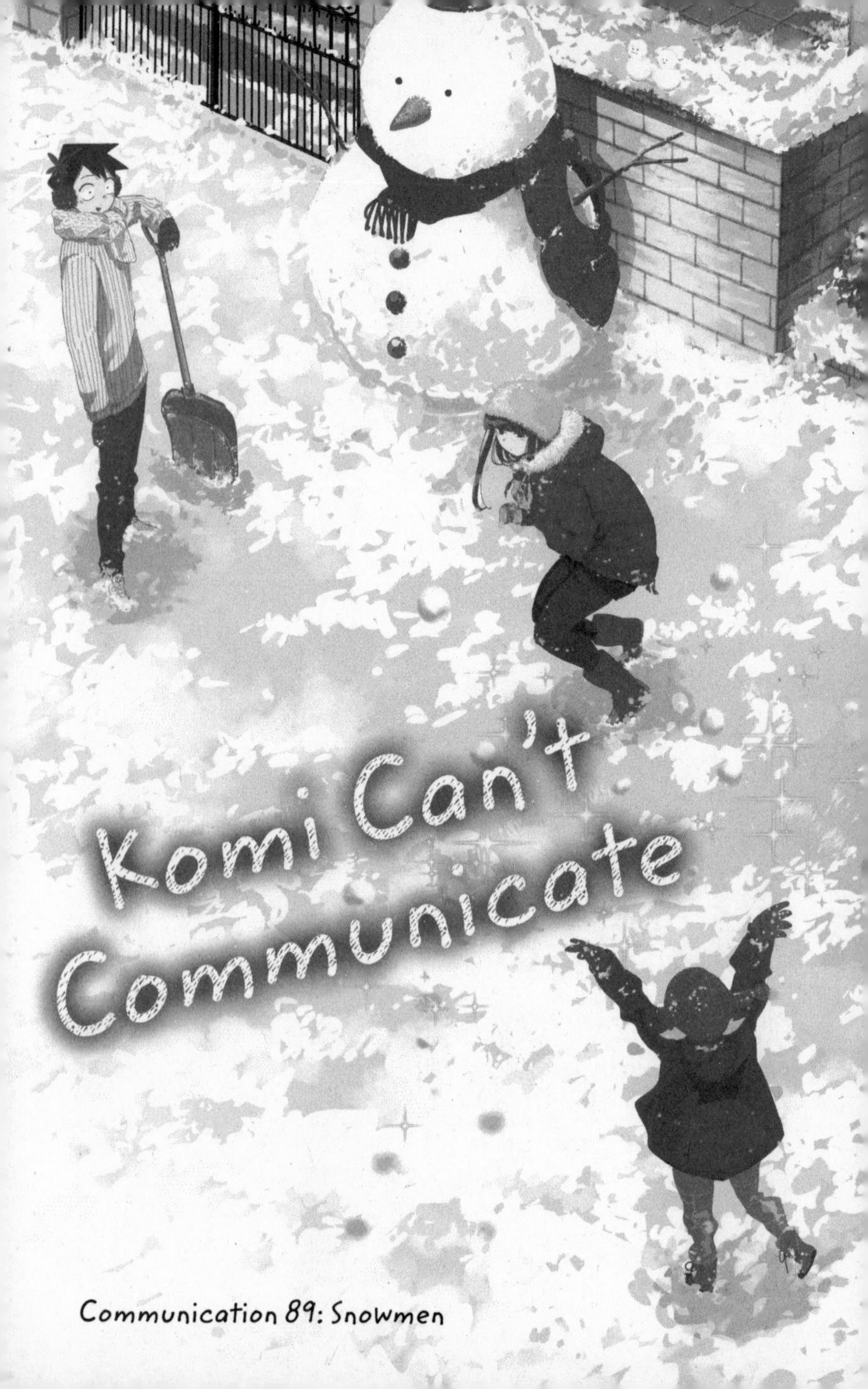
Komi Can't Communicate
Communication 89: Snowmen

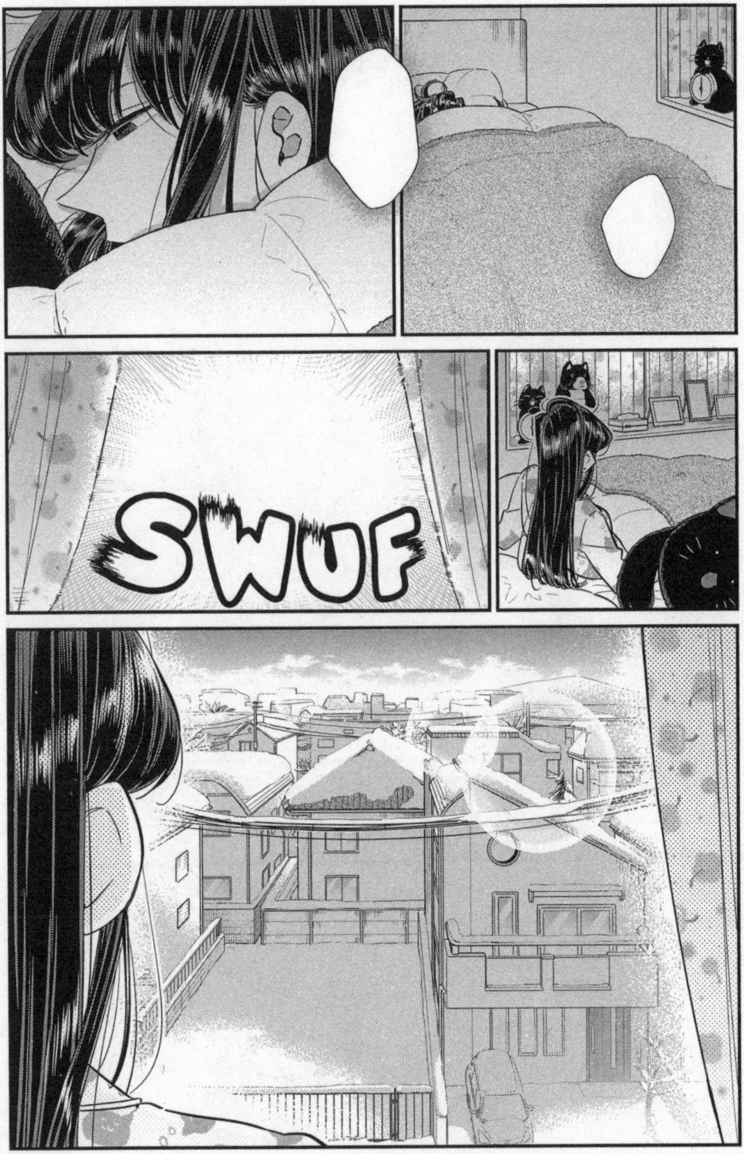
SWUF

!
HUSTLE
BUSTLE
FUMP
BUMP

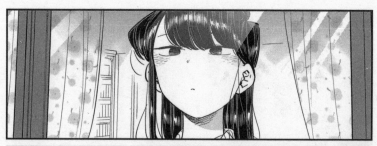

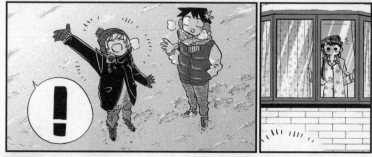

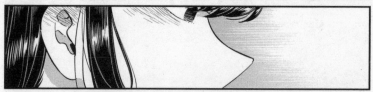

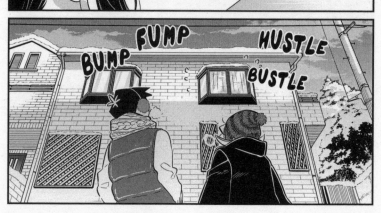

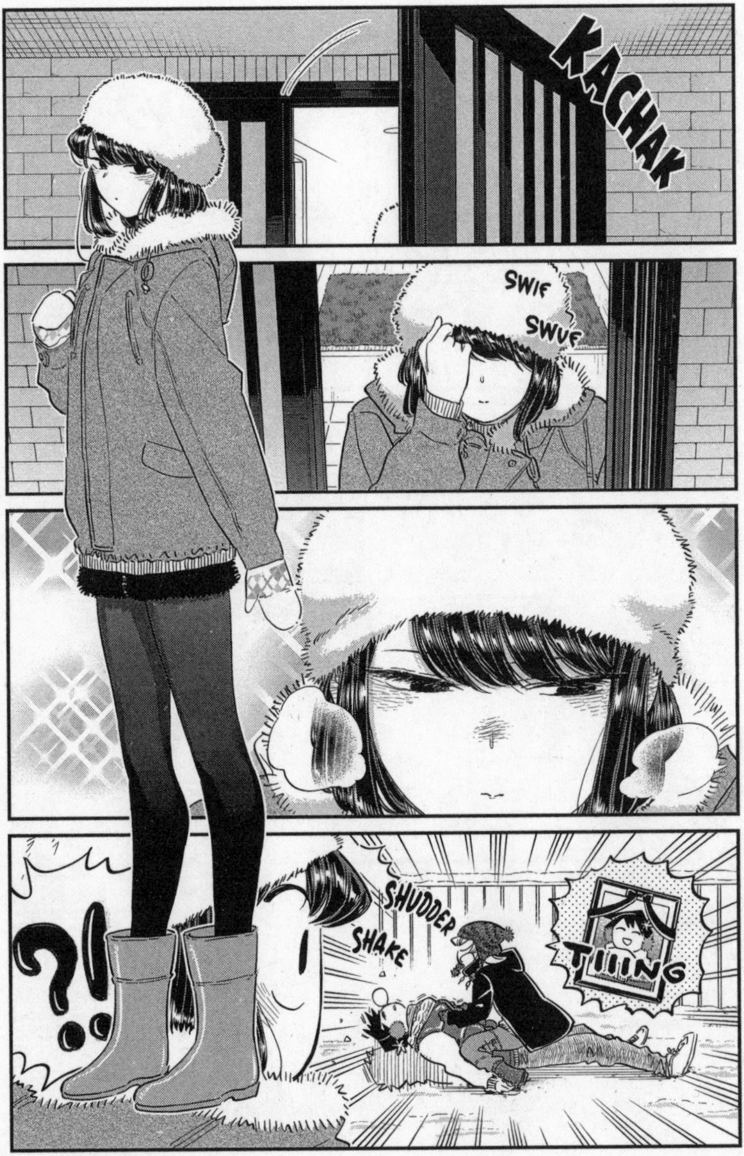
KACHAK
SWIF
SWUF
TIIING
SHUDDER
SHAKE
?!

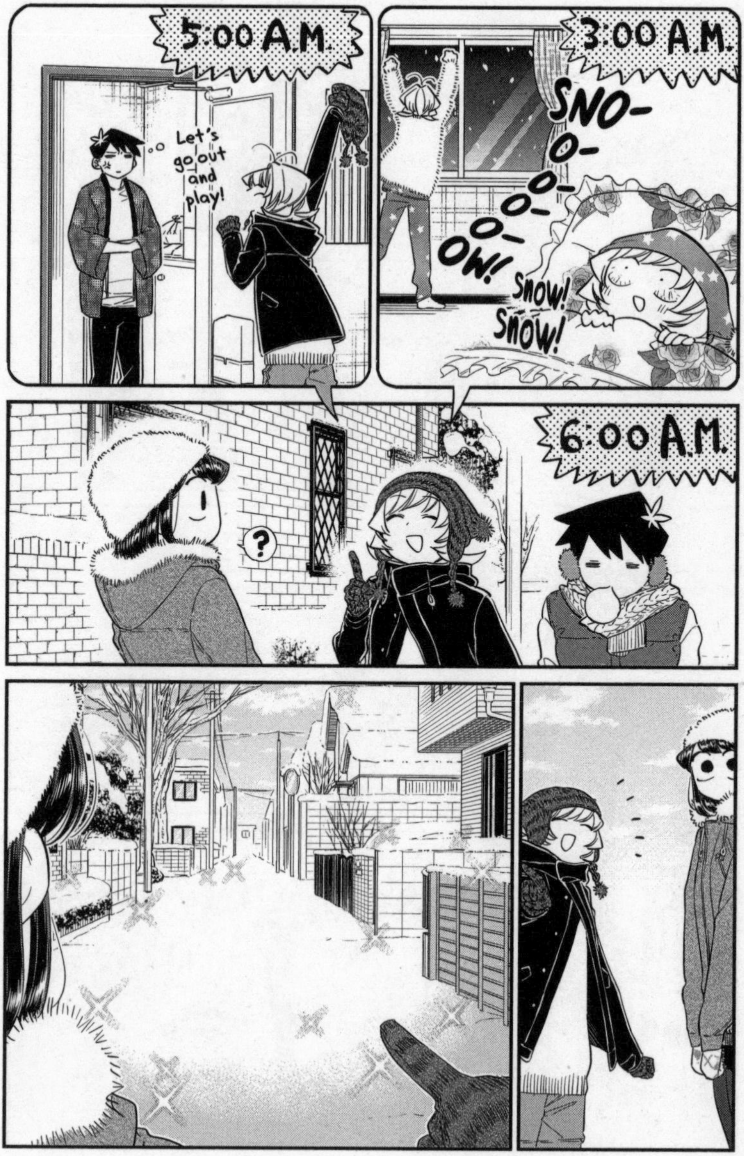
3:00 A.M.
SNO-O-O-O-O-OW!
SNOW! SNOW!
5:00 A.M.
Let's go out and play!
6:00 A.M.
?

!
!
SHUV
SHUV
?
?
CRNCH
CRNCH
CRNCH
CRNCH
CRNCH
CRNCH
!
!!
TRMBL
TRMBL
!!

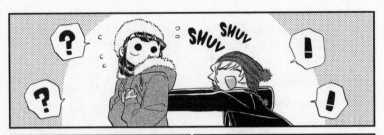

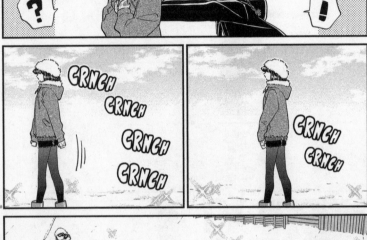

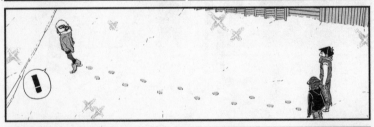

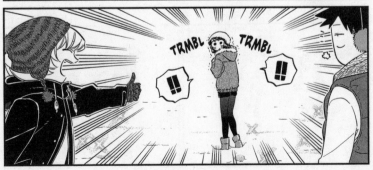

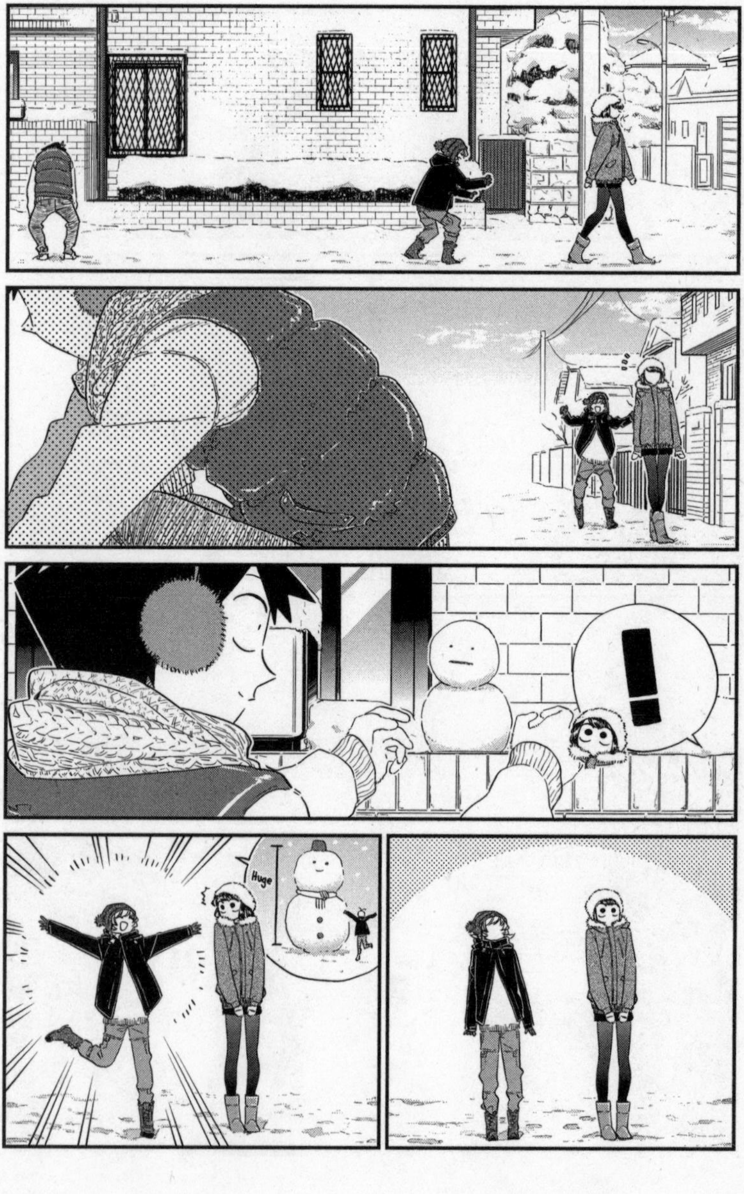
!
Huge

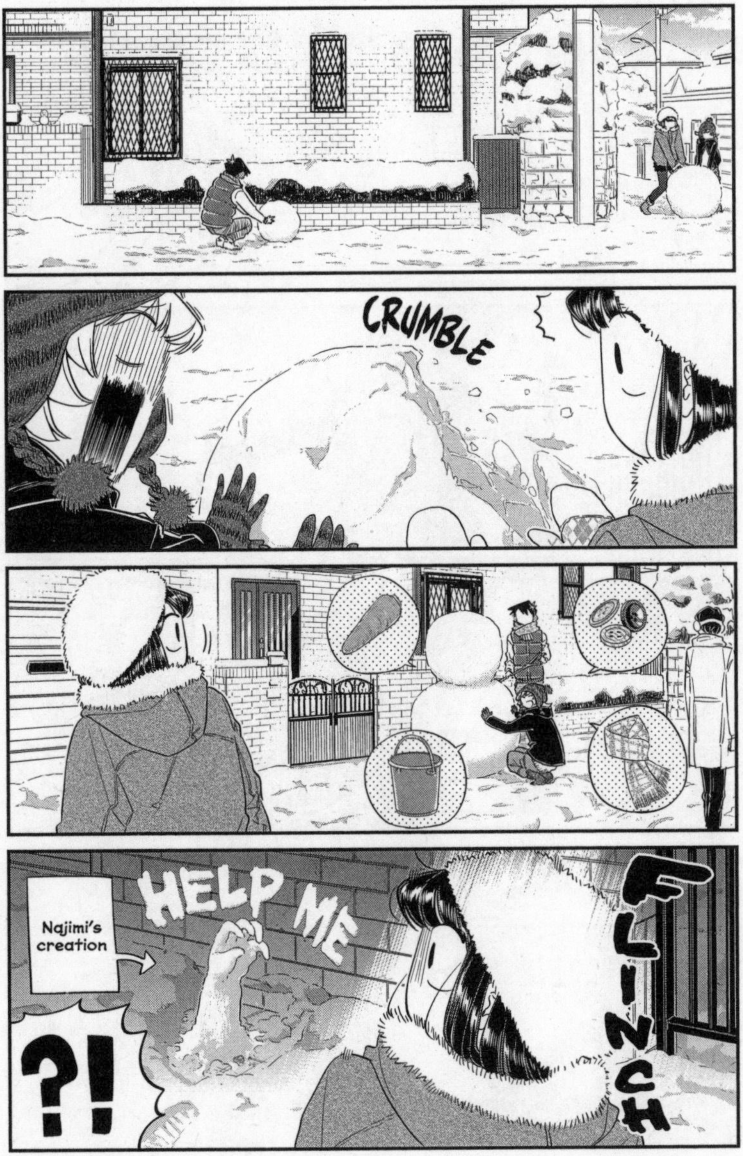
CRUMBLE
HELP ME
FLINCH
Najimi's creation
?!

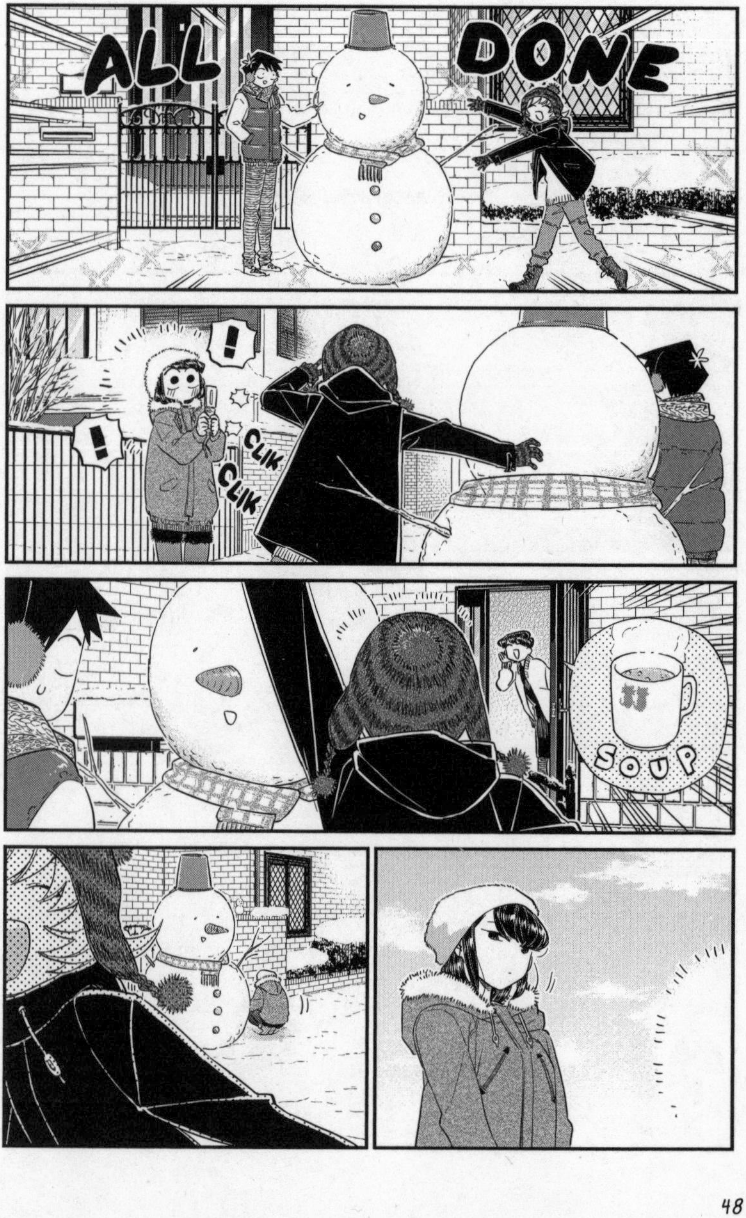
ALL DONE
!
!
CLIK
CLIK
SOUP

POUT
...
SWIK SWIK
SMI LE

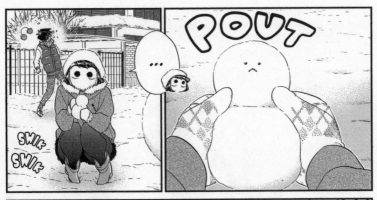

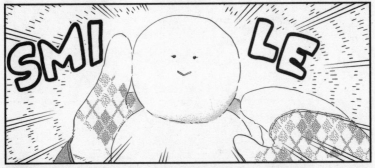

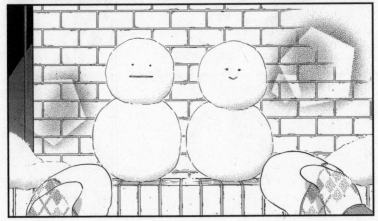

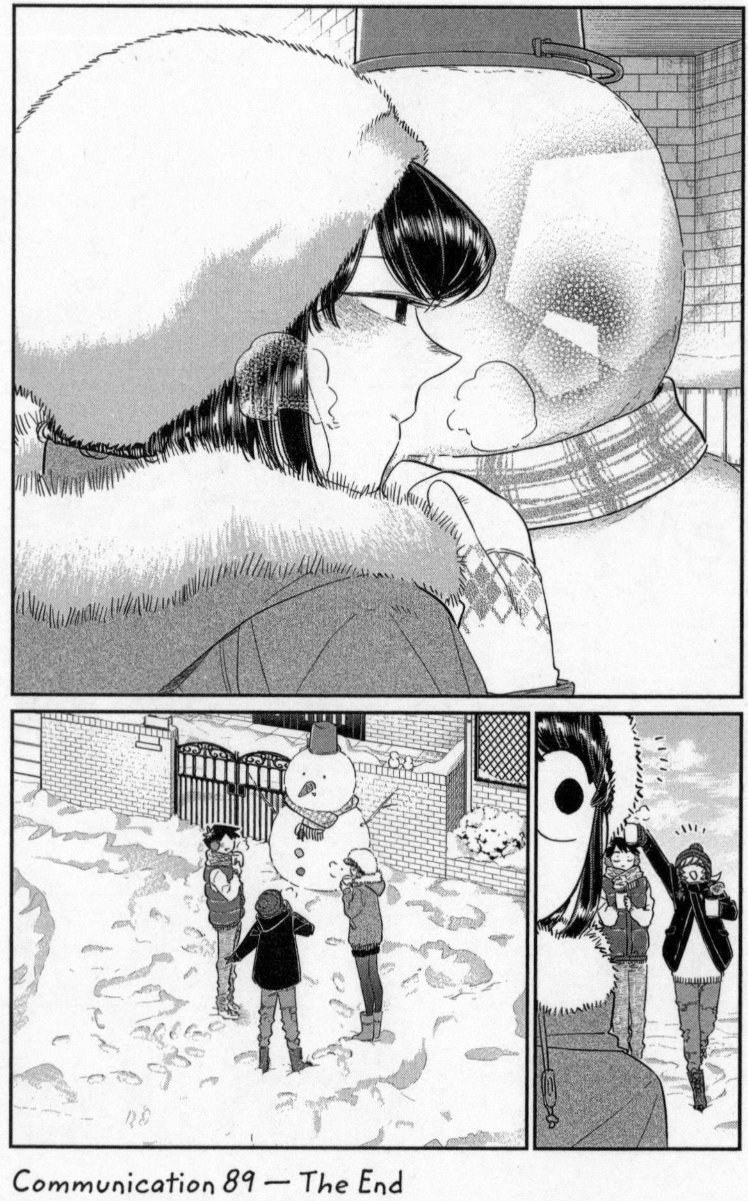

Communication 89 — The End

Komi Can't Communicate

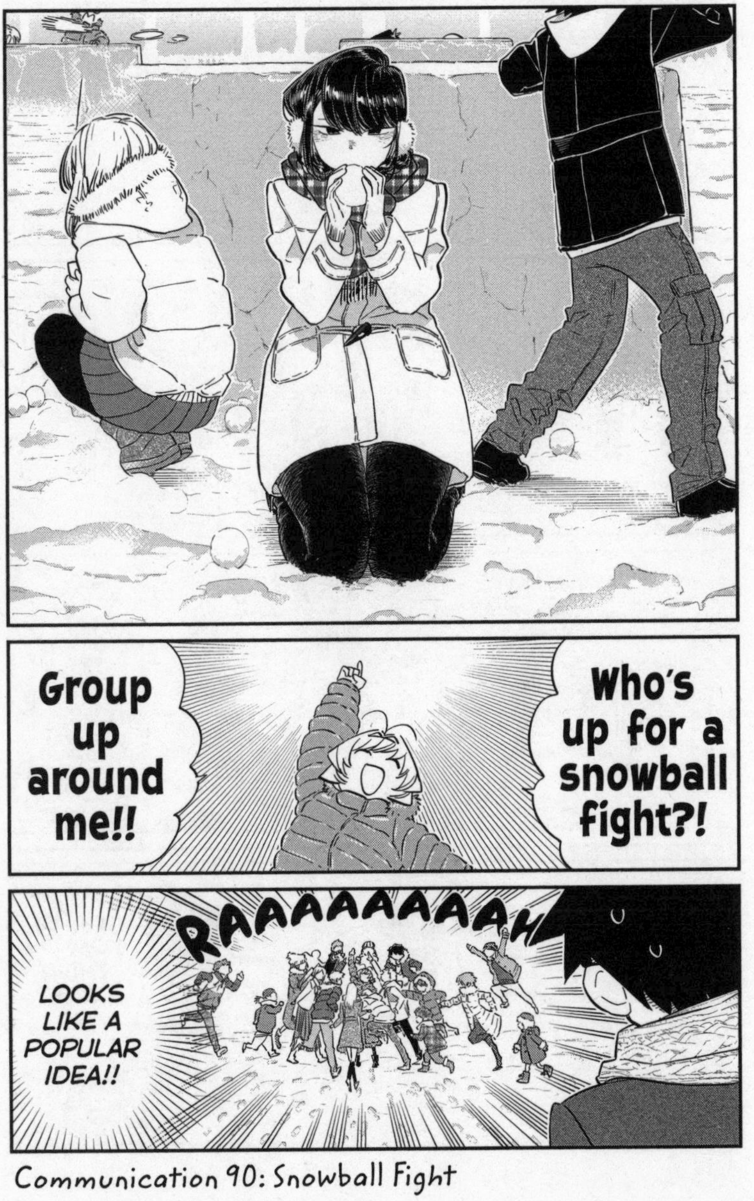
Who's up for a snowball fight?!
Group up around me!!
RAAAAAAAAH
LOOKS LIKE A POPULAR IDEA!!

Communication 90: Snowball Fight

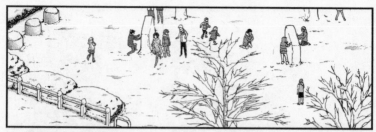

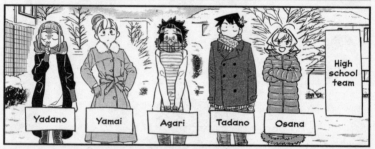

High school team
Osana
Tadano
Agari
Yamai
Yadano
Komi
Oki
Saiko
Michisato
Shiota
Elementary school team
WHY IS KOMI ON *THEIR* TEAM?
THEY WERE SHORT ONE PLAYER! AH HA HA!
Ebullient
TREMMMBLE
I SUSPECT THERE'S ANOTHER REASON ...

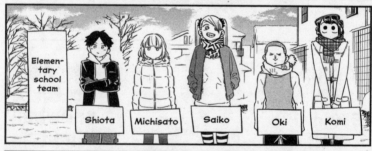

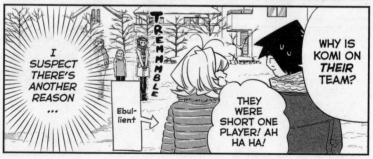

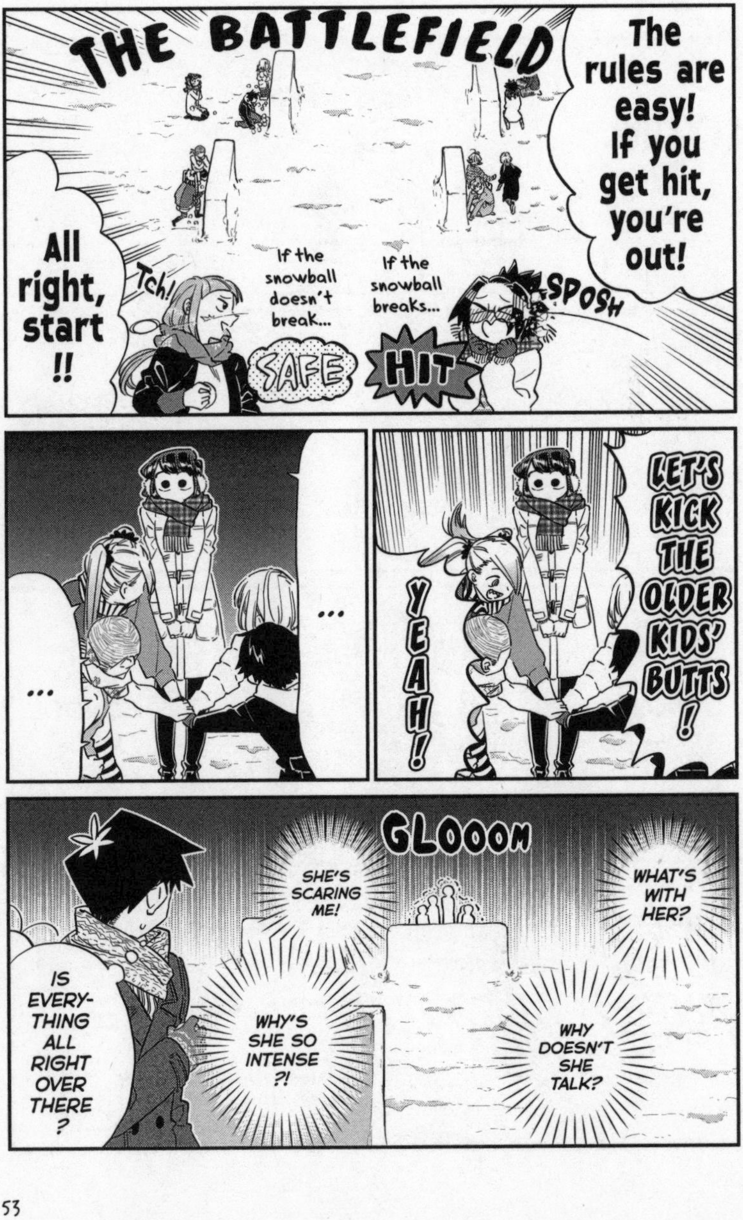
THE BATTLEFIELD
The rules are easy! If you get hit, you're out!
SPOSH
If the snowball breaks...
HIT
If the snowball doesn't break...
SAFE
Tch!
All right, start!!
LET'S KICK THE OLDER KIDS' BUTTS!
YEAH!
...
...
GLOOOM
WHAT'S WITH HER?
SHE'S SCARING ME!
WHY DOESN'T SHE TALK?
WHY'S SHE SO INTENSE?!
IS EVERY-THING ALL RIGHT OVER THERE?

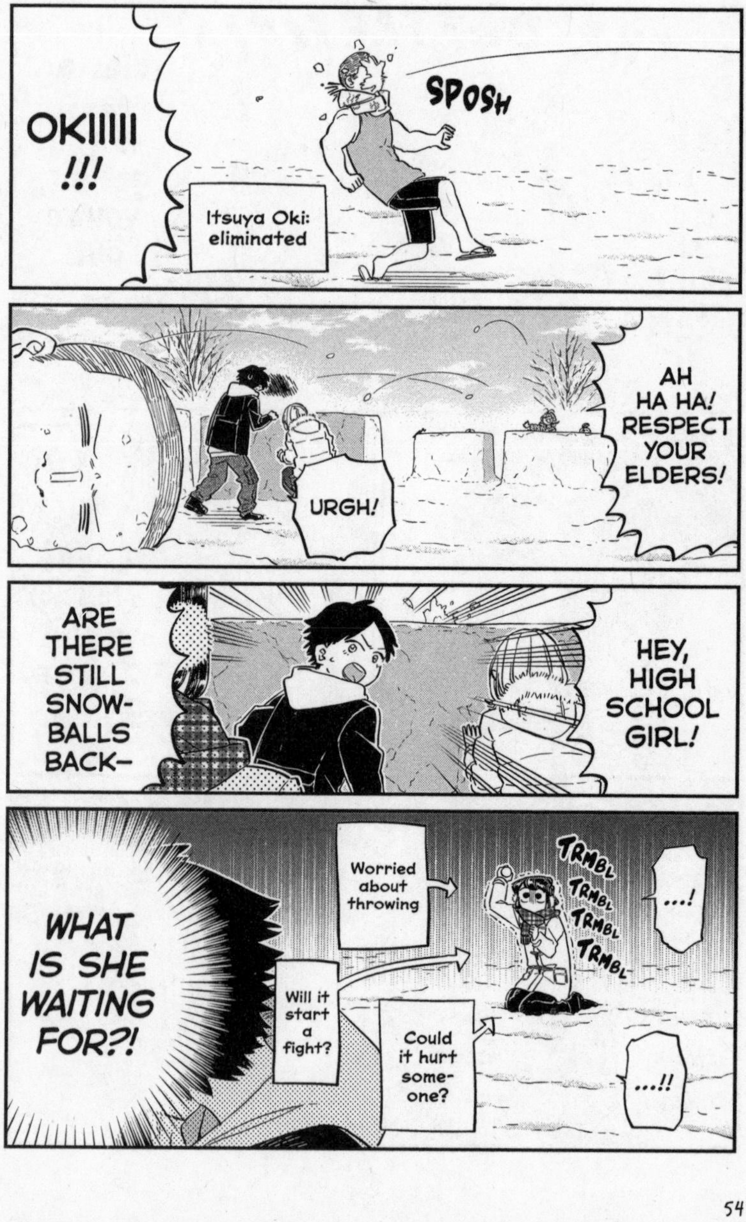
SPOSH
OKIIIII !!!
Itsuya Oki: eliminated
AH HA HA! RESPECT YOUR ELDERS!
URGH!
HEY, HIGH SCHOOL GIRL!
ARE THERE STILL SNOW-BALLS BACK–
...!
TRMBL TRMBL TRMBL TRMBL
Worried about throwing
...!!
Could it hurt some-one?
Will it start a fight?
WHAT IS SHE WAITING FOR?!

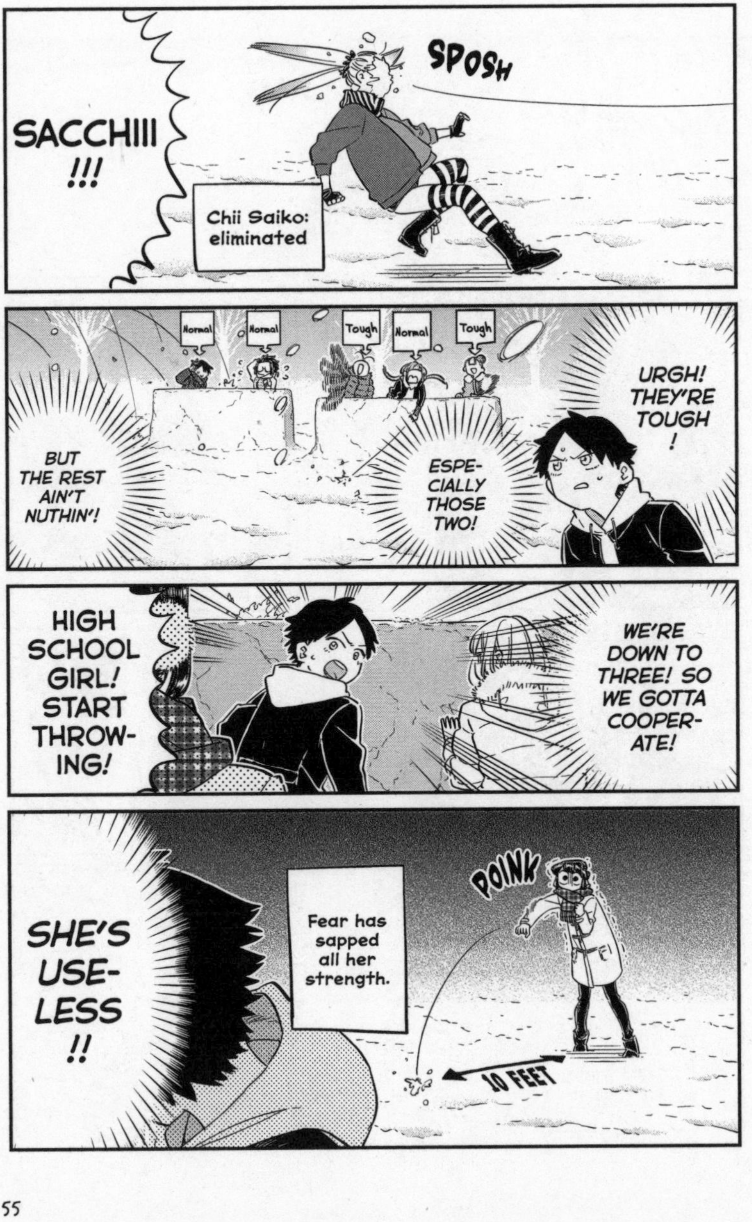
SPOSH
Chii Saiko: eliminated
SACCHIII !!!
Tough
Normal
Tough
Normal
Normal
URGH! THEY'RE TOUGH!
ESPECIALLY THOSE TWO!
BUT THE REST AIN'T NUTHIN'!
WE'RE DOWN TO THREE! SO WE GOTTA COOPERATE!
HIGH SCHOOL GIRL! START THROWING!
POINK
10 FEET
Fear has sapped all her strength.
SHE'S USELESS !!

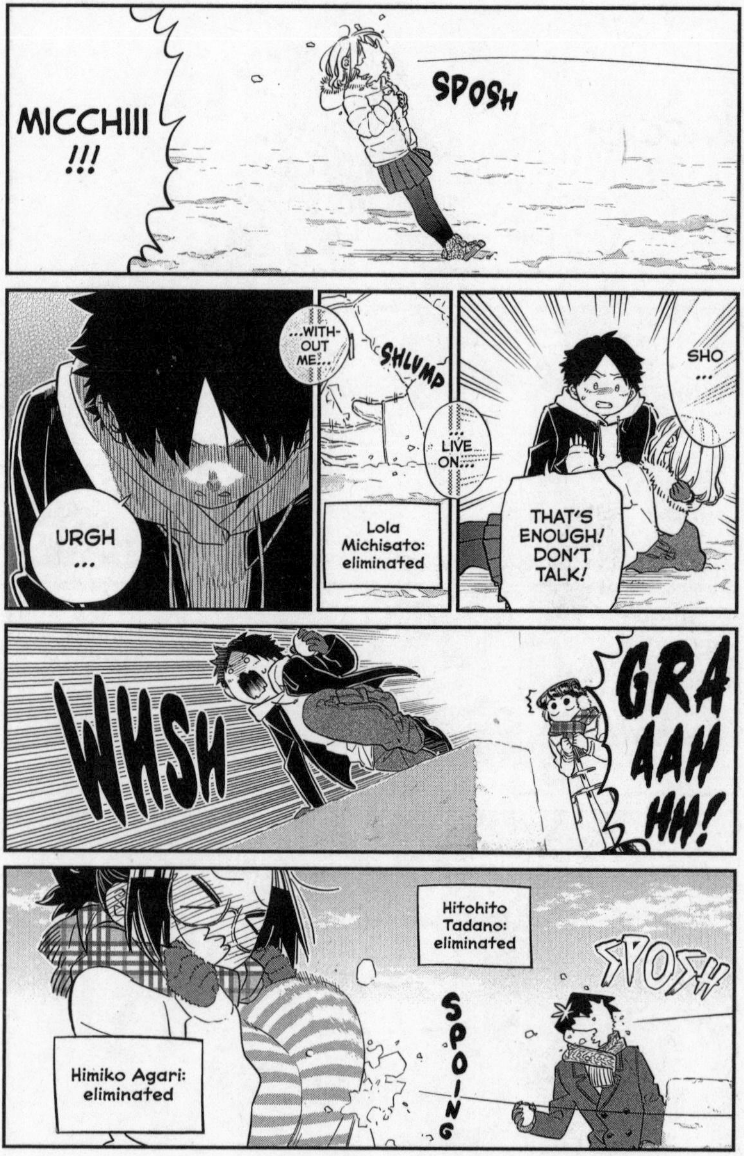
SPOSH
MICCHIII !!!
SHO ...
THAT'S ENOUGH! DON'T TALK!
SHLUMP
...WITH-OUT ME...
... LIVE ON...
Lola Michisato: eliminated
URGH ...
GRAAAHHH!
WHSH
SPOSH
Hitohito Tadano: eliminated
SPOING
Himiko Agari: eliminated

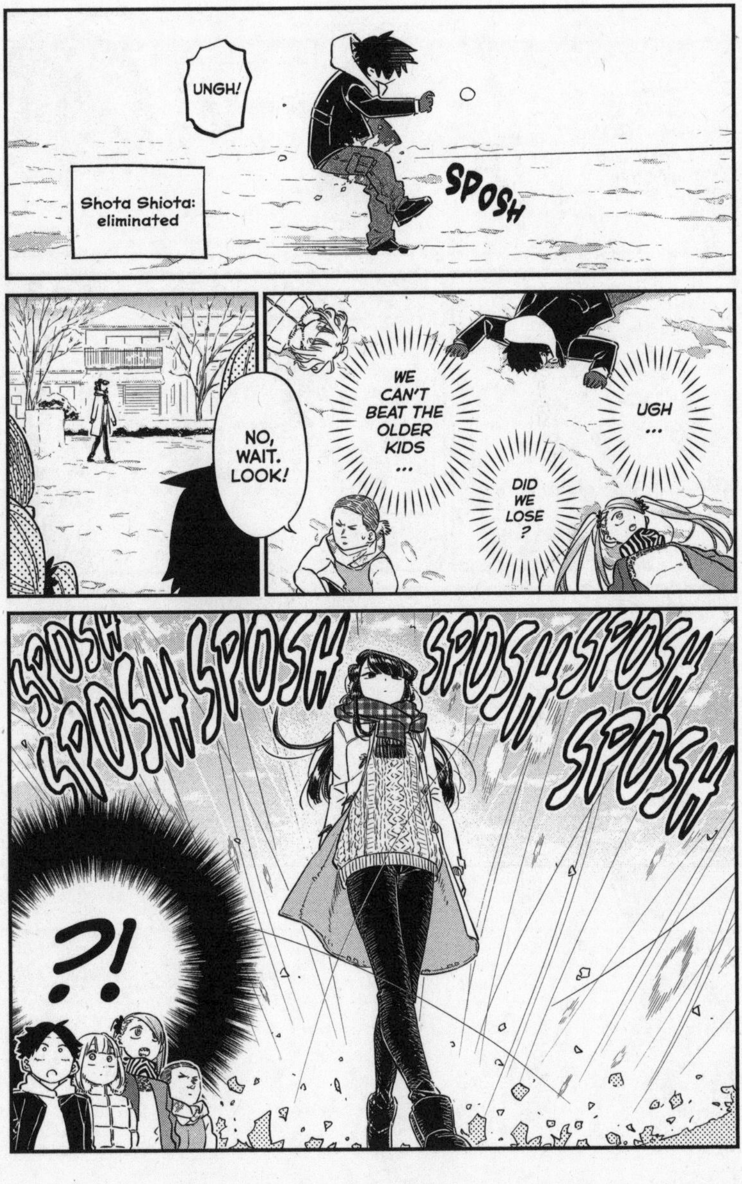
UNGH!
SPOSH
Shota Shiota: eliminated
UGH ...
WE CAN'T BEAT THE OLDER KIDS ...
DID WE LOSE ?
NO, WAIT. LOOK!
SPOSH SPOSH SPOSH
SPOSH SPOSH SPOSH SPOSH
SPOSH
?!

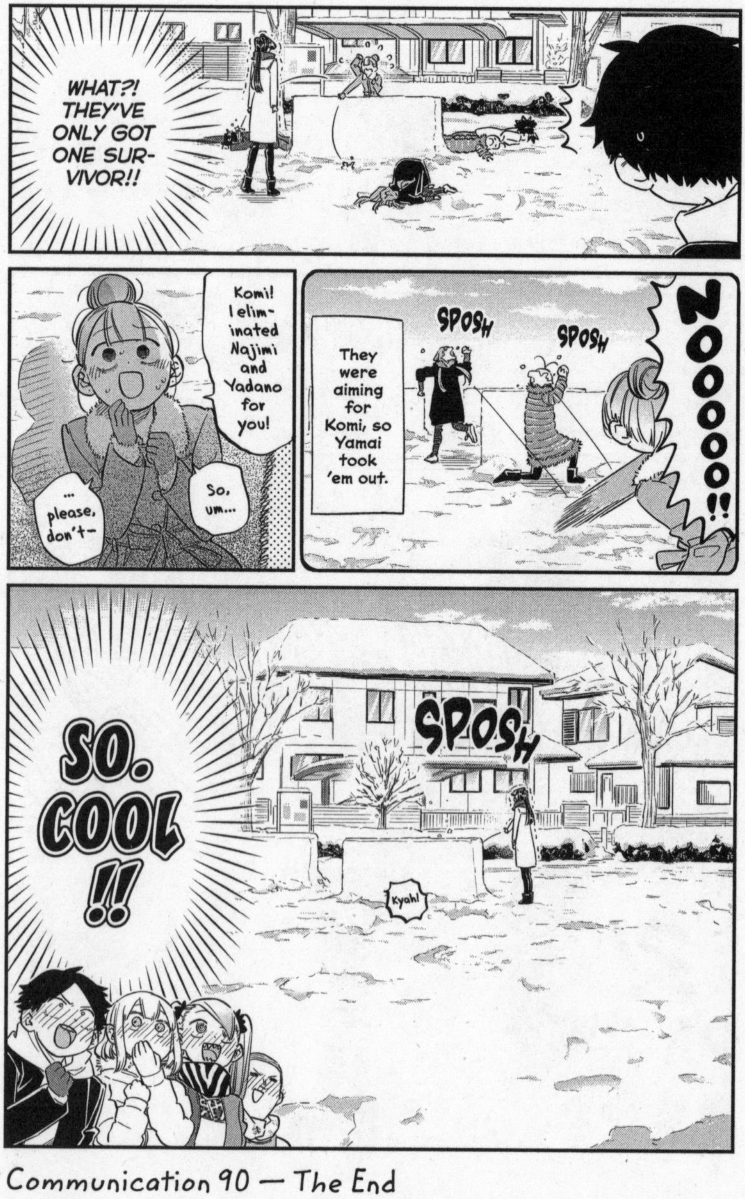
WHAT?! THEY'VE ONLY GOT ONE SUR-VIVOR!!
NOOOOOO!!
SPOSH
SPOSH
They were aiming for Komi, so Yamai took 'em out.
Komi! I elim-inated Najimi and Yadano for you!
So, um...
... please, don't-
SPOSH
SO. COOL!!
Kyah!

Communication 90 — The End

THE LITTLE KIDS' RELATIONSHIPS

Likes

A special feeling beyond mere friendship

Likes

Komi Can't
Communicate

Komi Can't Communicate

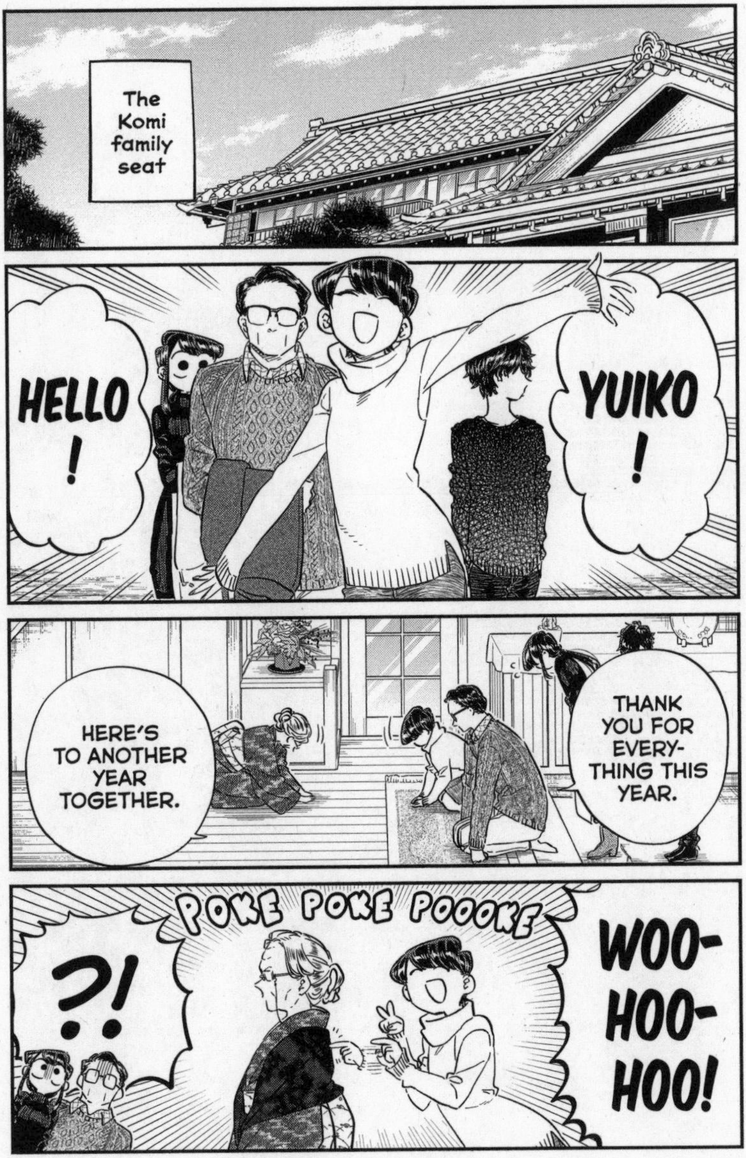
The Komi family seat
YUIKO!
HELLO!
THANK YOU FOR EVERYTHING THIS YEAR.
HERE'S TO ANOTHER YEAR TOGETHER.
WOO-HOO-HOO!
POKE POKE POOOKE
?!

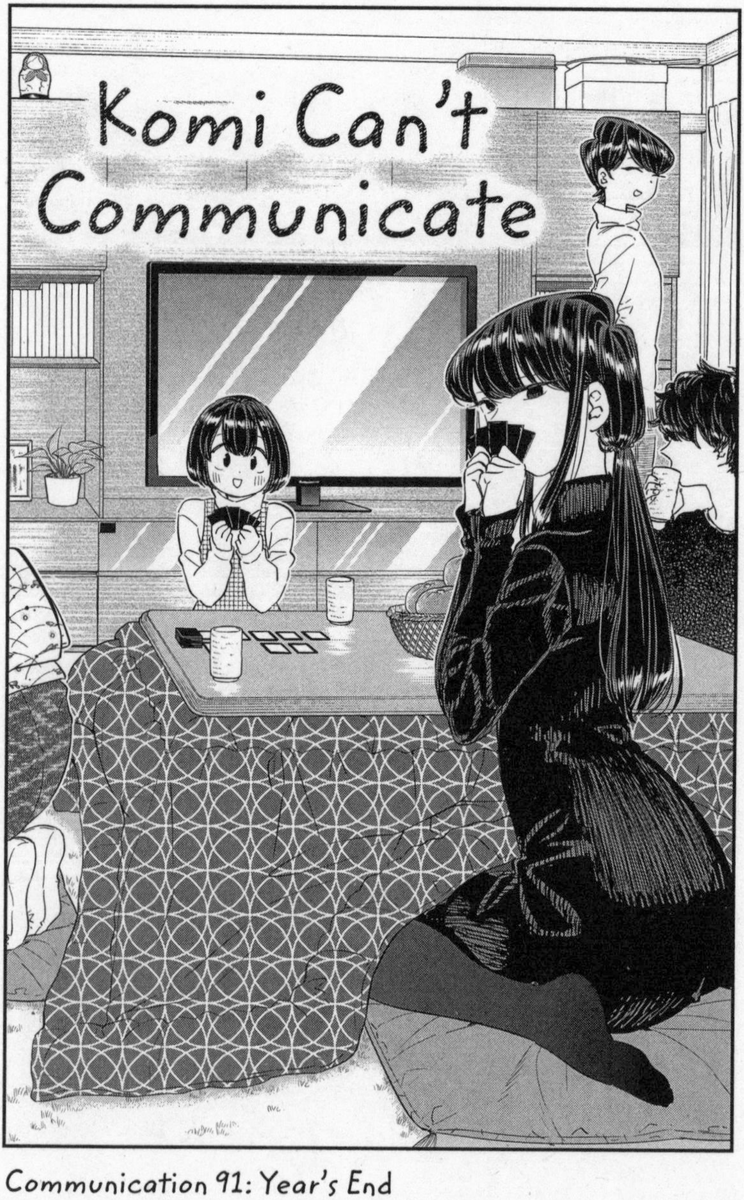
Komi Can't Communicate

Communication 91: Year's End

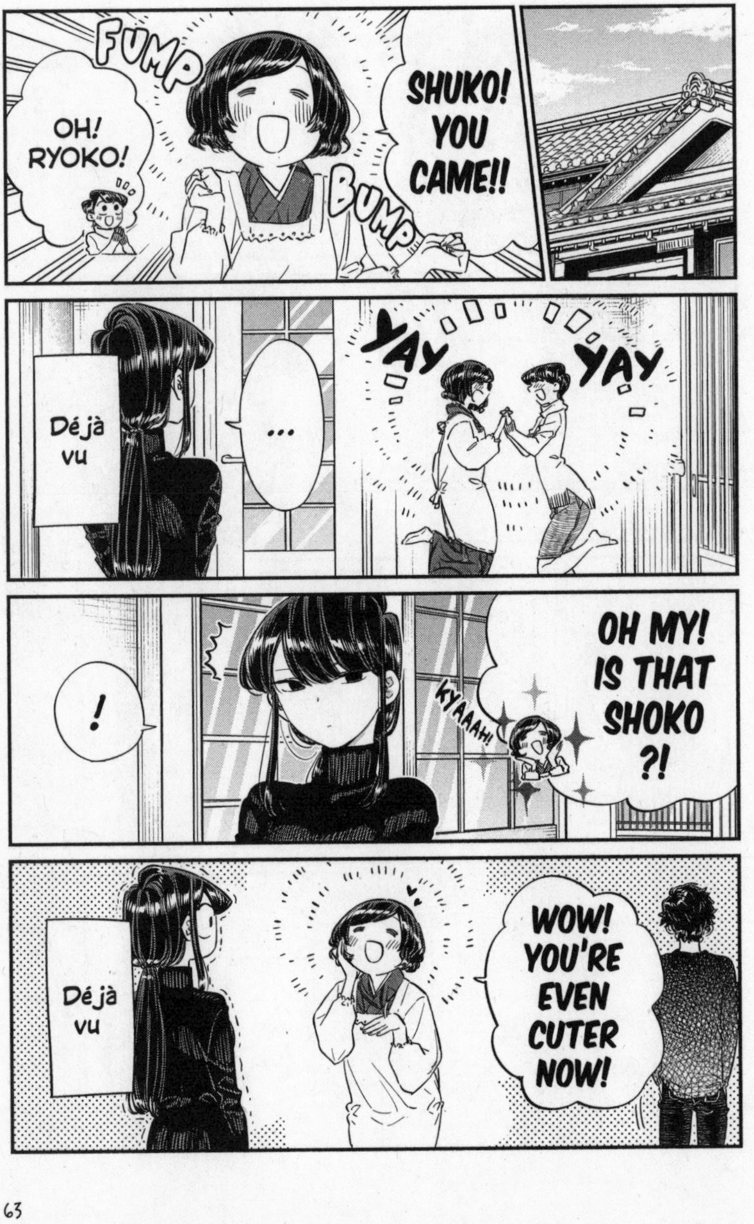
SHUKO! YOU CAME!!
FUMP
BUMP
OH! RYOKO!
YAY
YAY
...
Déjà vu
OH MY! IS THAT SHOKO ?!
KYAAAH!
!
WOW! YOU'RE EVEN CUTER NOW!
Déjà vu

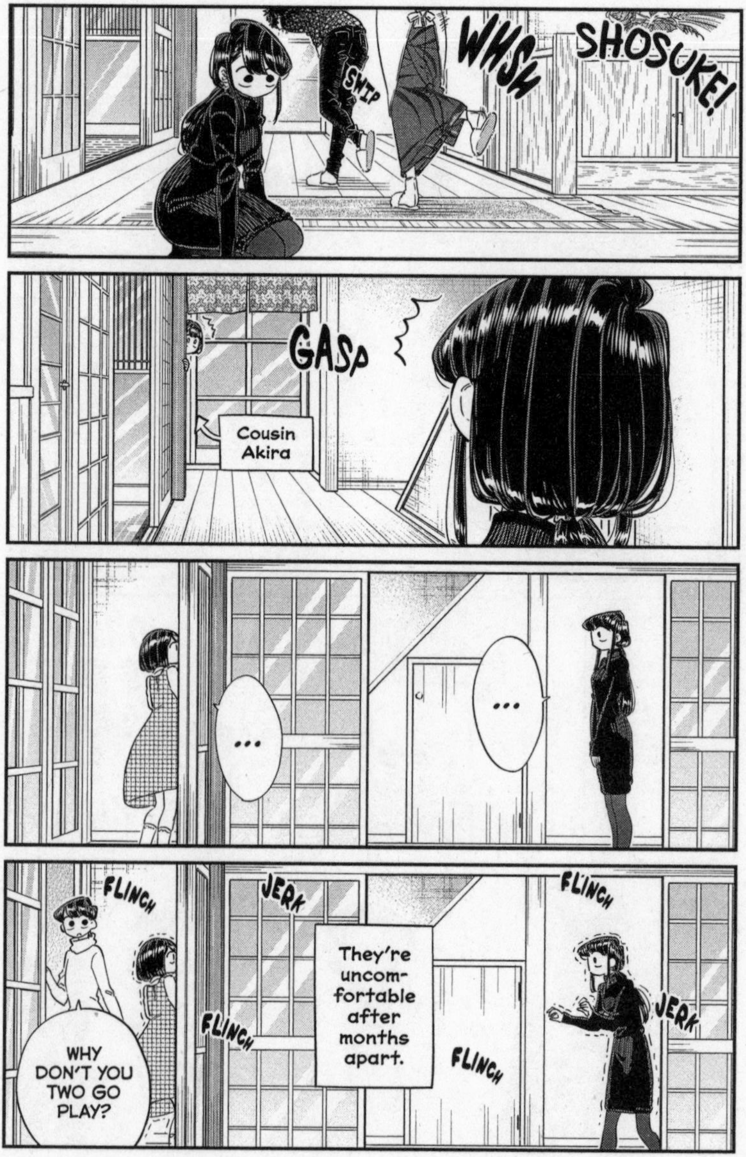
SHOSUKE!
WHSH
SWIP
GASP
Cousin Akira
...
...
FLINCH
JERK
They're uncomfortable after months apart.
FLINCH
FLINCH
JERK
FLINCH
WHY DON'T YOU TWO GO PLAY?

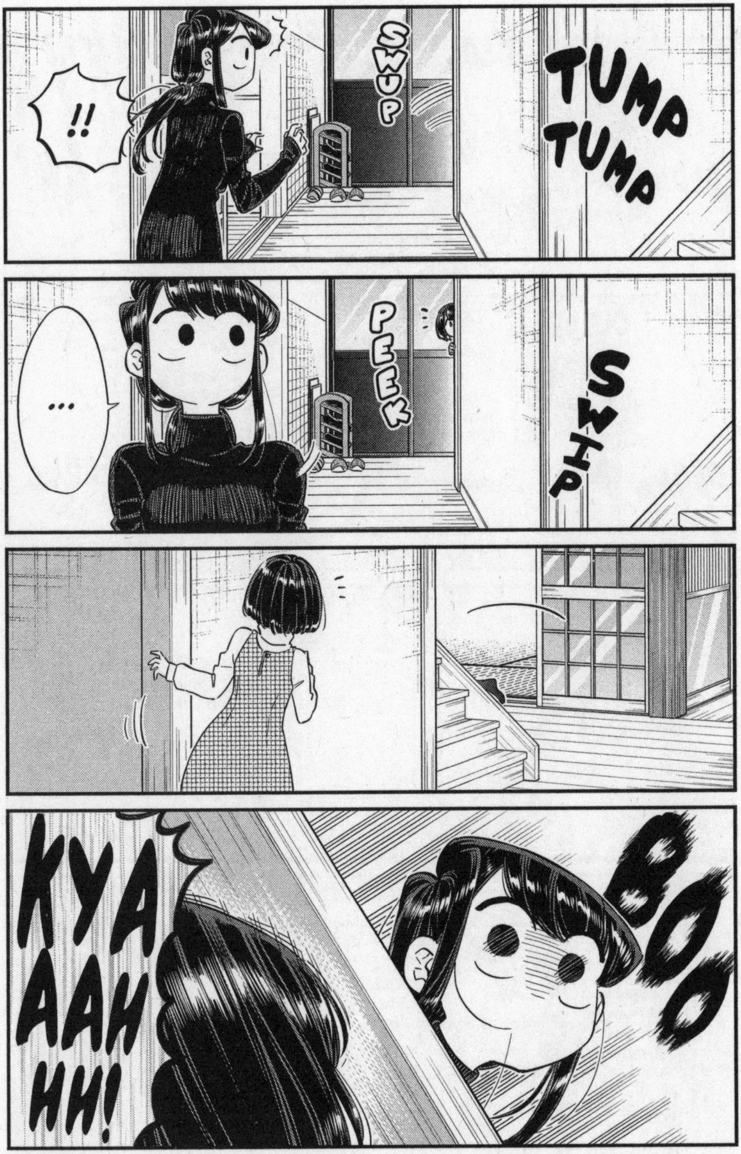
TUMP TUMP
SWUP
!!
SWIP
PEEK
...
BOO
KYAAAHHH!

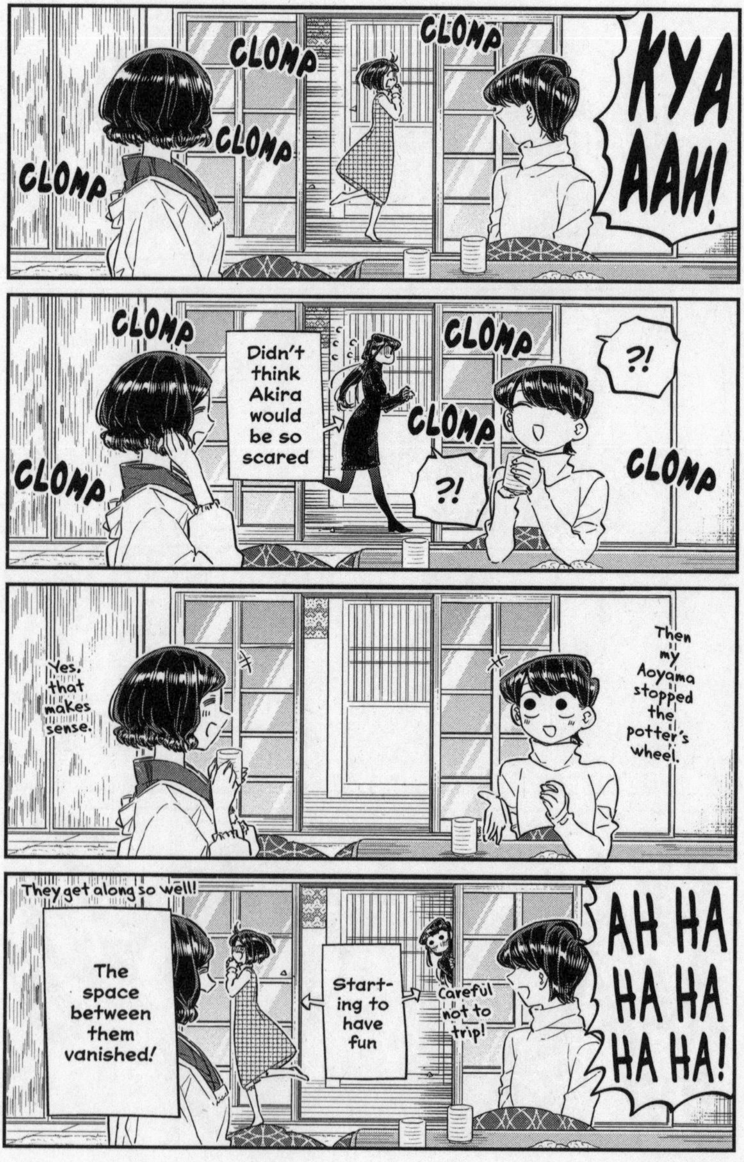
KYA AAH!
CLOMP
CLOMP
CLOMP
CLOMP
?!
CLOMP
CLOMP
CLOMP
?!
CLOMP
Didn't think Akira would be so scared
CLOMP
Then my Aoyama stopped the potter's wheel.
Yes, that makes sense.
AH HA HA HA HA HA!
Careful not to trip!
Start-ing to have fun
They get along so well!
The space between them vanished!

SHOKO! LET'S PLAY HANAFUDA CARDS!
BOUNCE BOUNCE
!
NOD
WA AAA AAH HH!
SUDDEN TEARS
?!
?!
?!
Waaaaah!
AKIRA CRIES WHEN SHE'S HAPPY.
Waaaaah!
Try to cheer her up.
?!
WA AAA AAH HH!
SWIP
SWIP
SWIP
SKILLED DEALER
?!

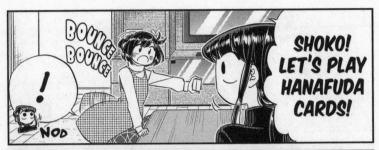

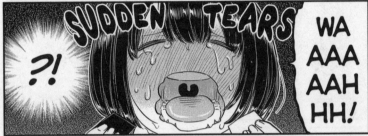

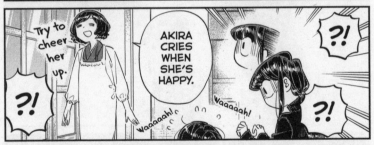

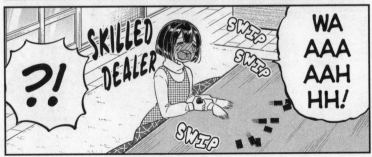

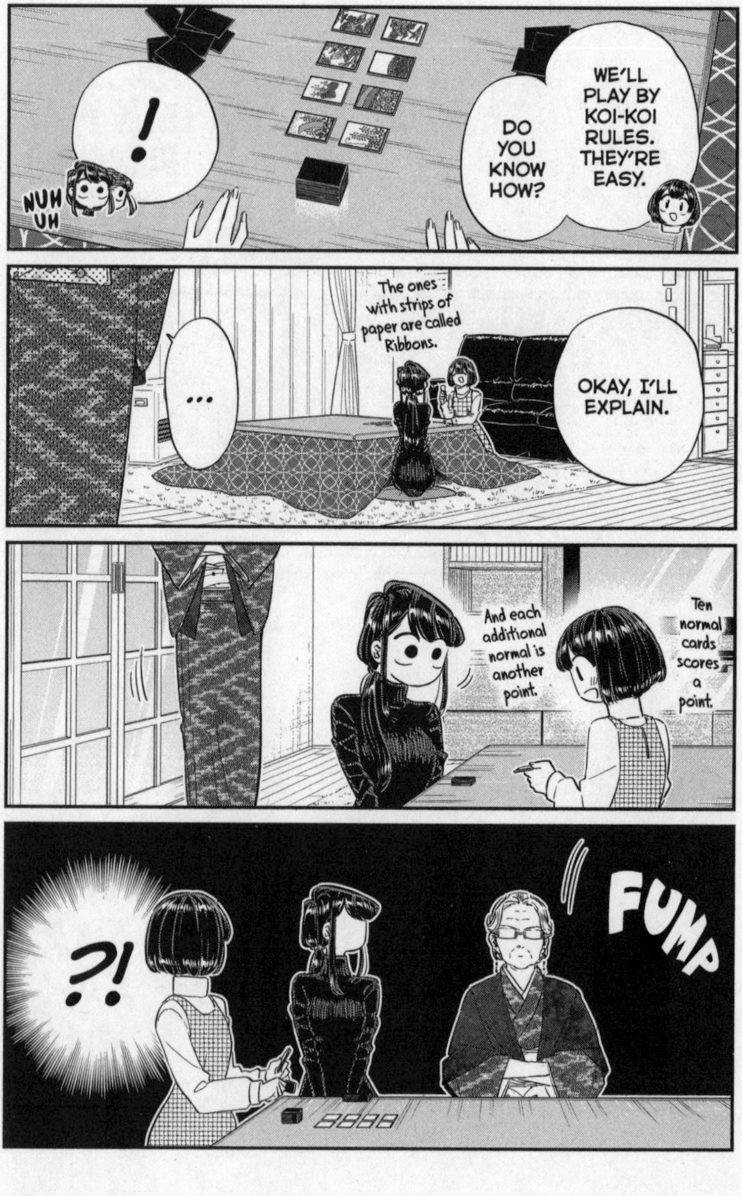
WE'LL PLAY BY KOI-KOI RULES. THEY'RE EASY.
DO YOU KNOW HOW?
!
NUH UH
OKAY, I'LL EXPLAIN.
The ones with strips of paper are called Ribbons.
...
Ten normal cards scores a point.
And each additional normal is another point.
FUMP
?!

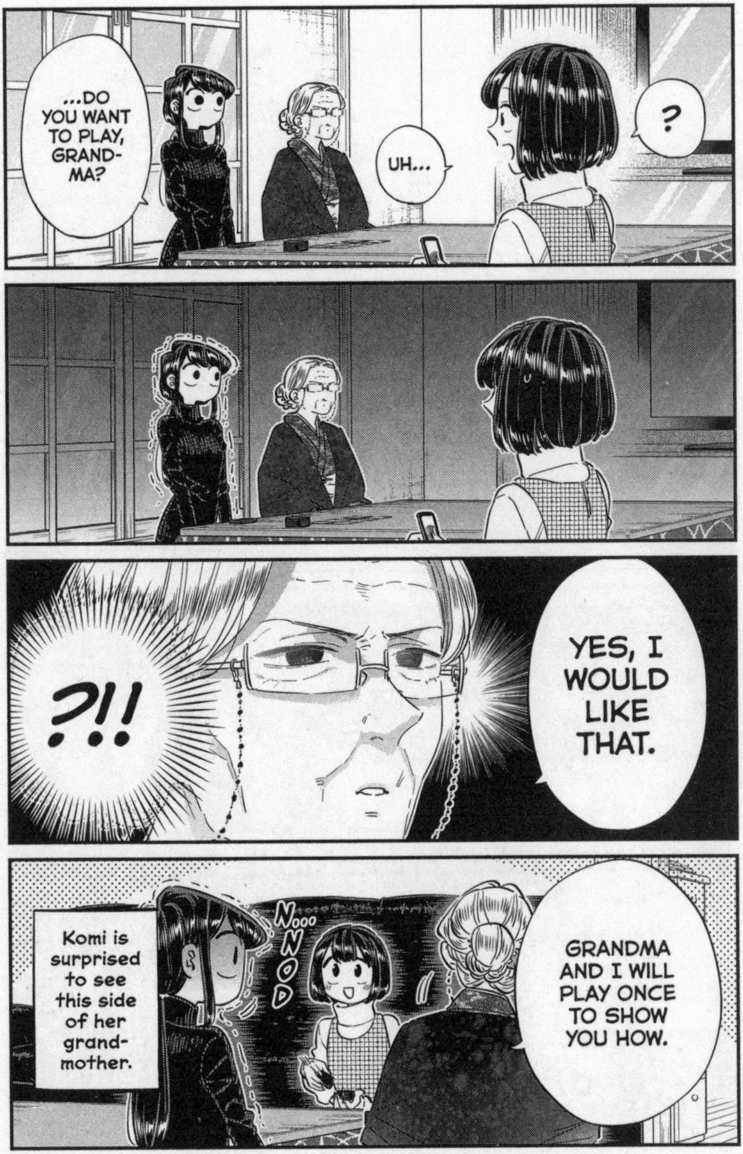
?
UH...
...DO YOU WANT TO PLAY, GRANDMA?
YES, I WOULD LIKE THAT.
?!!
GRANDMA AND I WILL PLAY ONCE TO SHOW YOU HOW.
NOOO NOD
Komi is surprised to see this side of her grandmother.

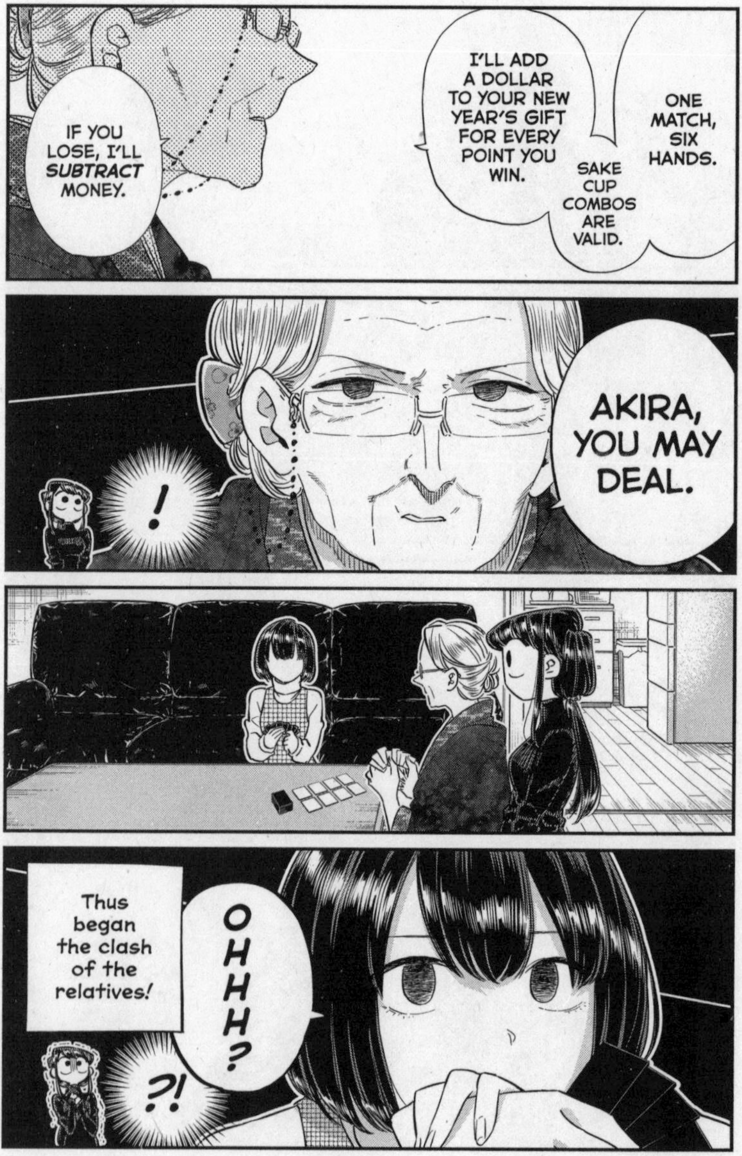
ONE MATCH, SIX HANDS.
SAKE CUP COMBOS ARE VALID.
I'LL ADD A DOLLAR TO YOUR NEW YEAR'S GIFT FOR EVERY POINT YOU WIN.
IF YOU LOSE, I'LL *SUBTRACT* MONEY.
AKIRA, YOU MAY DEAL.
!
OHHH?
Thus began the clash of the relatives!
?!

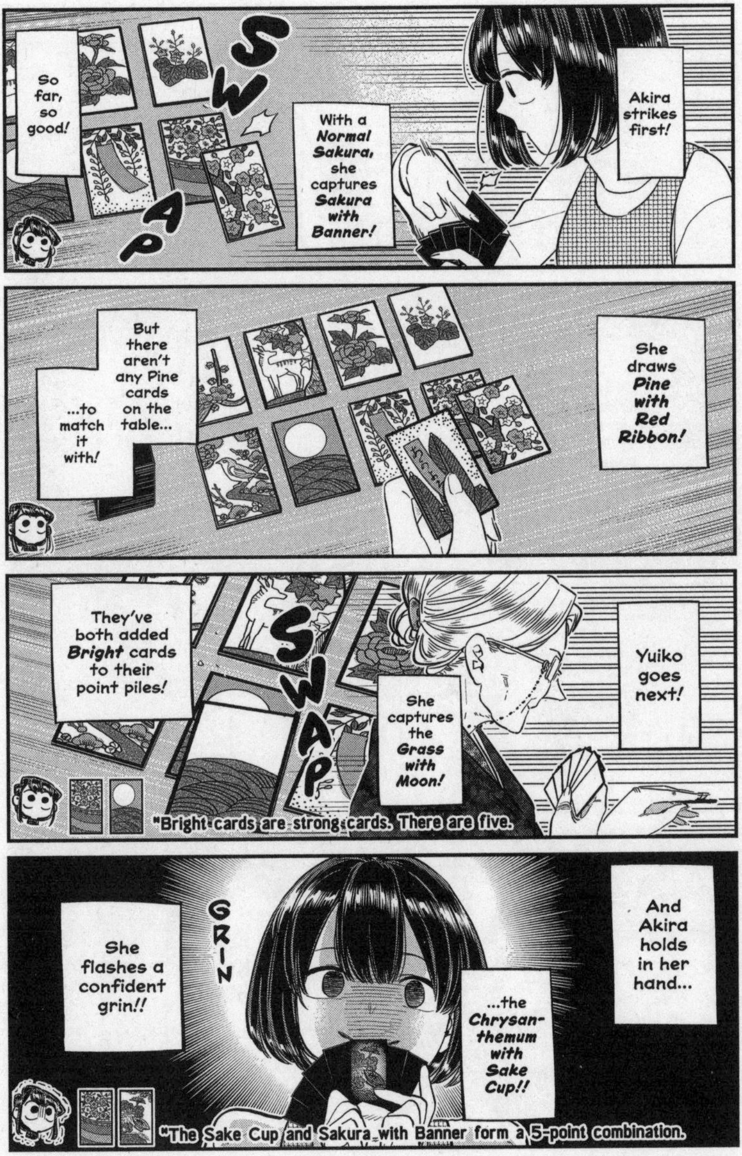
Akira strikes first!
With a *Normal Sakura*, she captures *Sakura with Banner*!
SWAP
So far, so good!
She draws *Pine with Red Ribbon*!
But there aren't any Pine cards on the table...
...to match it with!
Yuiko goes next!
She captures the *Grass with Moon*!
SWAP
They've both added *Bright* cards to their point piles!
*Bright cards are strong cards. There are five.
And Akira holds in her hand...
...the *Chrysanthemum with Sake Cup*!!
GRIN
She flashes a confident grin!!
*The Sake Cup and Sakura with Banner form a 5-point combination.

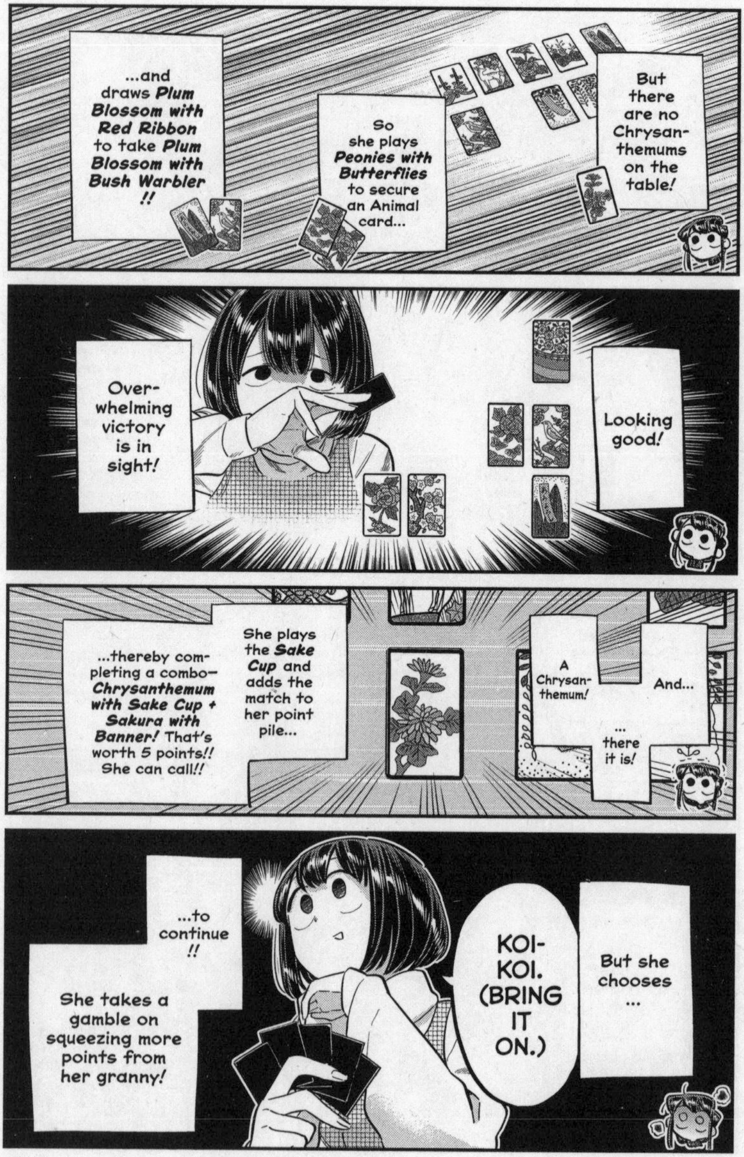
But there are no Chrysanthemums on the table!
So she plays Peonies with Butterflies to secure an Animal card...
...and draws Plum Blossom with Red Ribbon to take Plum Blossom with Bush Warbler!!
Looking good!
Overwhelming victory is in sight!
And...
...there it is!
A Chrysanthemum!
She plays the Sake Cup and adds the match to her point pile...
...thereby completing a combo—Chrysanthemum with Sake Cup + Sakura with Banner! That's worth 5 points!! She can call!!
But she chooses...
KOI-KOI. (BRING IT ON.)
...to continue!!
She takes a gamble on squeezing more points from her granny!

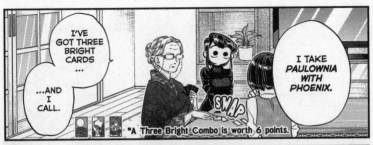

I TAKE PAULOWNIA WITH PHOENIX.
SWAP
I'VE GOT THREE BRIGHT CARDS ...
...AND I CALL.
*A Three Bright Combo is worth 6 points.
Defeat!
Sudden defeat!!
BDUMP
She got carried away and ignored her opponent's cards!
Pride goeth before the fall!
BUT THERE'S MORE TO IT...
GRANDMA'S GOT SKILLS!
SHE WON WITH THREE BRIGHTS!
THE NEXT FIVE HANDS WILL BE INTENSE!!
Here are the rules!
Um, I call.
SAFE
HAVE COMBOS
Koi-koi!
Bring it on!
When you have a combination, you may call or continue.
Choosing to continue means you intend to get more combinations.

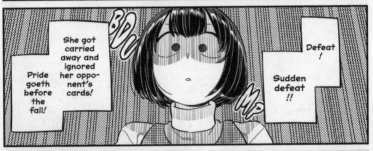

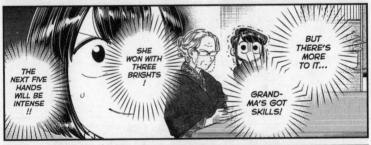

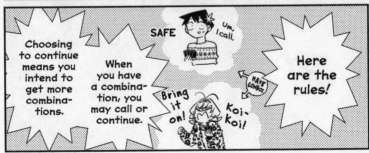

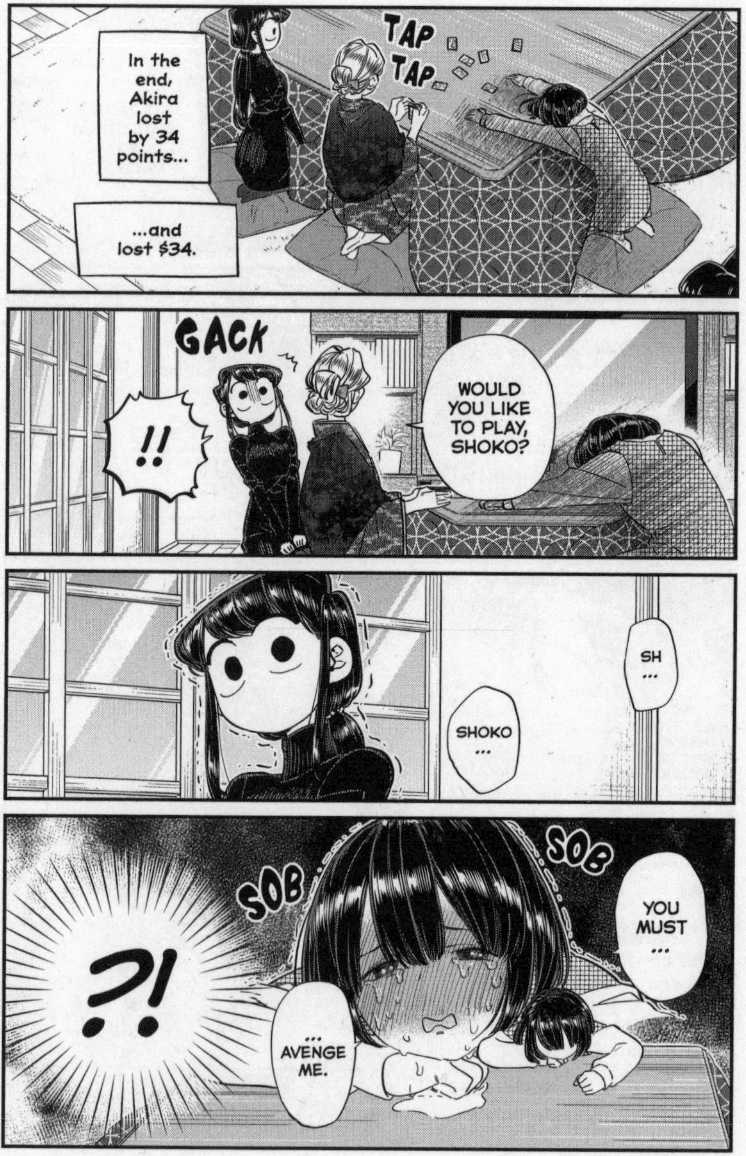
TAP
TAP
In the end, Akira lost by 34 points...
...and lost $34.
WOULD YOU LIKE TO PLAY, SHOKO?
GACK
!!
SH...
SHOKO...
SOB
YOU MUST...
SOB
?!
...AVENGE ME.

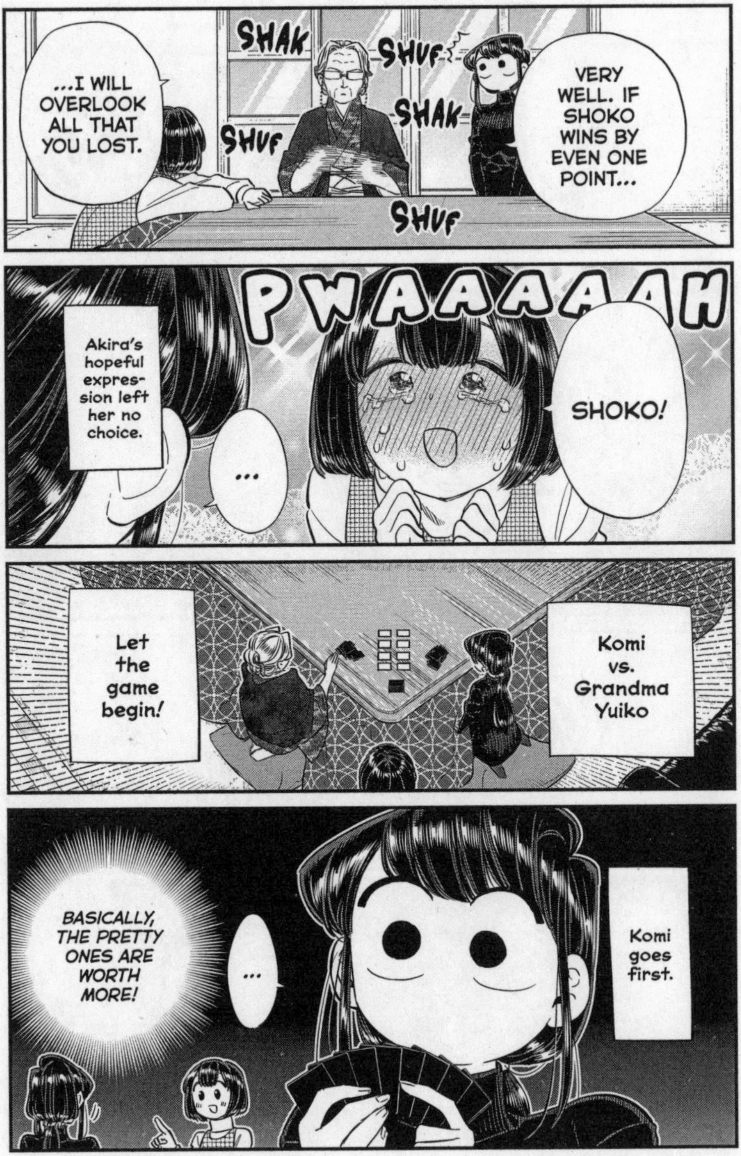
VERY WELL. IF SHOKO WINS BY EVEN ONE POINT...
SHUF
SHAK
SHUF
SHAK
SHUF
SHUF
...I WILL OVERLOOK ALL THAT YOU LOST.
PWAAAAAAH
SHOKO!
...
Akira's hopeful expression left her no choice.
Komi vs. Grandma Yuiko
Let the game begin!
Komi goes first.
...
BASICALLY, THE PRETTY ONES ARE WORTH MORE!

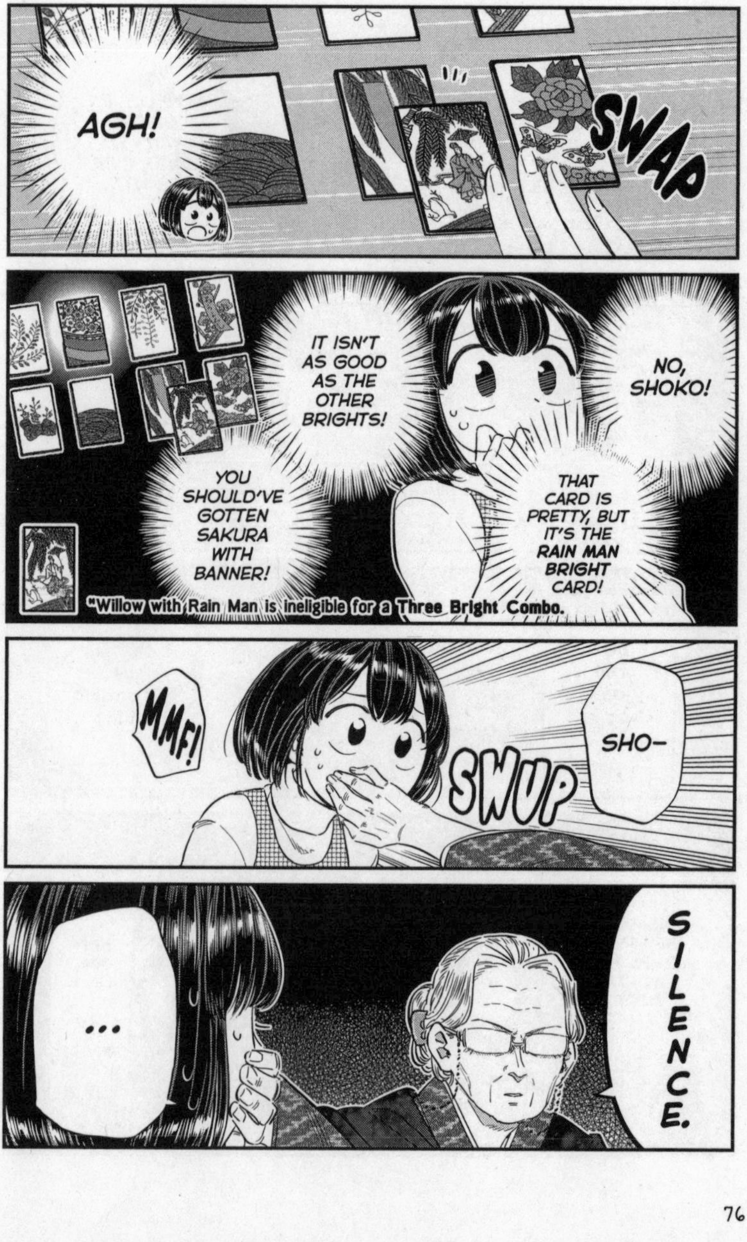
SWAP
AGH!
NO, SHOKO!
THAT CARD IS PRETTY, BUT IT'S THE RAIN MAN BRIGHT CARD!
IT ISN'T AS GOOD AS THE OTHER BRIGHTS!
YOU SHOULD'VE GOTTEN SAKURA WITH BANNER!
*Willow with Rain Man is ineligible for a Three Bright Combo.
SHO-
SWUP
MMF!
SILENCE.
...

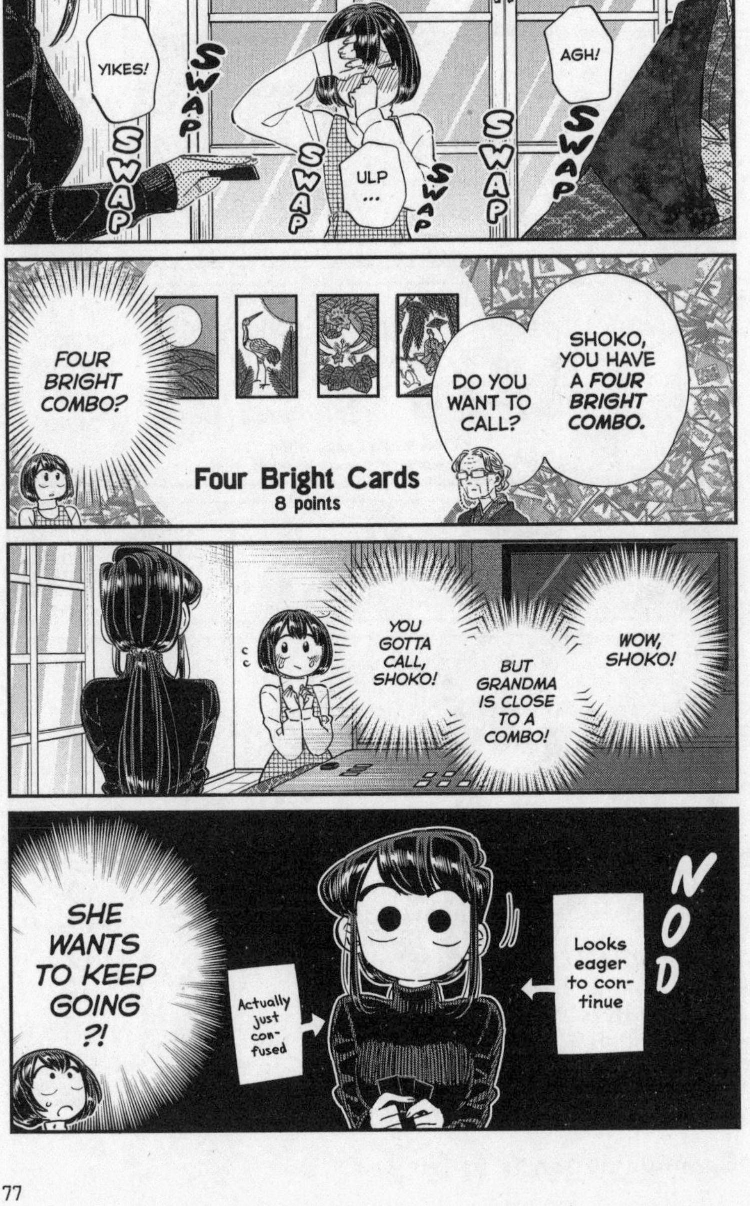
AGH!
SWAP
SWAP
SWAP
ULP...
SWAP
SWAP
YIKES!
SWAP
SHOKO, YOU HAVE A *FOUR BRIGHT COMBO.*
DO YOU WANT TO CALL?
FOUR BRIGHT COMBO?
Four Bright Cards
8 points
WOW, SHOKO!
BUT GRANDMA IS CLOSE TO A COMBO!
YOU GOTTA CALL, SHOKO!
NOD
Looks eager to continue
Actually just confused
SHE WANTS TO KEEP GOING?!

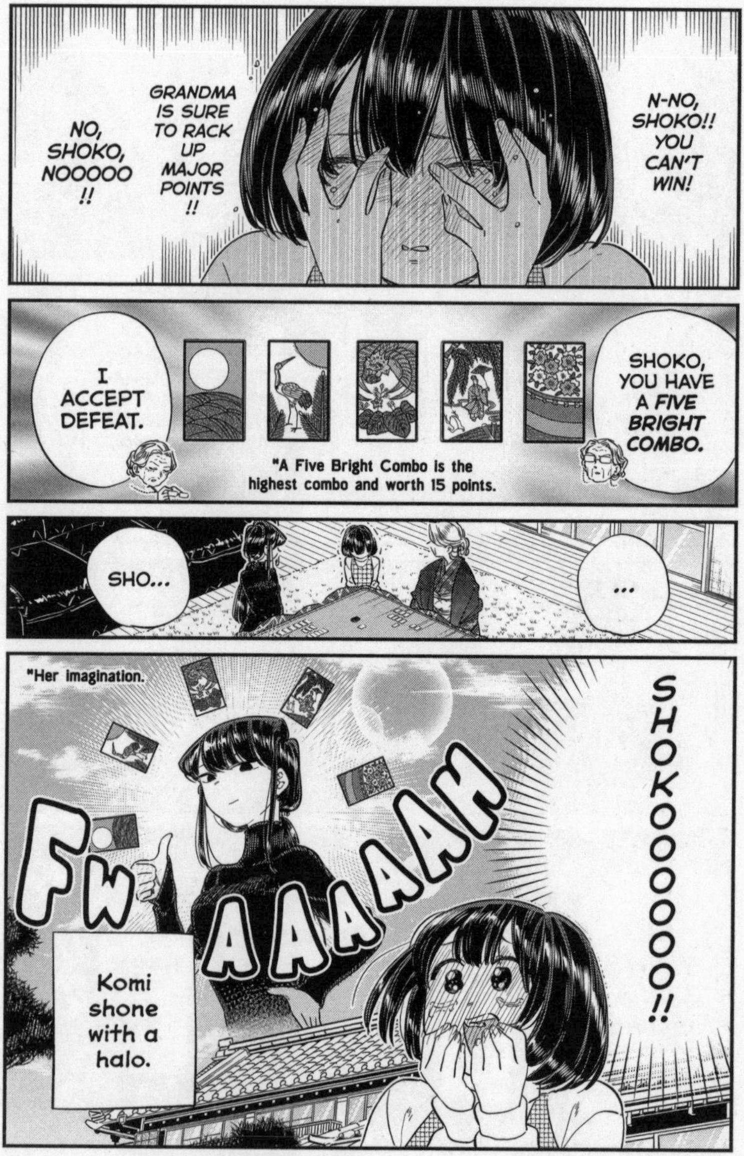
N-NO, SHOKO!! YOU CAN'T WIN!
GRANDMA IS SURE TO RACK UP MAJOR POINTS!!
NO, SHOKO, NOOOOO!!
SHOKO, YOU HAVE A *FIVE BRIGHT* COMBO.
I ACCEPT DEFEAT.
*A Five Bright Combo is the highest combo and worth 15 points.
...
SHO...
SHOKOOOOOOOO!!
*Her imagination.
FWAAAAAAH
Komi shone with a halo.

Communication 91 — The End

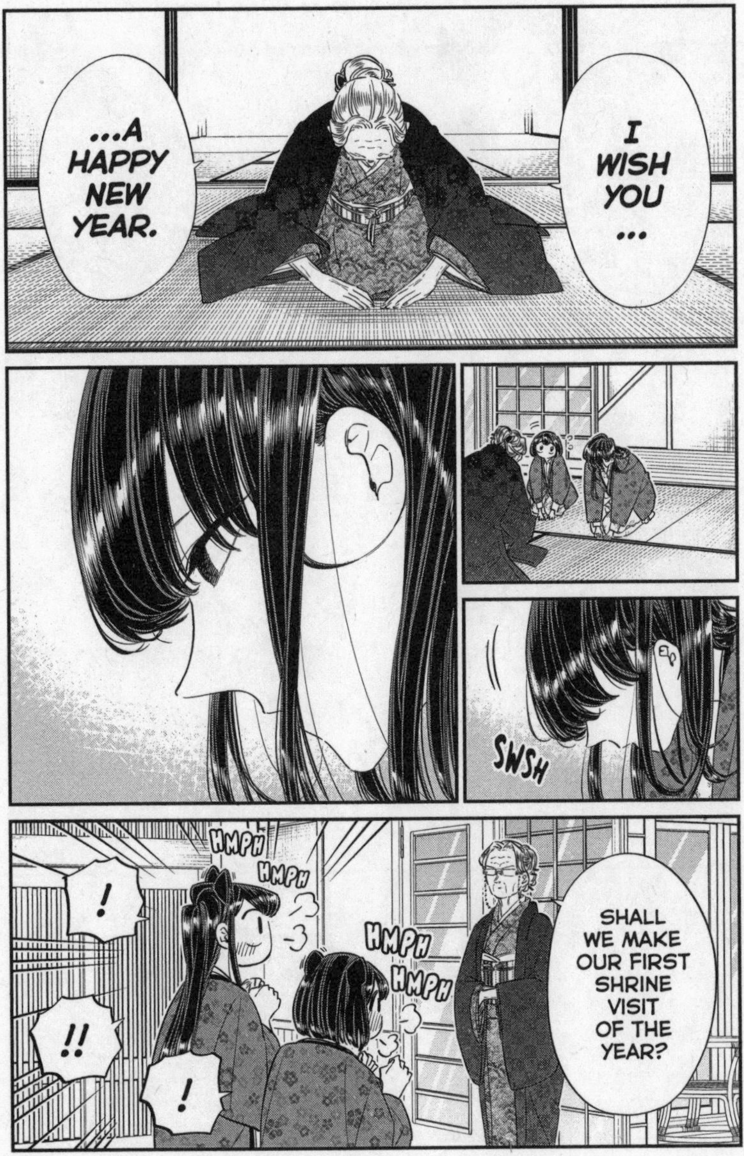
I WISH YOU ...
...A HAPPY NEW YEAR.
SWSH
SHALL WE MAKE OUR FIRST SHRINE VISIT OF THE YEAR?
HMPH HMPH
!
HMPH HMPH
!!
!

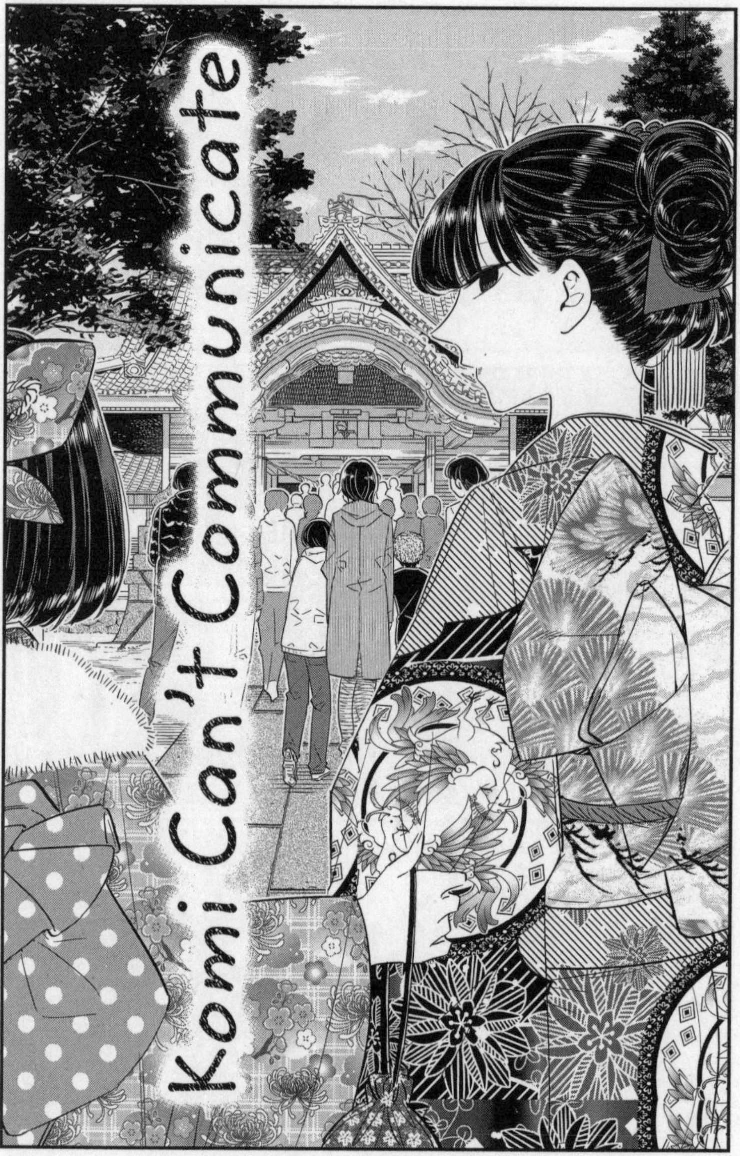
Komi Can't Communicate

Communication 92: New Year's Day

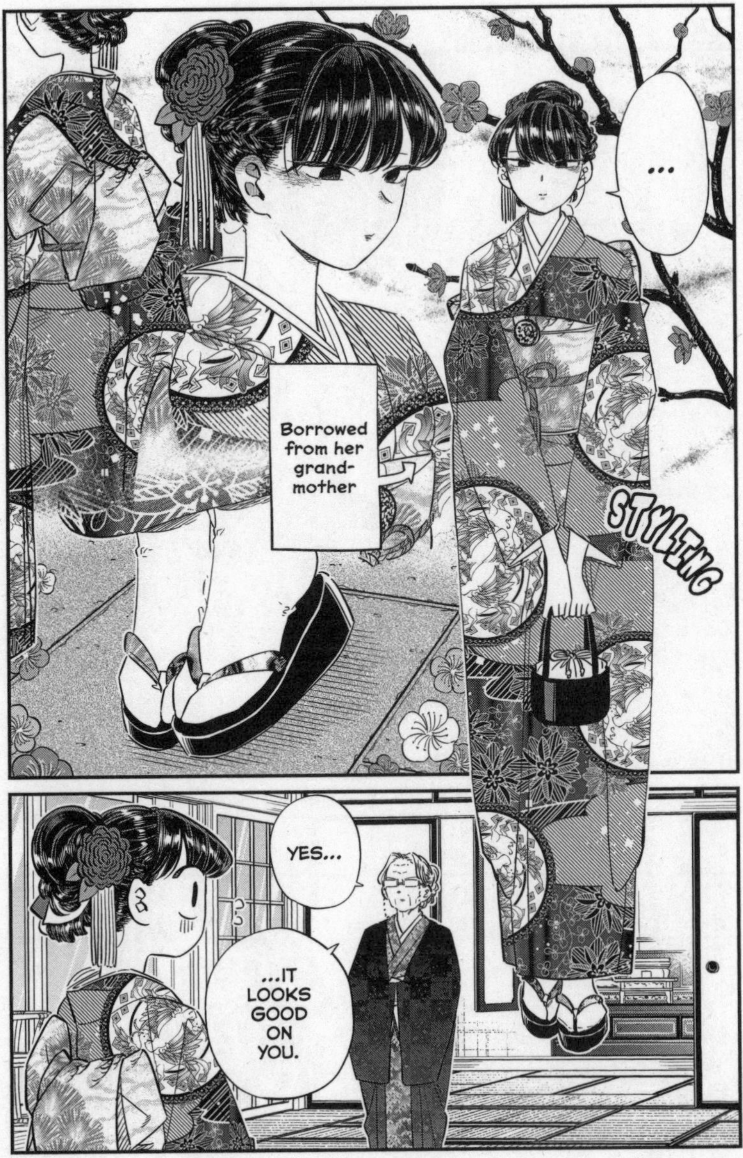
...
STYLING
Borrowed from her grand-mother
YES...
...IT LOOKS GOOD ON YOU.

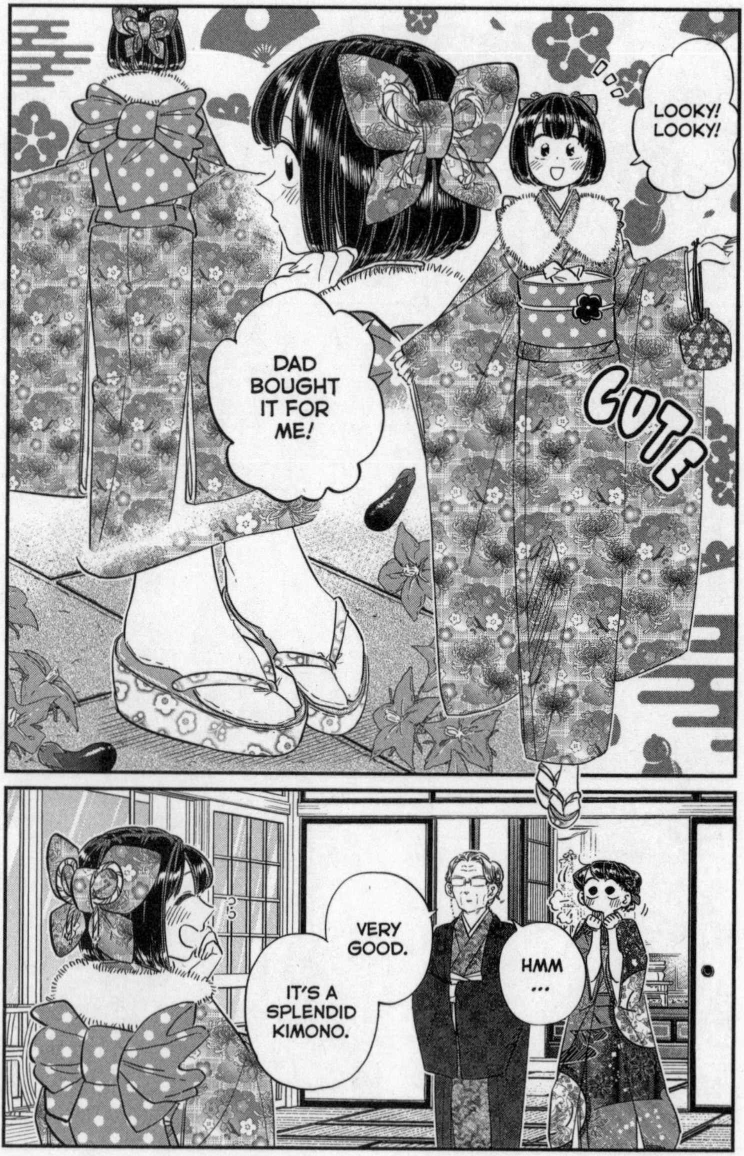
LOOKY! LOOKY!
CUTE
DAD BOUGHT IT FOR ME!
HMM ...
VERY GOOD.
IT'S A SPLENDID KIMONO.

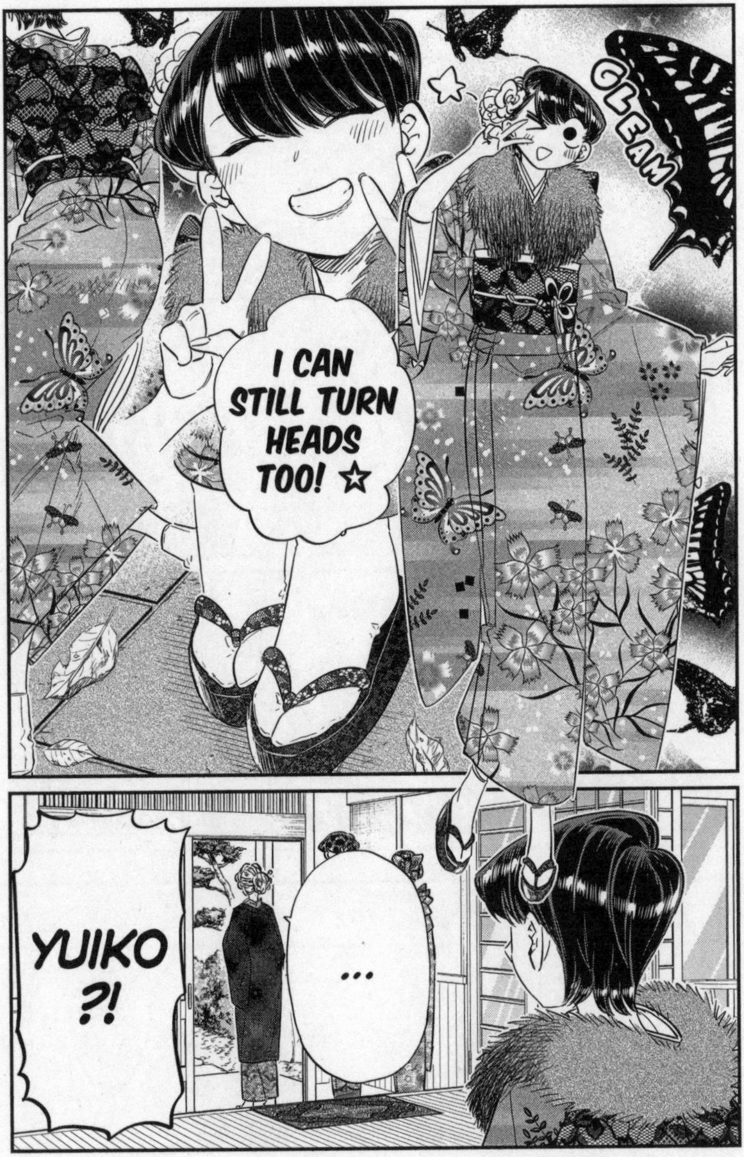
GLEAM
I CAN STILL TURN HEADS TOO! ☆
...
YUIKO ?!

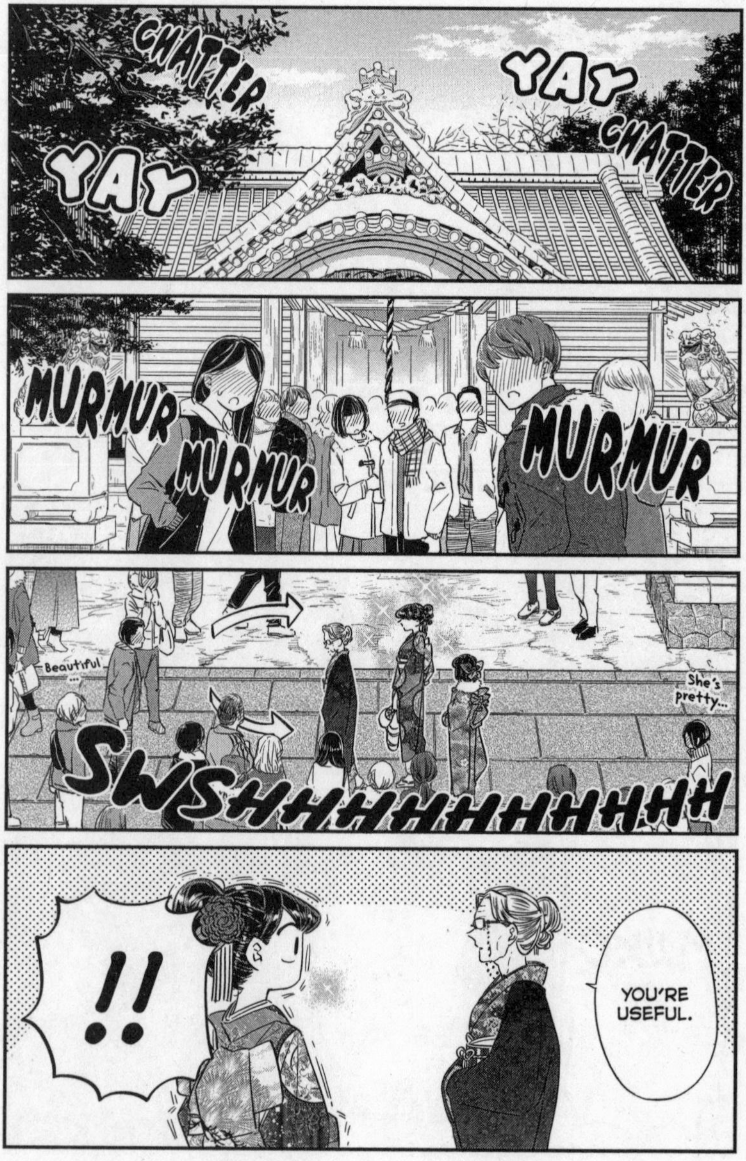
YAY
CHATTER
CHATTER
YAY
MURMUR
MURMUR
MURMUR
She's pretty...
SWSHHHHHHHHHH
Beautiful...
YOU'RE USEFUL.
!!

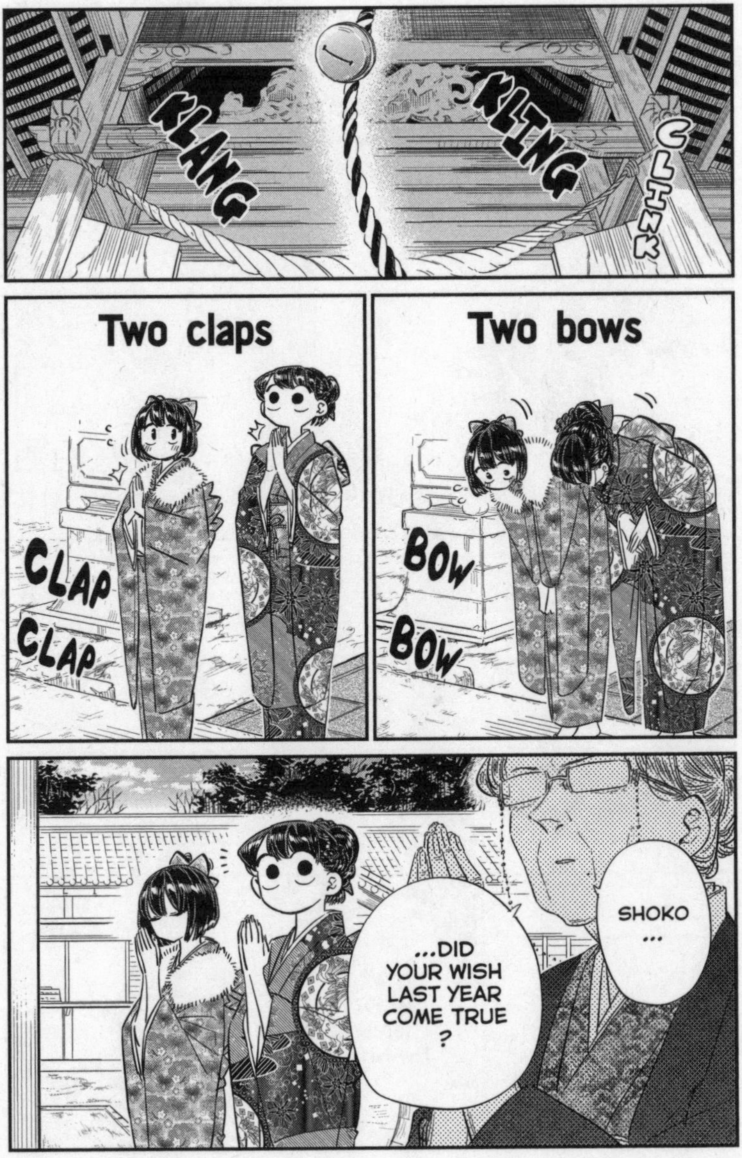
CLINK
KLING
KLANG
Two bows
BOW
BOW
Two claps
CLAP
CLAP
SHOKO ...
...DID YOUR WISH LAST YEAR COME TRUE ?

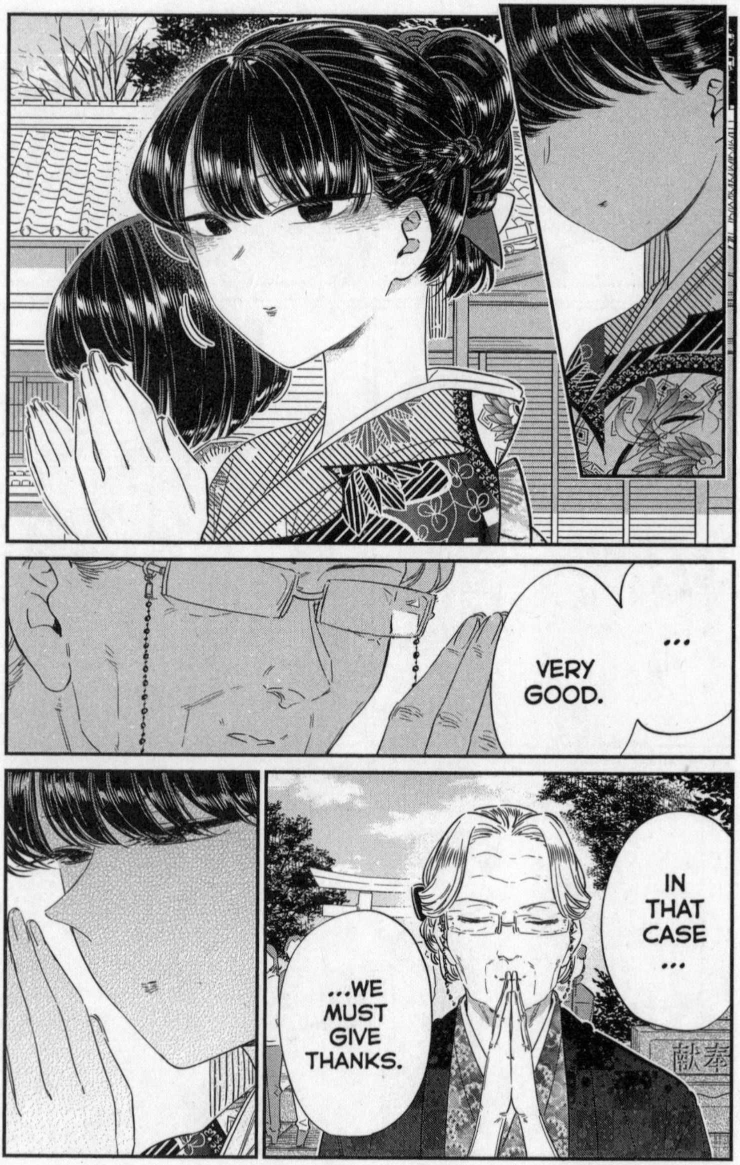
...
VERY GOOD.
IN THAT CASE ...
...WE MUST GIVE THANKS.
献奉

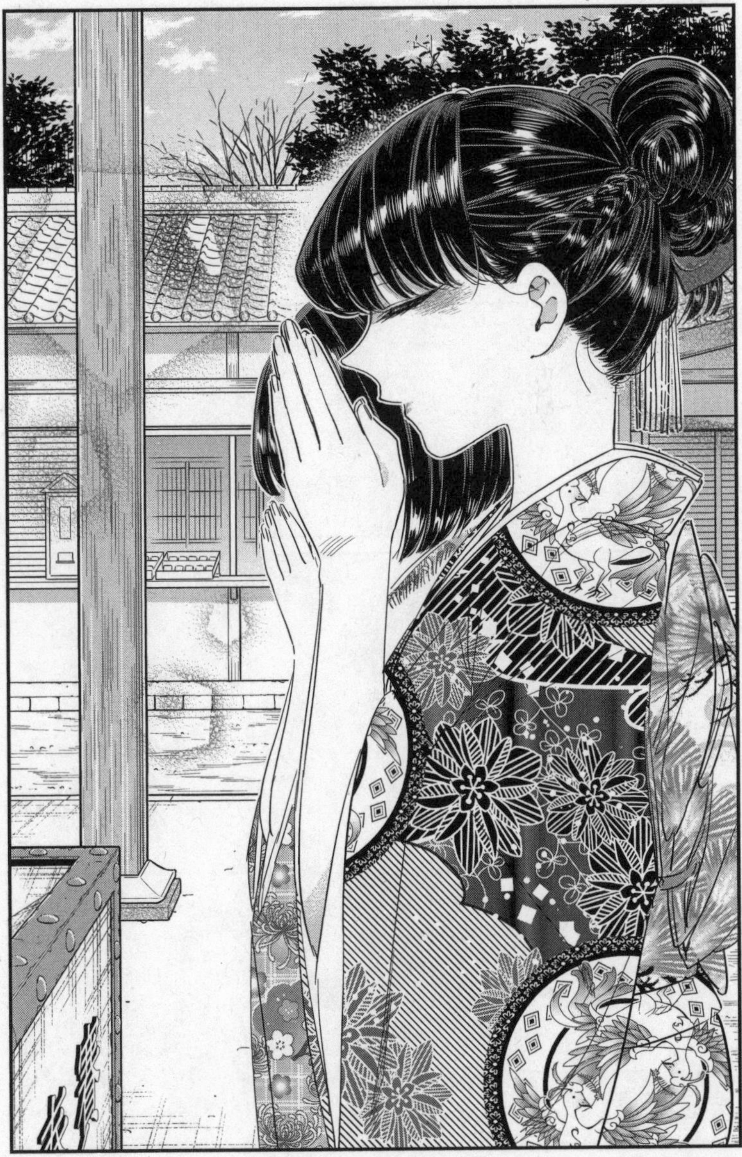

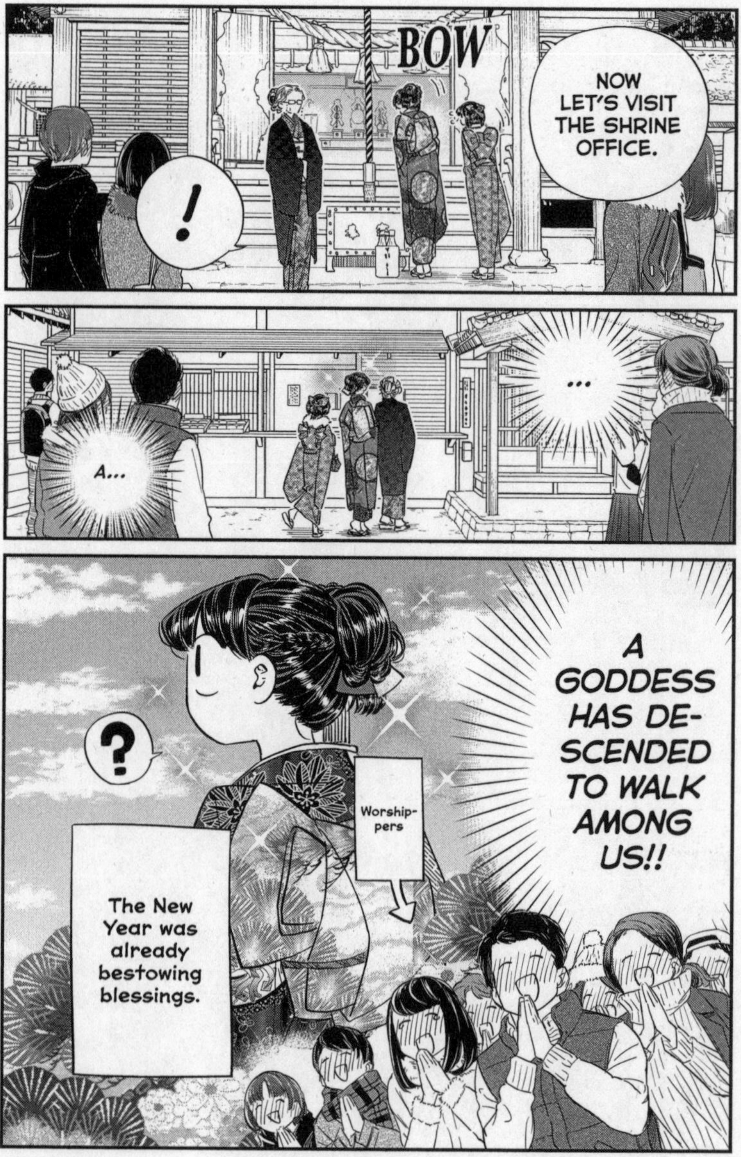
NOW LET'S VISIT THE SHRINE OFFICE.
BOW
!
...
A...
A GODDESS HAS DE-SCENDED TO WALK AMONG US!!
Worship-pers
?
The New Year was already bestowing blessings.

Communication 92 — The End

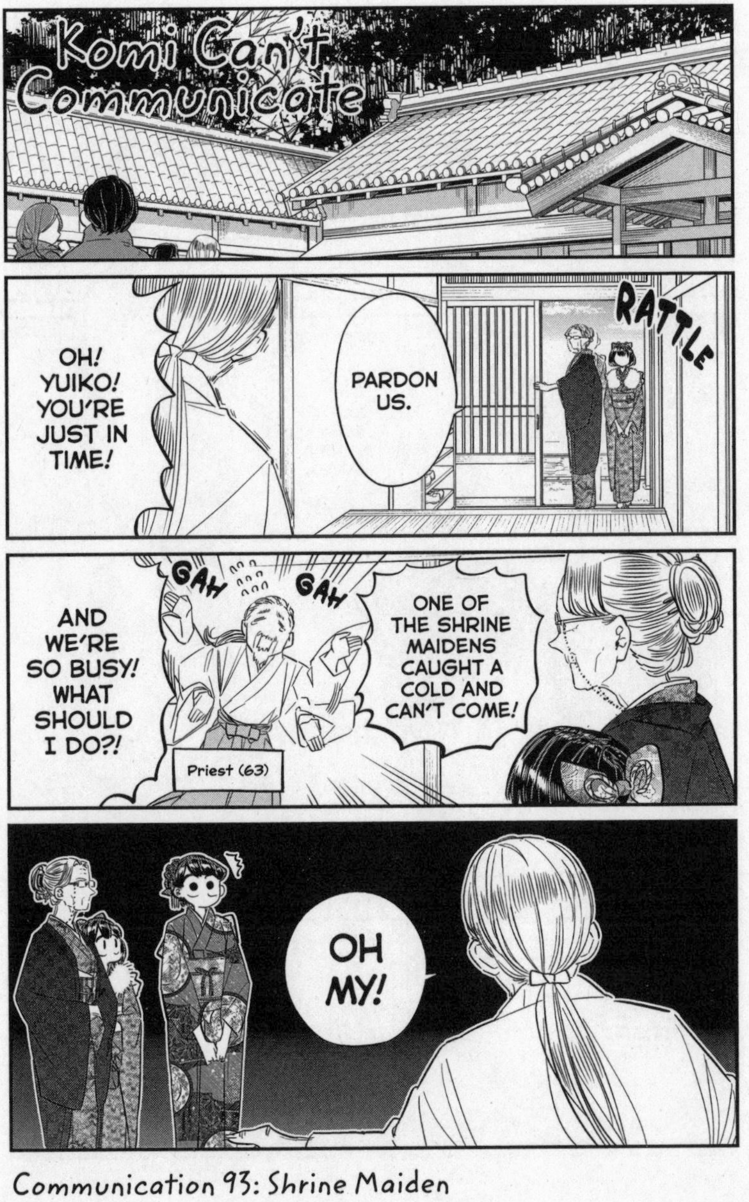
Komi Can't Communicate
RATTLE
PARDON US.
OH! YUIKO! YOU'RE JUST IN TIME!
ONE OF THE SHRINE MAIDENS CAUGHT A COLD AND CAN'T COME!
GAH GAH
AND WE'RE SO BUSY! WHAT SHOULD I DO?!
Priest (63)
OH MY!

Communication 93: Shrine Maiden

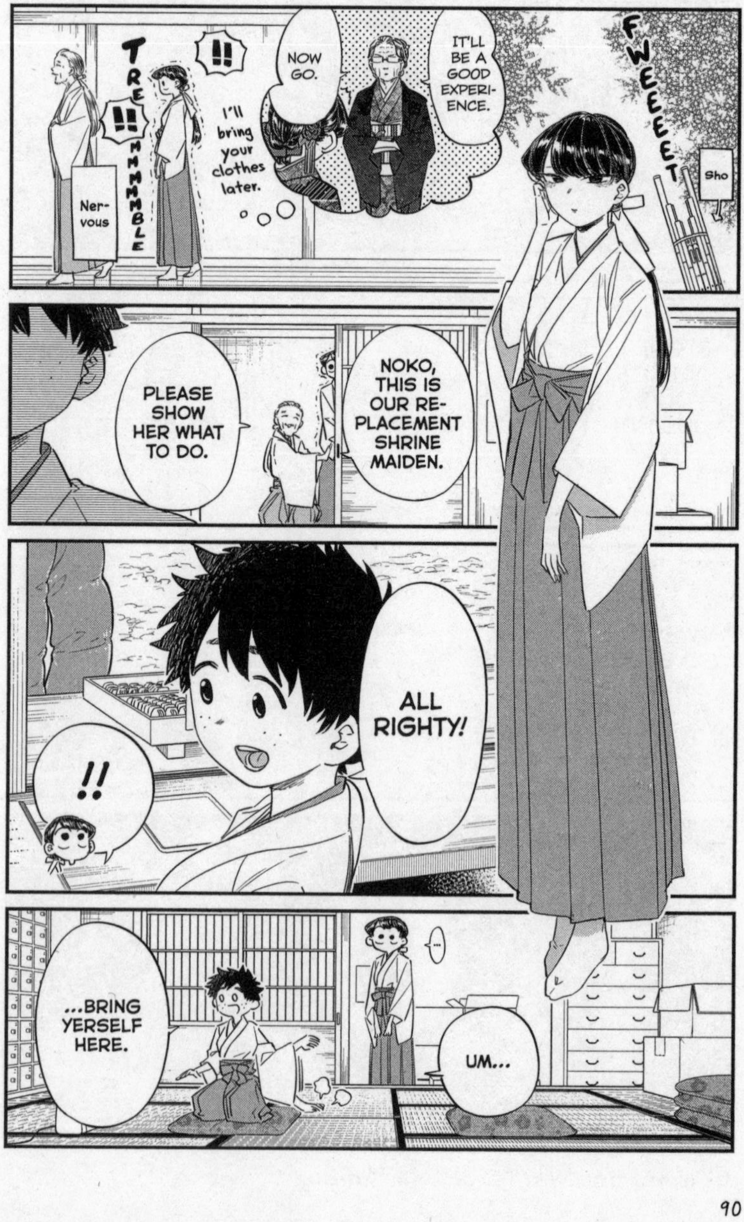
FWEEEEET
Sho
IT'LL BE A GOOD EXPERIENCE.
NOW GO.
!!
TREMMMMBLE
I'll bring your clothes later.
!!
Nervous
NOKO, THIS IS OUR REPLACEMENT SHRINE MAIDEN.
PLEASE SHOW HER WHAT TO DO.
ALL RIGHTY!
!!
...
UM...
...BRING YERSELF HERE.

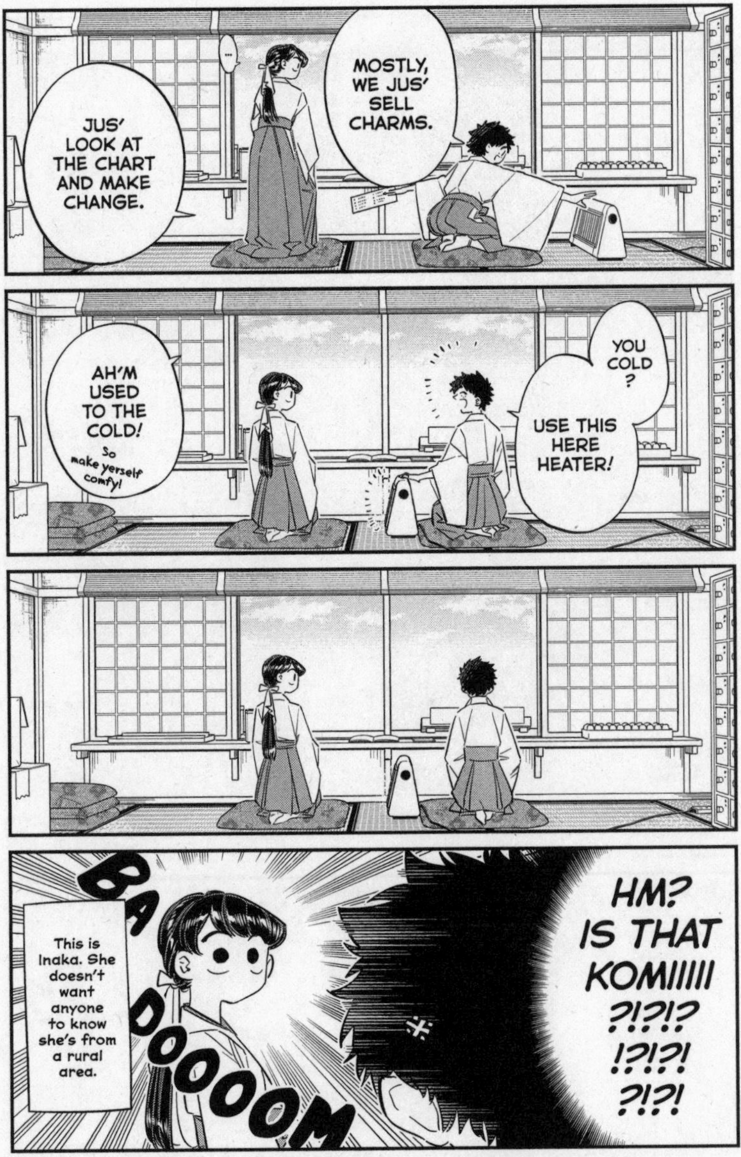
MOSTLY, WE JUS' SELL CHARMS.
...
JUS' LOOK AT THE CHART AND MAKE CHANGE.
YOU COLD?
USE THIS HERE HEATER!
AH'M USED TO THE COLD!
So make yerself comfy!
HM? IS THAT KOMIIIIII ?!?!? !?!?! ?!?!
BADOOOOM
This is Inaka. She doesn't want anyone to know she's from a rural area.

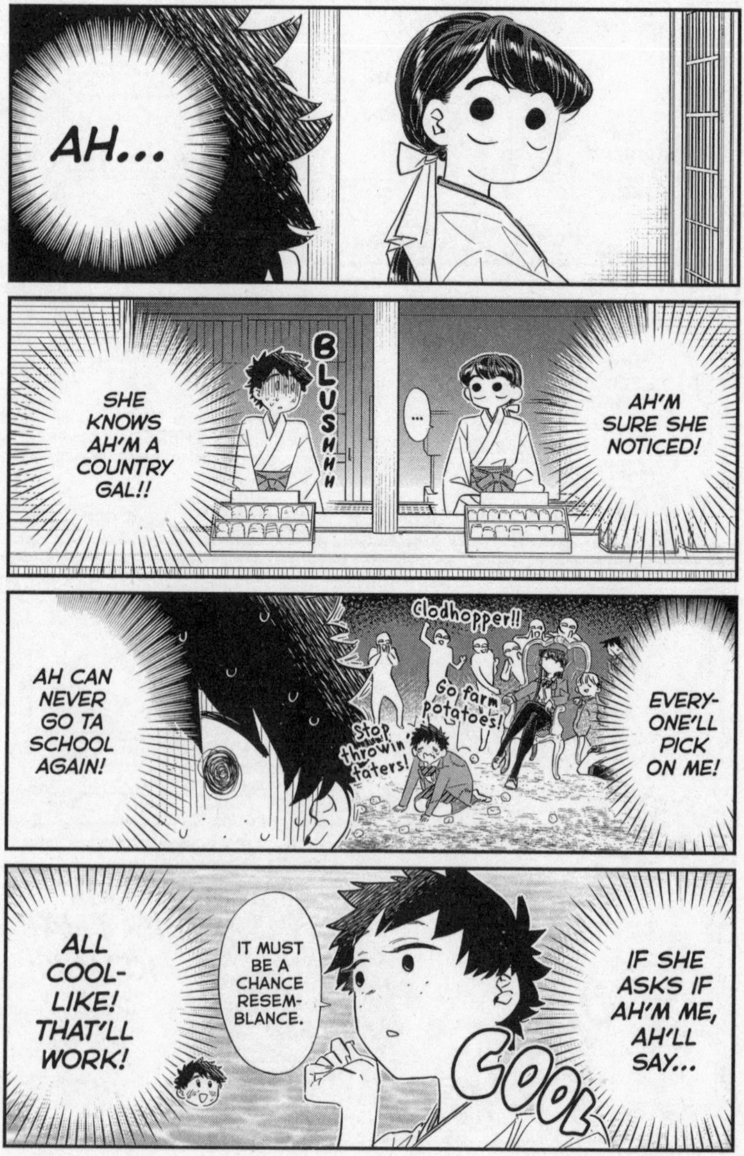
AH...
AH'M SURE SHE NOTICED!
...
BLUSHHH
SHE KNOWS AH'M A COUNTRY GAL!!
EVERY-ONE'LL PICK ON ME!
Clodhopper!!
Go farm potatoes!
Stop throwin' taters!
AH CAN NEVER GO TA SCHOOL AGAIN!
IF SHE ASKS IF AH'M ME, AH'LL SAY...
COOL
IT MUST BE A CHANCE RESEM-BLANCE.
ALL COOL-LIKE! THAT'LL WORK!

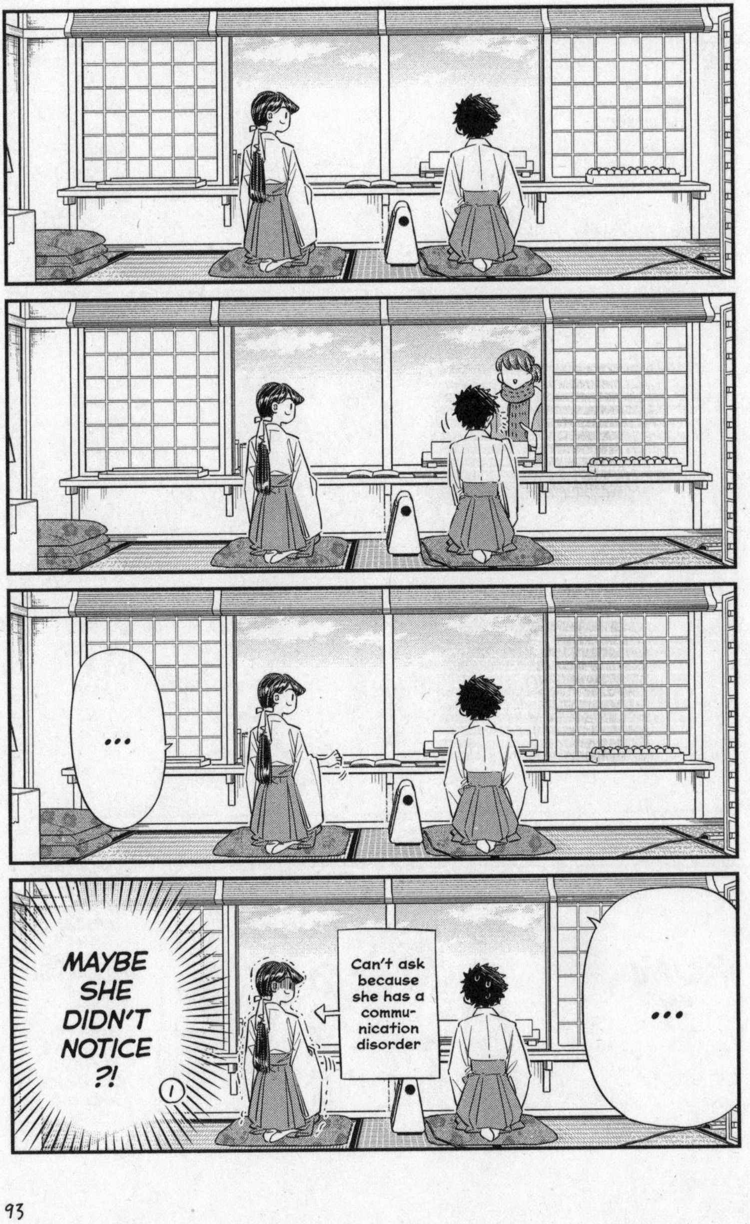
...
...
Can't ask because she has a communication disorder
MAYBE SHE DIDN'T NOTICE?!

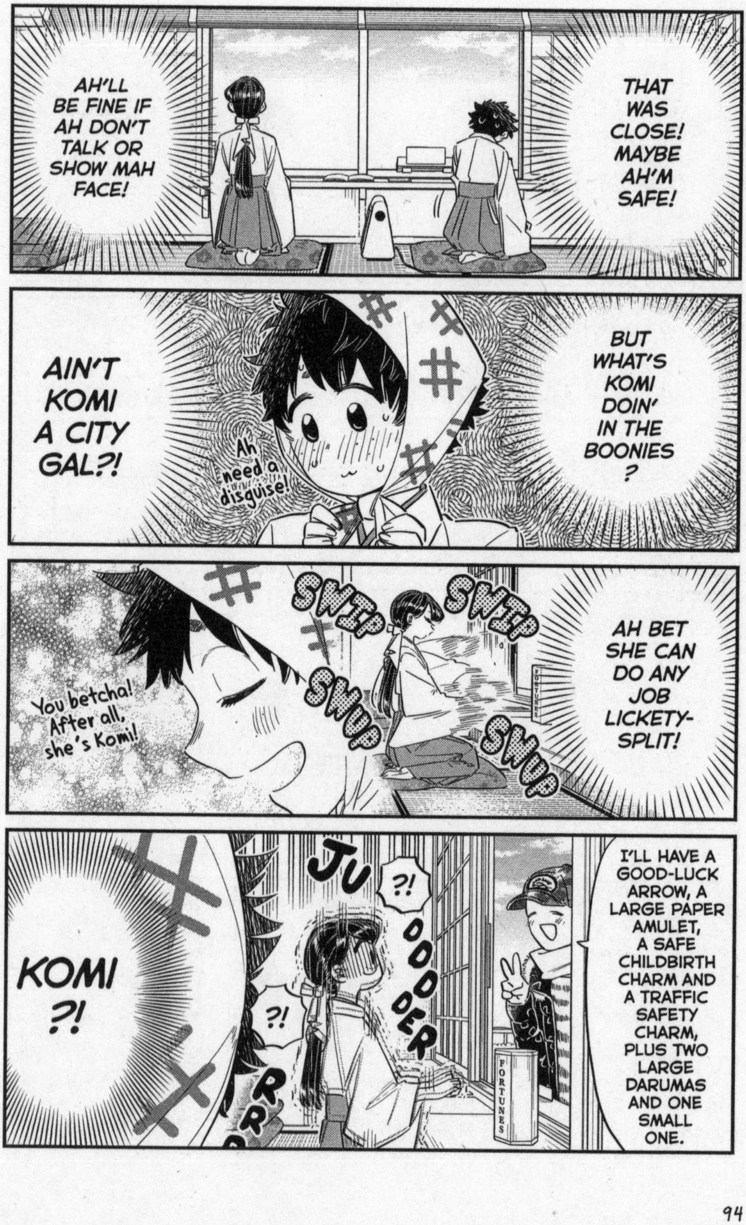
THAT WAS CLOSE! MAYBE AH'M SAFE!
AH'LL BE FINE IF AH DON'T TALK OR SHOW MAH FACE!
BUT WHAT'S KOMI DOIN' IN THE BOONIES?
Ah need a disguise!
AIN'T KOMI A CITY GAL?!
AH BET SHE CAN DO ANY JOB LICKETY-SPLIT!
SWIP
SWIP
SWUP
SWUP
FORTUNES
You betcha! After all, she's Komi!
I'LL HAVE A GOOD-LUCK ARROW, A LARGE PAPER AMULET, A SAFE CHILDBIRTH CHARM AND A TRAFFIC SAFETY CHARM, PLUS TWO LARGE DARUMAS AND ONE SMALL ONE.
FORTUNES
JU
DODDODER
RR
?!
?!
KOMI ?!

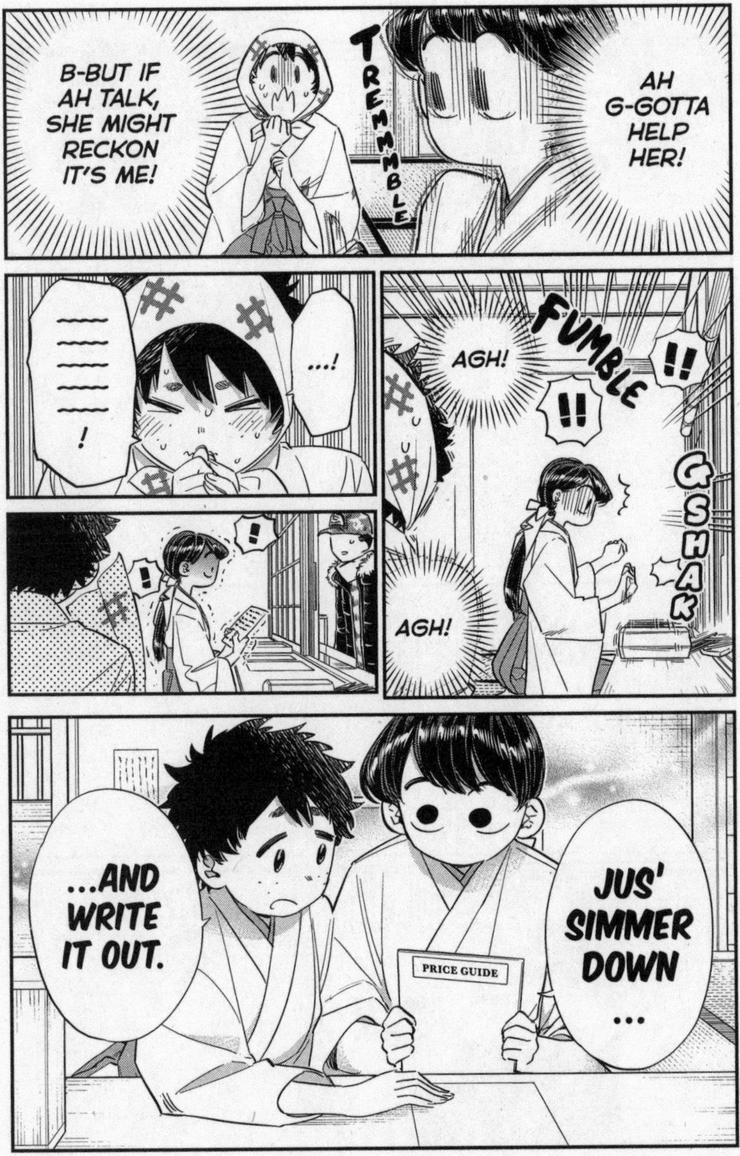
AH G-GOTTA HELP HER!
TREMMMBLE
B-BUT IF AH TALK, SHE MIGHT RECKON IT'S ME!
!!
FUMBLE
AGH!
!!
GSHAK
AGH!
...!
—————!
!
!
JUS' SIMMER DOWN ...
PRICE GUIDE
...AND WRITE IT OUT.

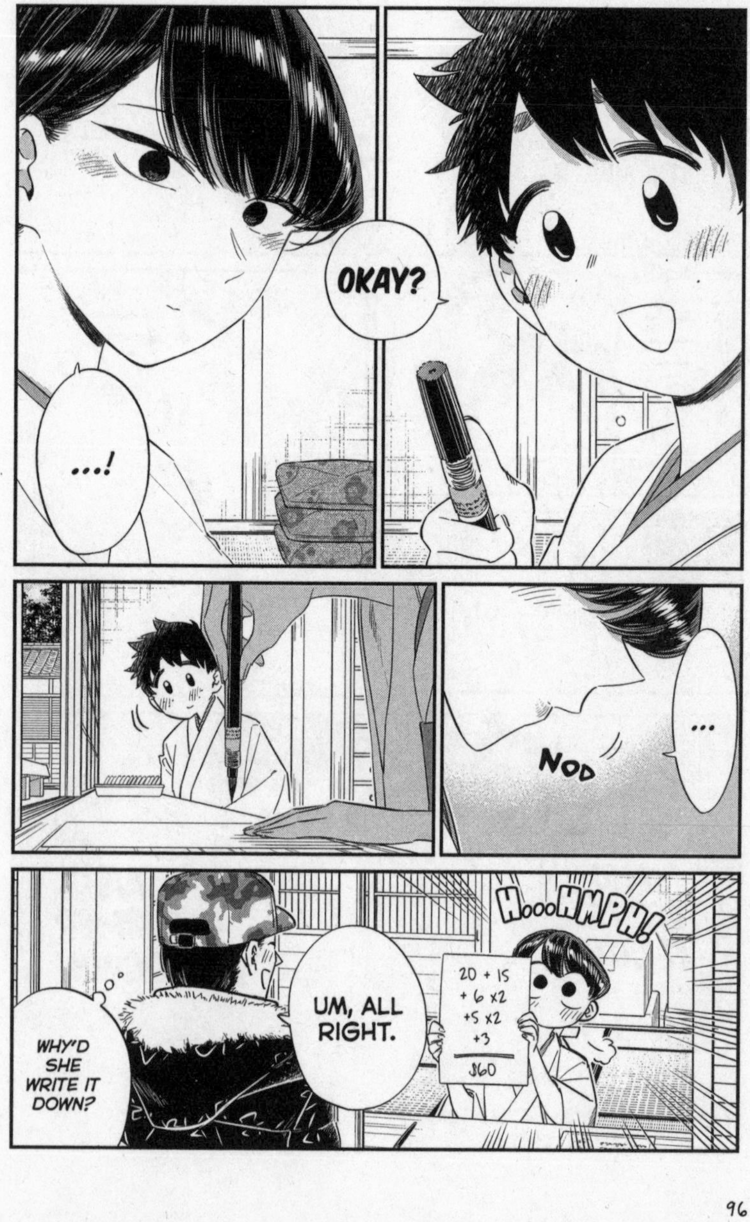
OKAY?
...!
...
NOD
H...HMPH!
20 + 15
+ 6 x2
+5 x2
+3
$60
UM, ALL RIGHT.
WHY'D SHE WRITE IT DOWN?

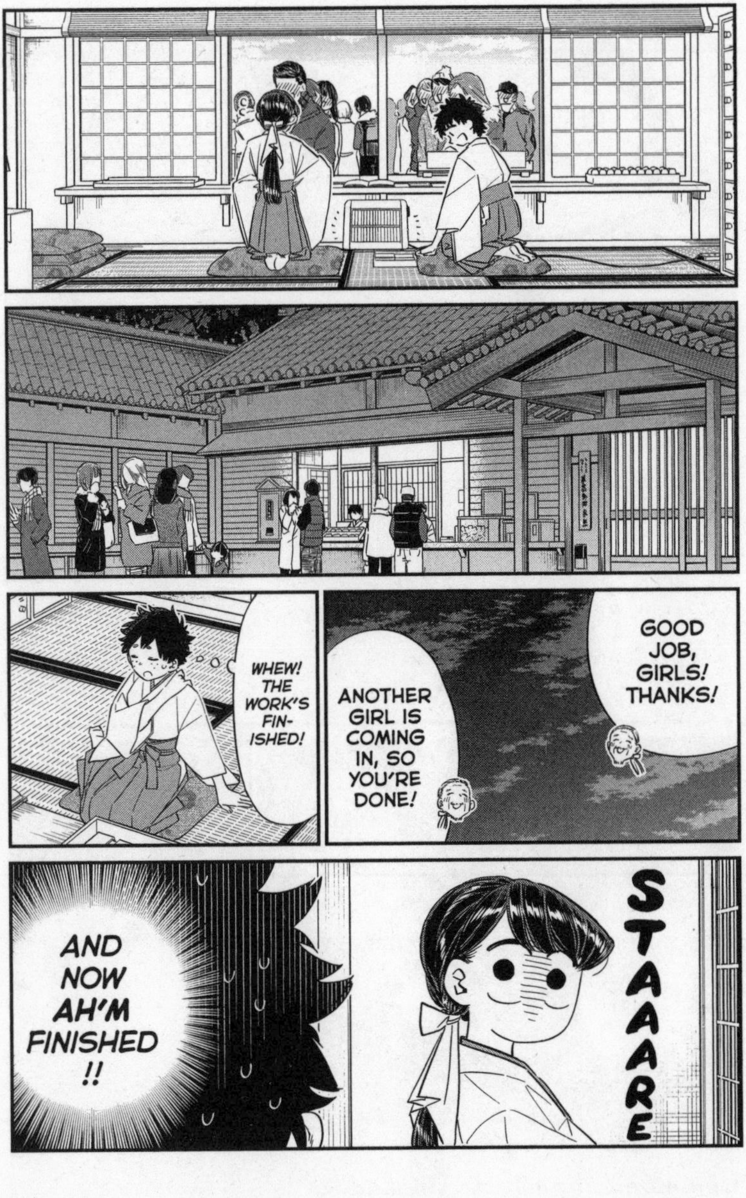
GOOD JOB, GIRLS! THANKS!
ANOTHER GIRL IS COMING IN, SO YOU'RE DONE!
WHEW! THE WORK'S FIN-ISHED!
STAAARE
AND NOW AH'M FINISHED !!

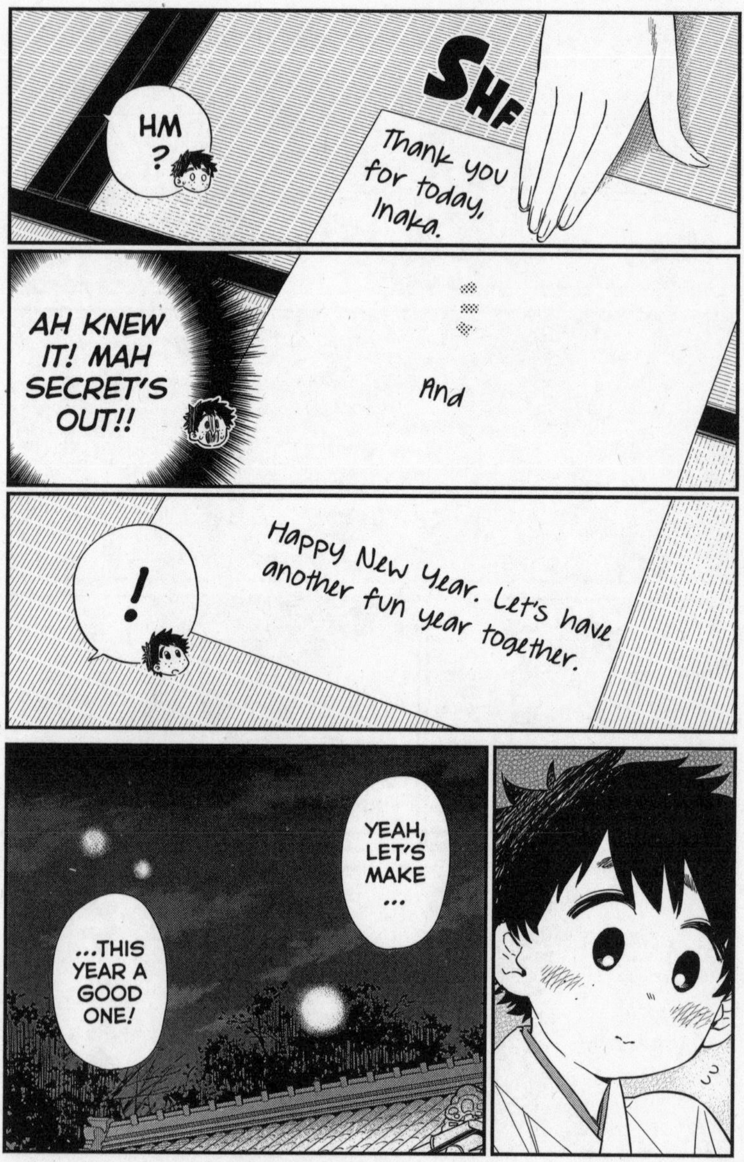
SHF
Thank you for today, Inaka.
HM?
...
And
AH KNEW IT! MAH SECRET'S OUT!!
Happy New Year. Let's have another fun year together.
!
YEAH, LET'S MAKE...
...THIS YEAR A GOOD ONE!

Communication 93 — The End

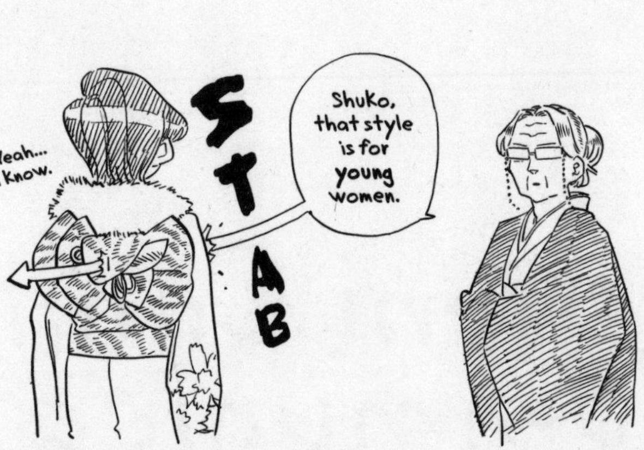
Shuko, that style is for young women.
STAB
Yeah... I know.

Komi Can't
Communicate

Komi Can't Communicate

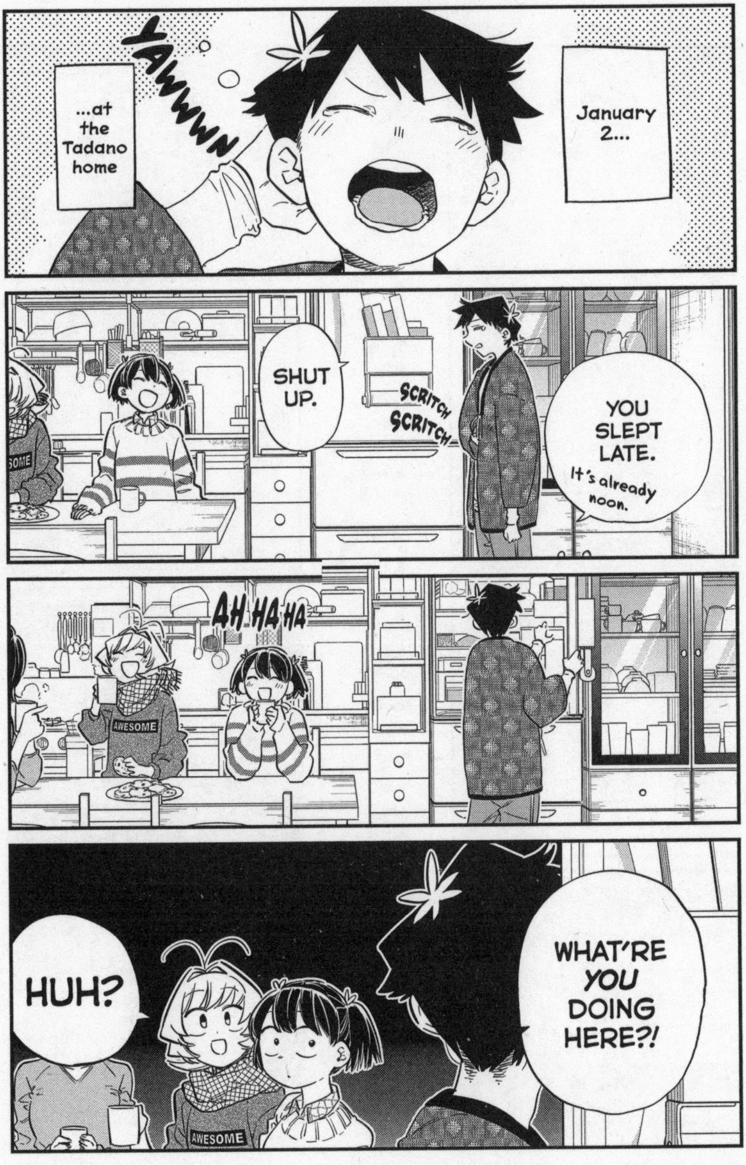

January 2...
...at the Tadano home
YAWWWN
YOU SLEPT LATE. It's already noon.
SCRITCH SCRITCH
SHUT UP.
AH HA HA
AWESOME
WHAT'RE *YOU* DOING HERE?!
HUH?
AWESOME

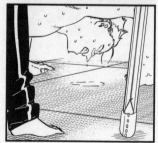

Komi Can't Communicate

Communication 94: Various New Year's Holidays

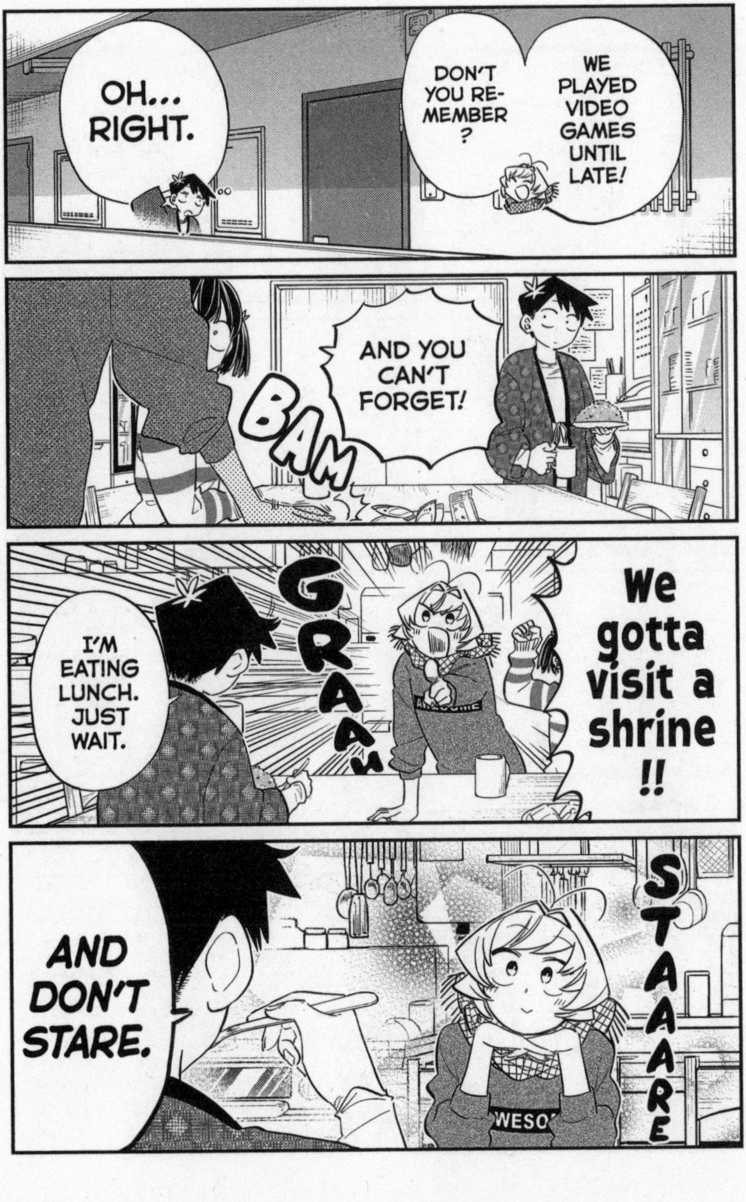
WE PLAYED VIDEO GAMES UNTIL LATE!
DON'T YOU RE-MEMBER?
OH... RIGHT.
AND YOU CAN'T FORGET!
BAM
We gotta visit a shrine!!
GRAAH
I'M EATING LUNCH. JUST WAIT.
STAAARE
AND DON'T STARE.

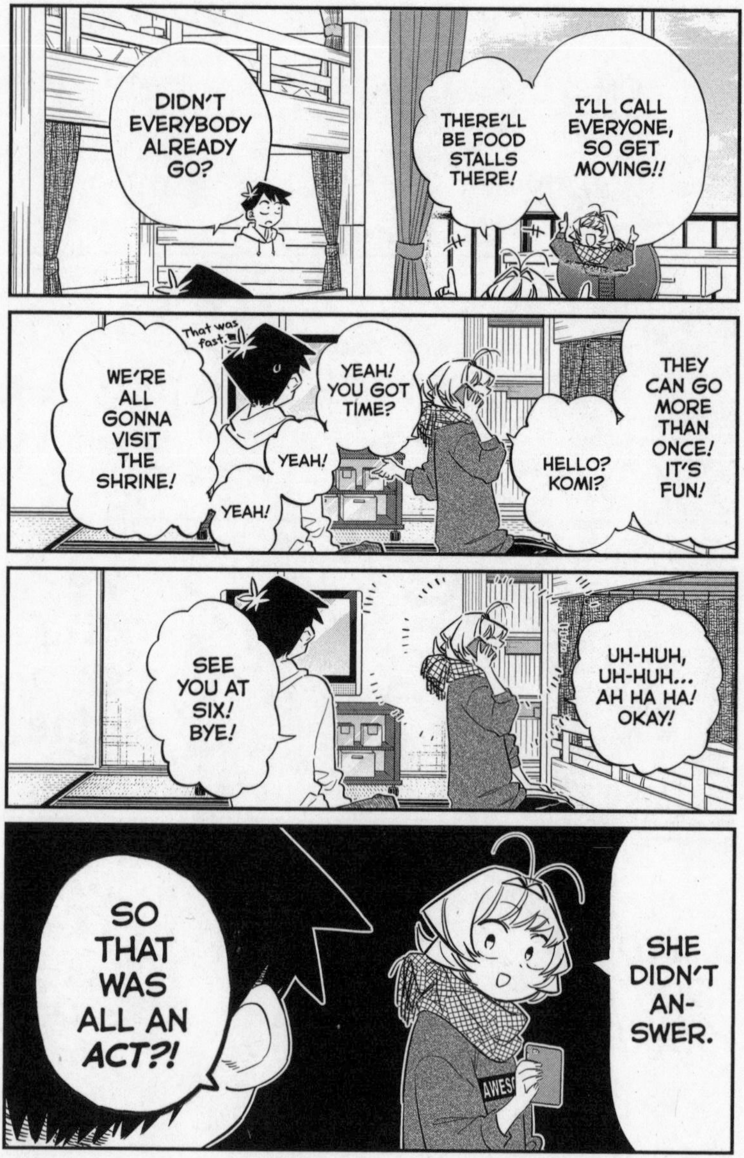
I'LL CALL EVERYONE, SO GET MOVING!!
THERE'LL BE FOOD STALLS THERE!
DIDN'T EVERYBODY ALREADY GO?
THEY CAN GO MORE THAN ONCE! IT'S FUN!
HELLO? KOMI?
YEAH! YOU GOT TIME?
YEAH!
YEAH!
That was fast.
WE'RE ALL GONNA VISIT THE SHRINE!
UH-HUH, UH-HUH... AH HA HA! OKAY!
SEE YOU AT SIX! BYE!
SHE DIDN'T AN-SWER.
SO THAT WAS ALL AN ACT?!

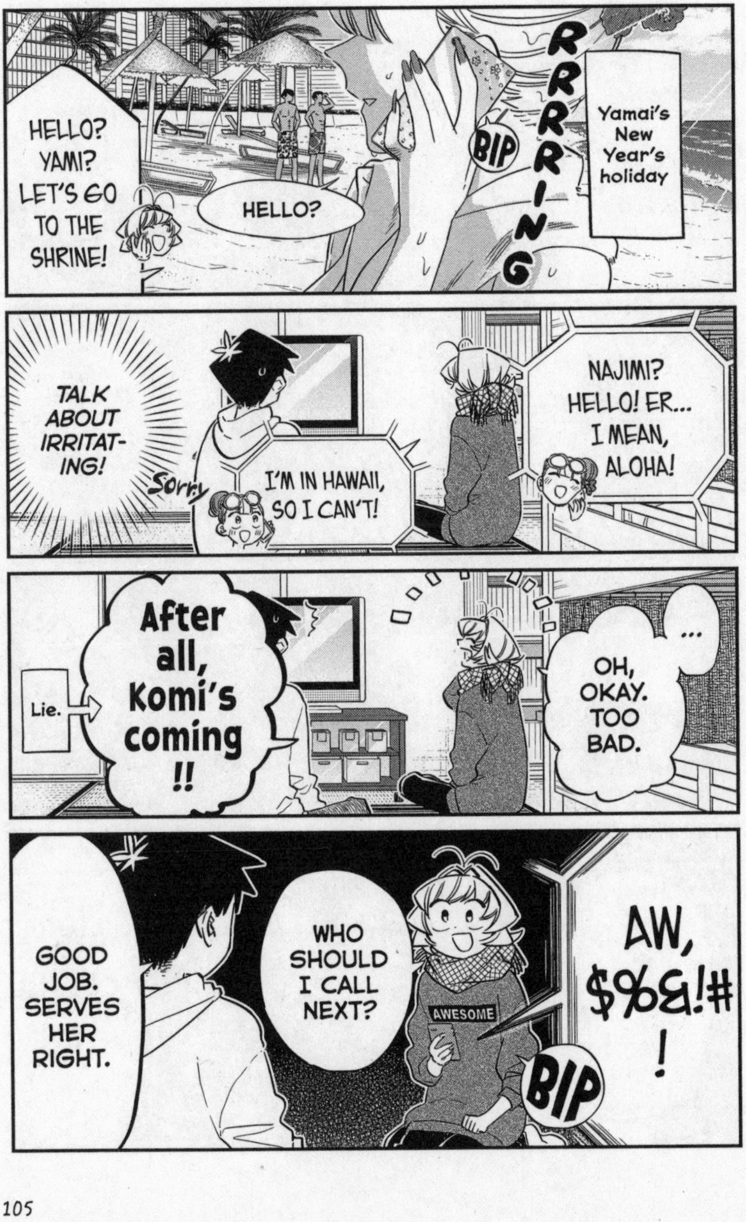
Yamai's New Year's holiday
RRRRING
BIP
HELLO?
HELLO? YAMI? LET'S GO TO THE SHRINE!
NAJIMI? HELLO! ER... I MEAN, ALOHA!
I'M IN HAWAII, SO I CAN'T!
Sorry
TALK ABOUT IRRITAT-ING!
...
OH, OKAY. TOO BAD.
After all, Komi's coming!!
Lie.
AW, $%B!# !
BIP
WHO SHOULD I CALL NEXT?
AWESOME
GOOD JOB. SERVES HER RIGHT.

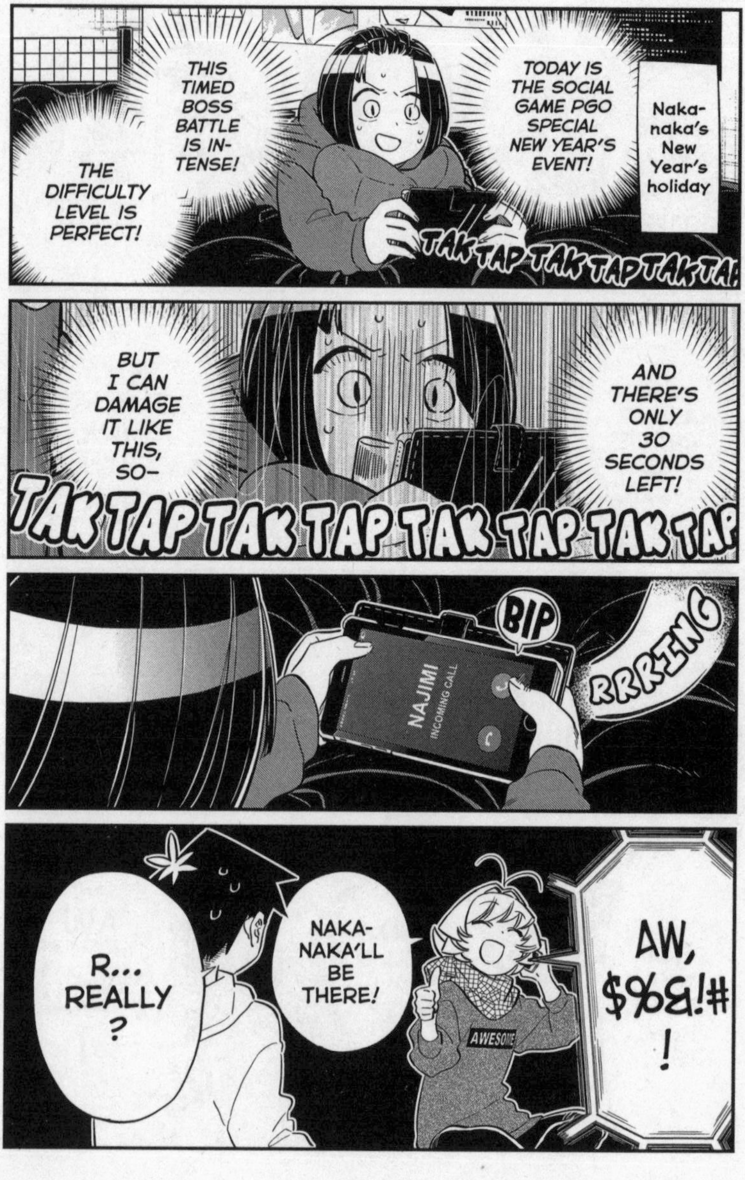
Naka-naka's New Year's holiday
TODAY IS THE SOCIAL GAME PGO SPECIAL NEW YEAR'S EVENT!
THIS TIMED BOSS BATTLE IS IN-TENSE!
THE DIFFICULTY LEVEL IS PERFECT!
TAK TAP TAK TAP TAK TAP
AND THERE'S ONLY 30 SECONDS LEFT!
BUT I CAN DAMAGE IT LIKE THIS, SO—
TAK TAP TAK TAP TAK TAP TAK TAP
RRRING
BIP
NAJIMI
INCOMING CALL
AW, $%&!#!
NAKA-NAKA'LL BE THERE!
R... REALLY?
AWESOME

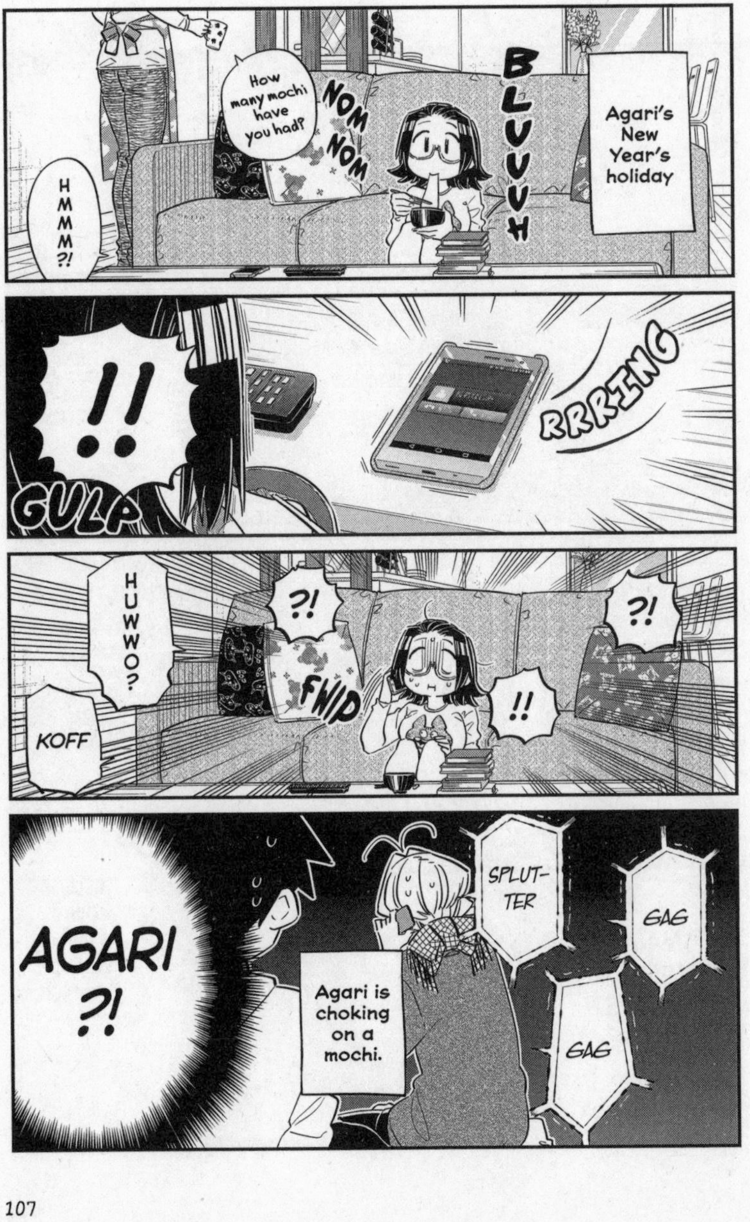
Agari's New Year's holiday
BLUUUH
NOM NOM
How many mochi have you had?
HMMMM?!
RRRING
!!
GULP
?!
!!
FWIP
?!
HUWWO?
KOFF
GAG
SPLUT-TER
GAG
Agari is choking on a mochi.
AGARI?!

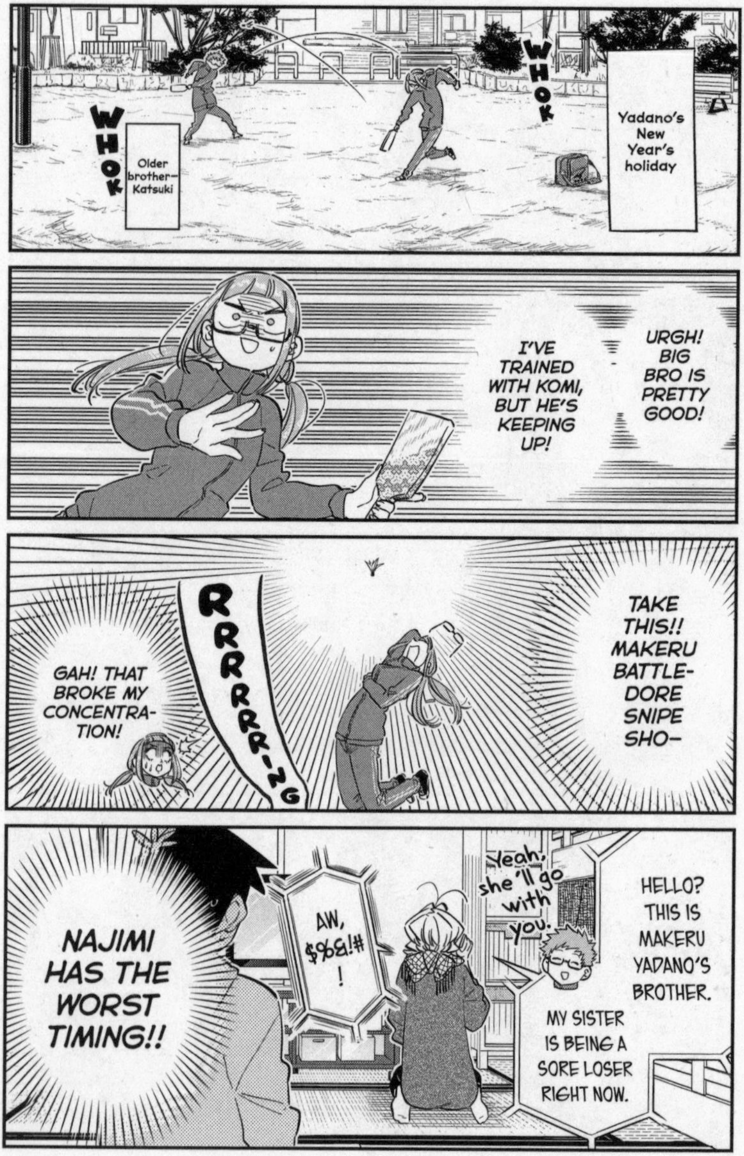
Yadano's New Year's holiday
WHOK
WHOK
Older brother-Katsuki
URGH! BIG BRO IS PRETTY GOOD!
I'VE TRAINED WITH KOMI, BUT HE'S KEEPING UP!
TAKE THIS!! MAKERU BATTLE-DORE SNIPE SHO–
RRRRRRING
GAH! THAT BROKE MY CONCENTRA-TION!
HELLO? THIS IS MAKERU YADANO'S BROTHER.
MY SISTER IS BEING A SORE LOSER RIGHT NOW.
Yeah, she'll go with you.
AW, #$%!
NAJIMI HAS THE WORST TIMING!!

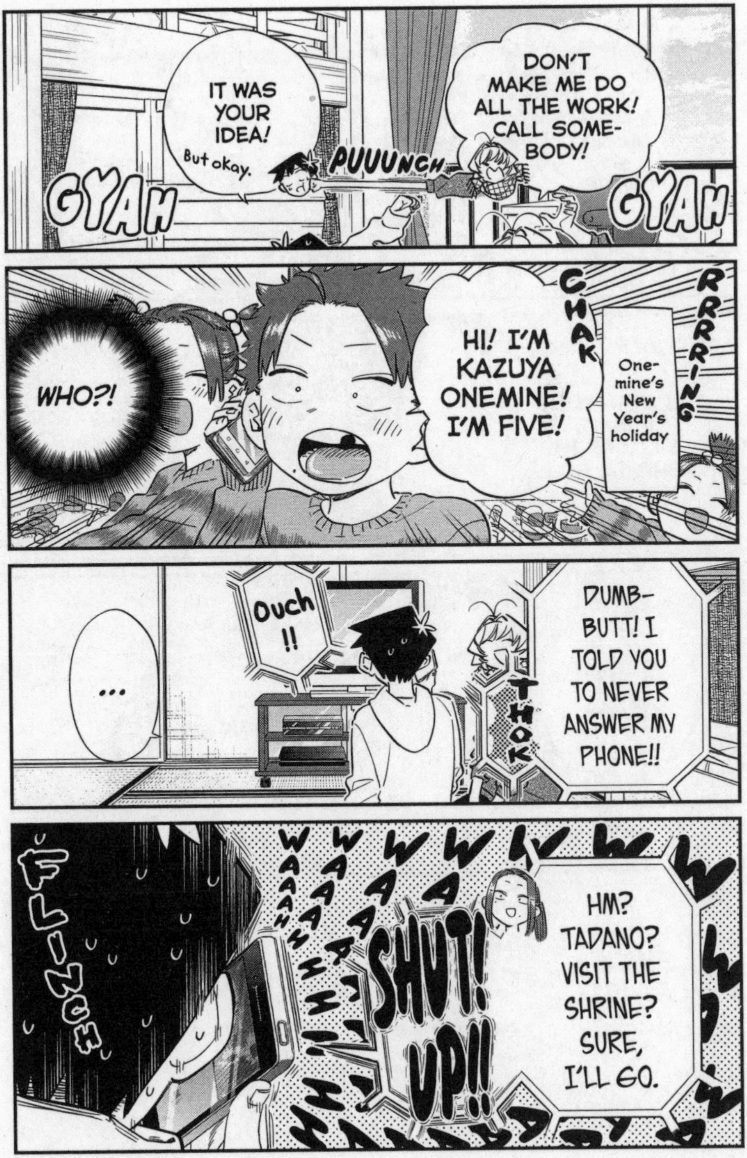
GYAH
DON'T MAKE ME DO ALL THE WORK! CALL SOME-BODY!
PUUUNCH
IT WAS YOUR IDEA!
But okay.
GYAH
RRRRING
One-mine's New Year's holiday
CHAK
HI! I'M KAZUYA ONEMINE! I'M FIVE!
WHO?!
DUMB-BUTT! I TOLD YOU TO NEVER ANSWER MY PHONE!!
THOK
Ouch !!
...
HM? TADANO? VISIT THE SHRINE? SURE, I'LL GO.
SHUT! UP!!
WAAAAH
FLINCH

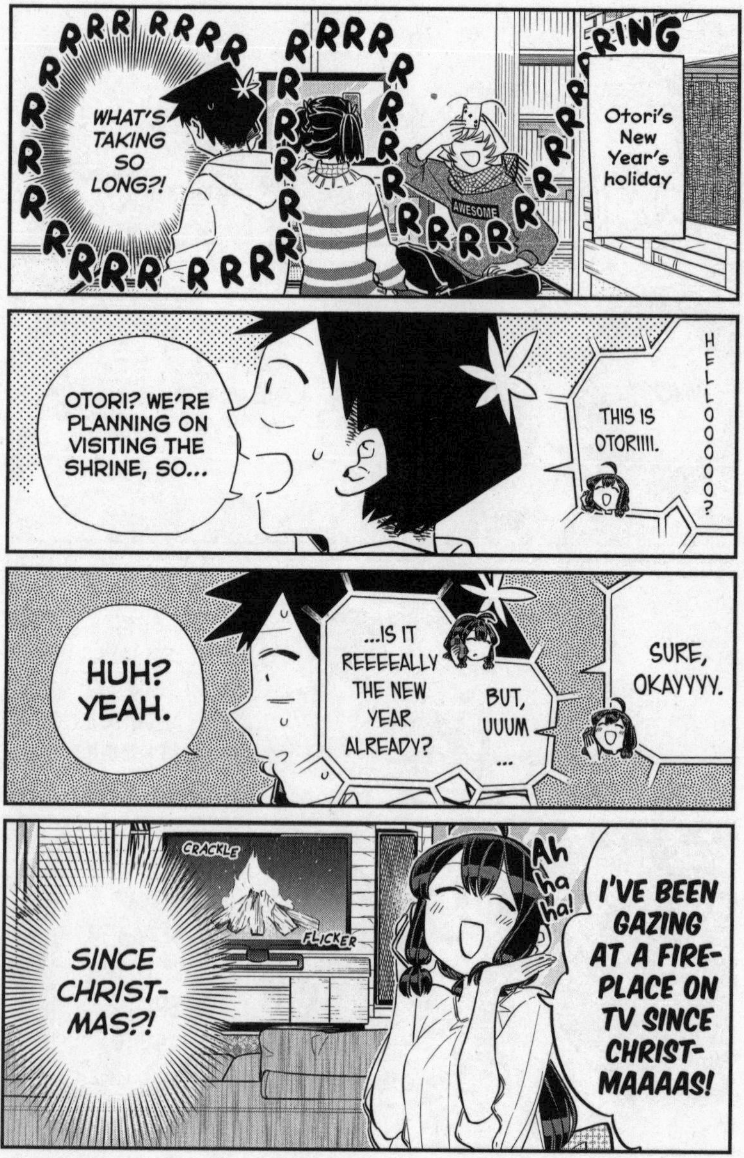
Otori's New Year's holiday
RRRRRING
AWESOME
WHAT'S TAKING SO LONG?!
HELLOOOOOO?
THIS IS OTORIIII.
OTORI? WE'RE PLANNING ON VISITING THE SHRINE, SO...
SURE, OKAYYYY.
BUT, UUUM ...
...IS IT REEEEALLY THE NEW YEAR ALREADY?
HUH? YEAH.
I'VE BEEN GAZING AT A FIRE-PLACE ON TV SINCE CHRIST-MAAAAS!
Ah ha ha!
CRACKLE
FLICKER
SINCE CHRIST-MAS?!

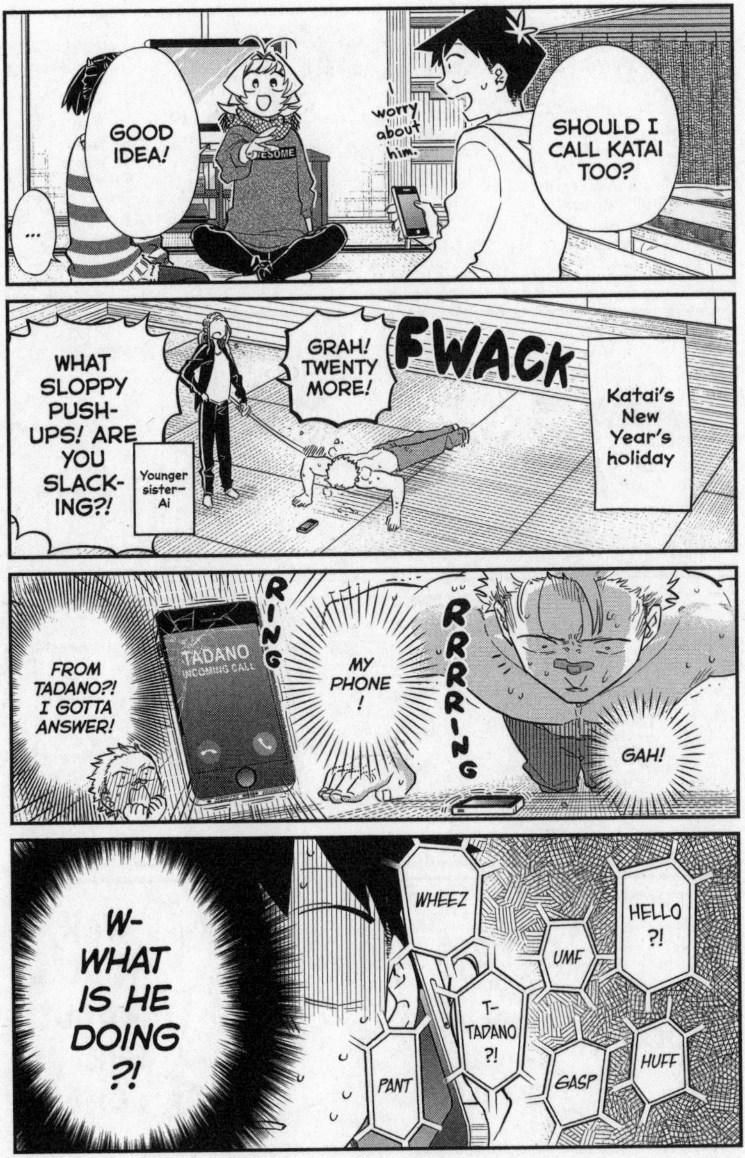
SHOULD I CALL KATAI TOO?
I worry about him.
GOOD IDEA!
...
Katai's New Year's holiday
FWACK
GRAH! TWENTY MORE!
WHAT SLOPPY PUSH-UPS! ARE YOU SLACKING?!
Younger sister—Ai
GAH!
RRRRING
RING
MY PHONE!
TADANO
INCOMING CALL
FROM TADANO?! I GOTTA ANSWER!
HELLO?!
UMF
WHEEZ
T-TADANO?!
HUFF
GASP
PANT
W-WHAT IS HE DOING?!

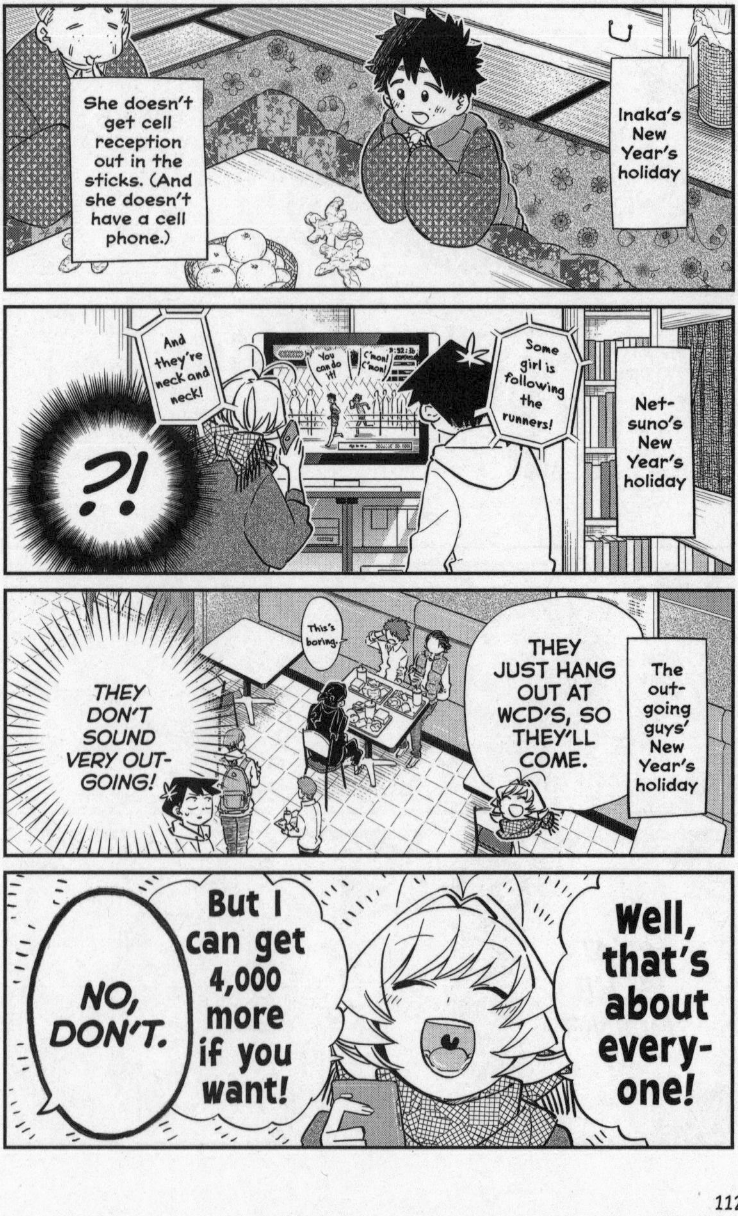
Inaka's New Year's holiday
She doesn't get cell reception out in the sticks. (And she doesn't have a cell phone.)
Net-suno's New Year's holiday
Some girl is following the runners!
C'mon! C'mon!
You can do it!
And they're neck and neck!
?!
The out-going guys' New Year's holiday
THEY JUST HANG OUT AT WCD'S, SO THEY'LL COME.
This's boring.
THEY DON'T SOUND VERY OUT-GOING!
Well, that's about every-one!
But I can get 4,000 more if you want!
NO, DON'T.

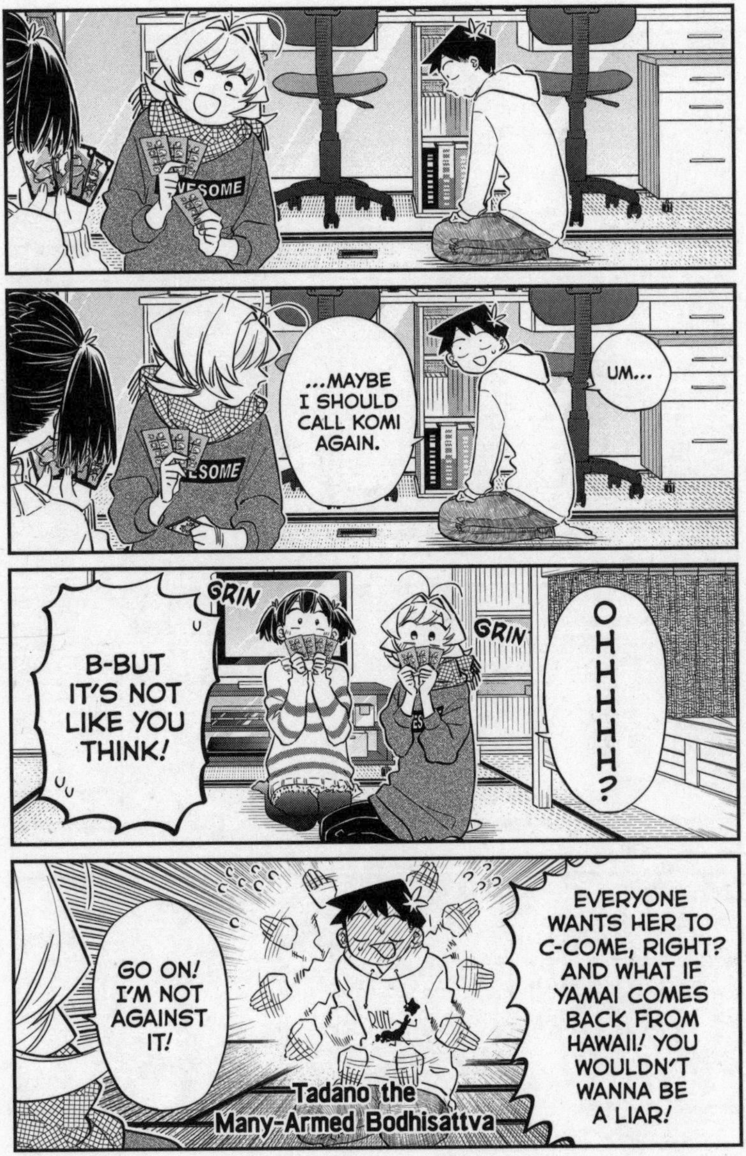
WESOME
UM...
...MAYBE I SHOULD CALL KOMI AGAIN.
OHHHHH?
GRIN
GRIN
B-BUT IT'S NOT LIKE YOU THINK!
EVERYONE WANTS HER TO C-COME, RIGHT? AND WHAT IF YAMAI COMES BACK FROM HAWAII! YOU WOULDN'T WANNA BE A LIAR!
Tadano the Many-Armed Bodhisattva
GO ON! I'M NOT AGAINST IT!

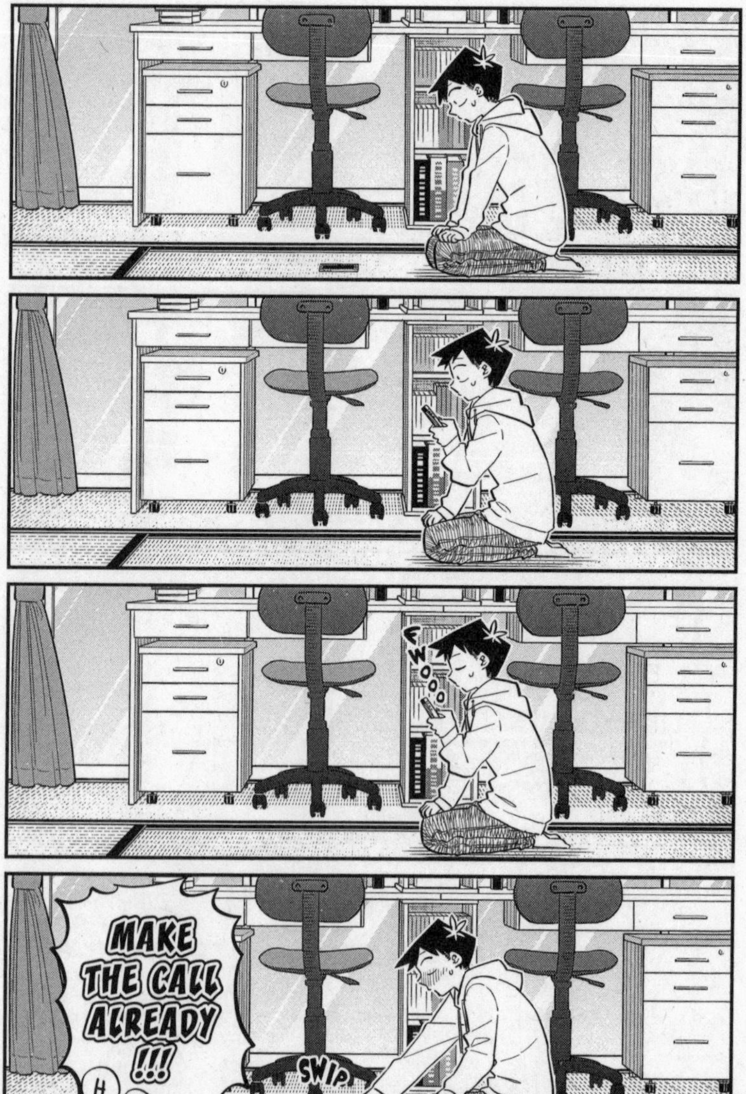
FWOOO
MAKE THE CALL ALREADY !!!
H
N
SWIP

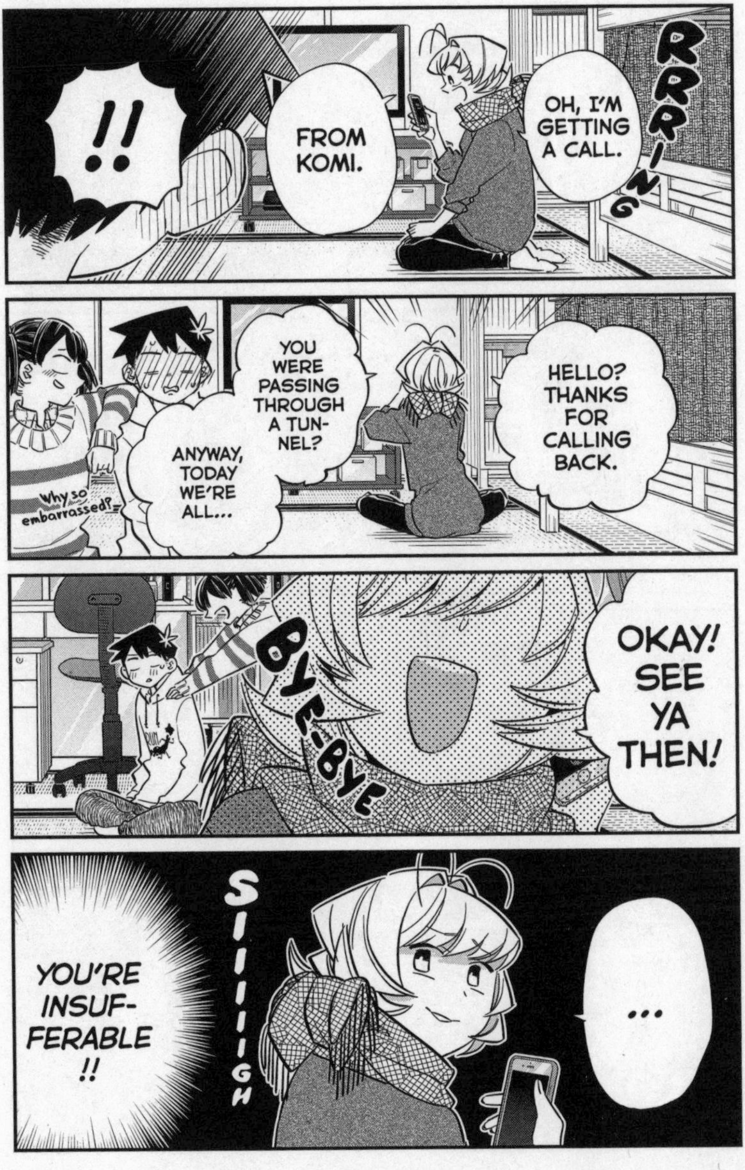
RRRING
OH, I'M GETTING A CALL.
FROM KOMI.
!!
HELLO? THANKS FOR CALLING BACK.
YOU WERE PASSING THROUGH A TUN-NEL?
ANYWAY, TODAY WE'RE ALL...
Why so embarrassed?
OKAY! SEE YA THEN!
BYE-BYE
...
SIIIIIGH
YOU'RE INSUF-FERABLE !!

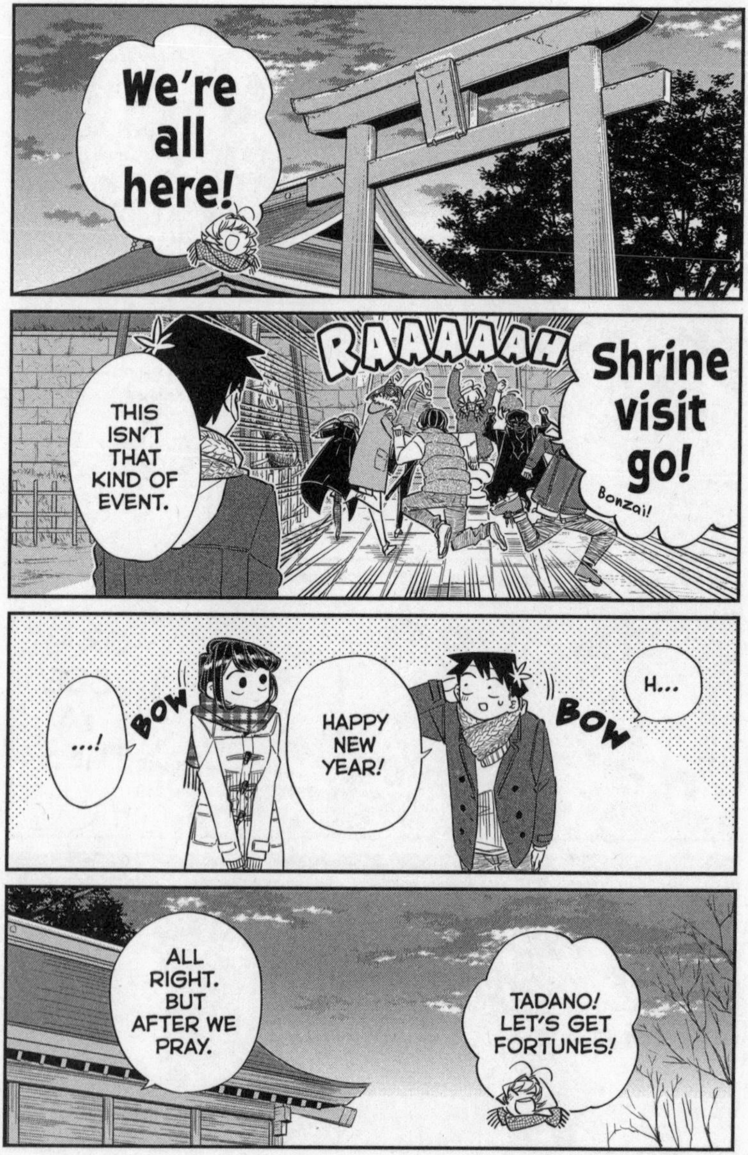
We're all here!
Shrine visit go!
Bonzai!
RAAAAAAH
THIS ISN'T THAT KIND OF EVENT.
H...
BOW
HAPPY NEW YEAR!
BOW
...!
TADANO! LET'S GET FORTUNES!
ALL RIGHT. BUT AFTER WE PRAY.

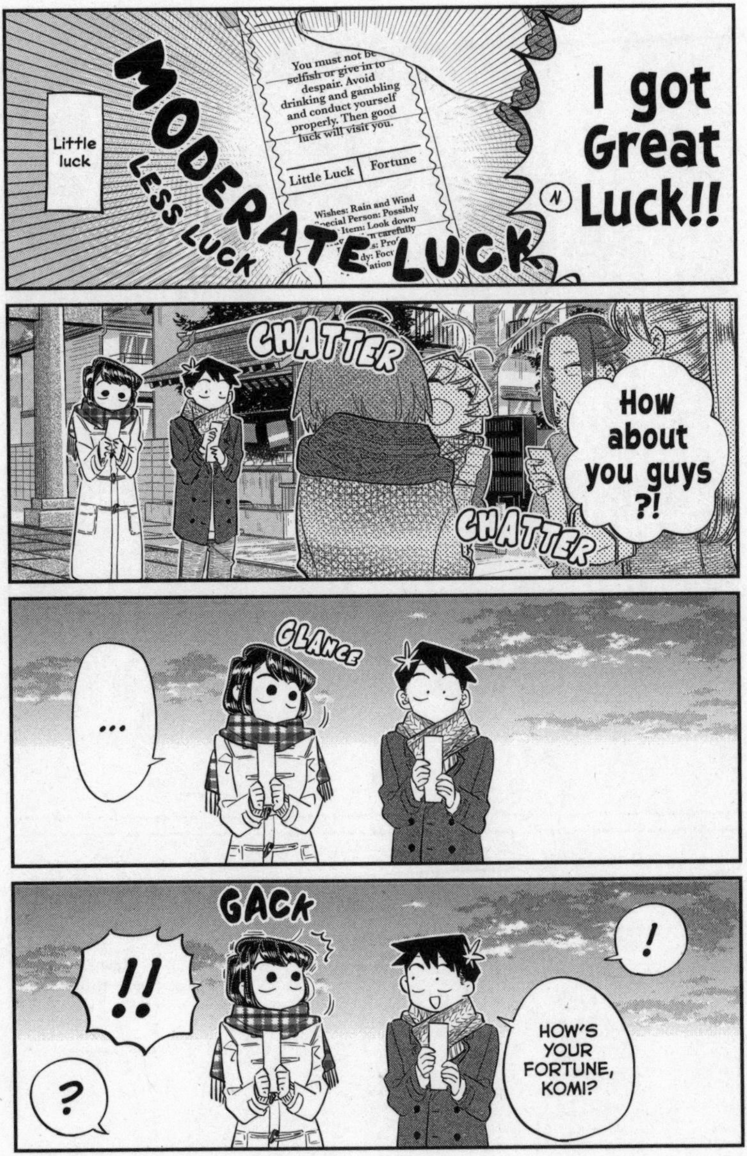
I got Great Luck!!
You must not be selfish or give in to despair. Avoid drinking and gambling and conduct yourself properly. Then good luck will visit you.
Fortune
Little Luck
Wishes: Rain and Wind
MODERATE LUCK
LESS LUCK
Little luck
How about you guys ?!
CHATTER
CHATTER
GLANCE
...
!
HOW'S YOUR FORTUNE, KOMI?
GACK
!!
?

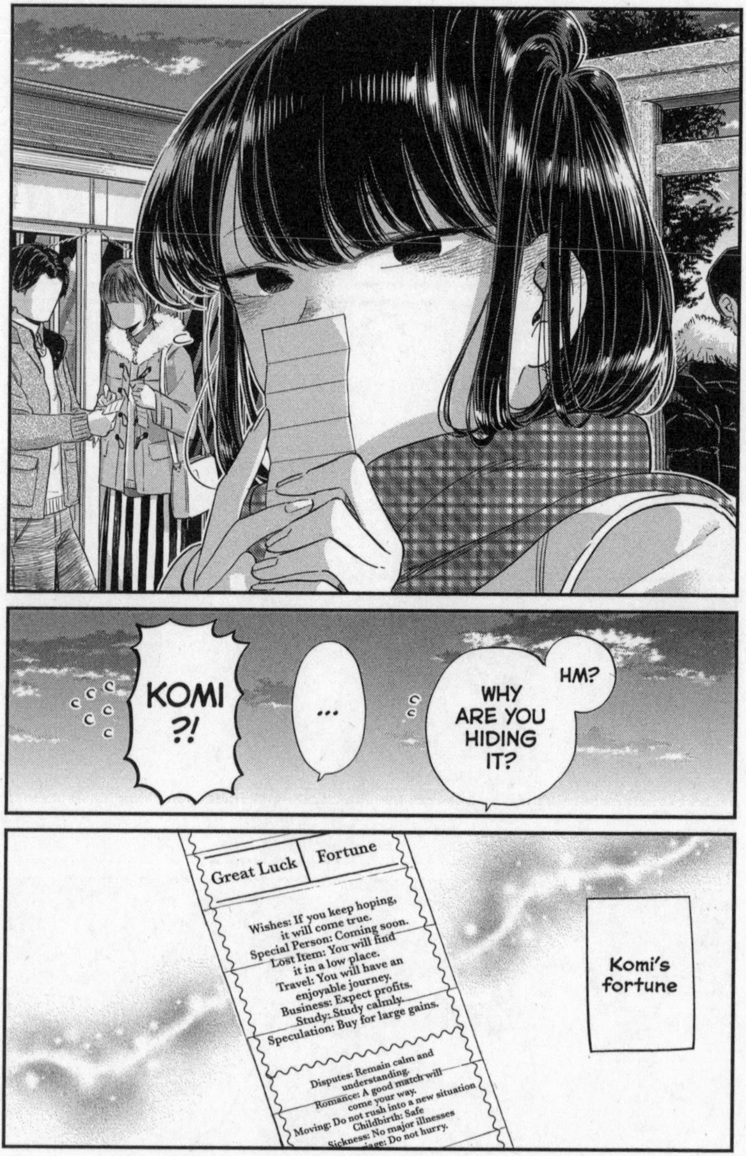
HM?
WHY ARE YOU HIDING IT?
...
KOMI ?!
Komi's fortune
Great Luck
Fortune
Wishes: If you keep hoping, it will come true.
Special Person: Coming soon.
Lost Item: You will find it in a low place.
Travel: You will have an enjoyable journey.
Business: Expect profits.
Study: Study calmly.
Speculation: Buy for large gains.
Disputes: Remain calm and understanding.
Romance: A good match will come your way.
Moving: Do not rush into a new situation
Childbirth: Safe
Sickness: No major illnesses

Communication 94 — The End

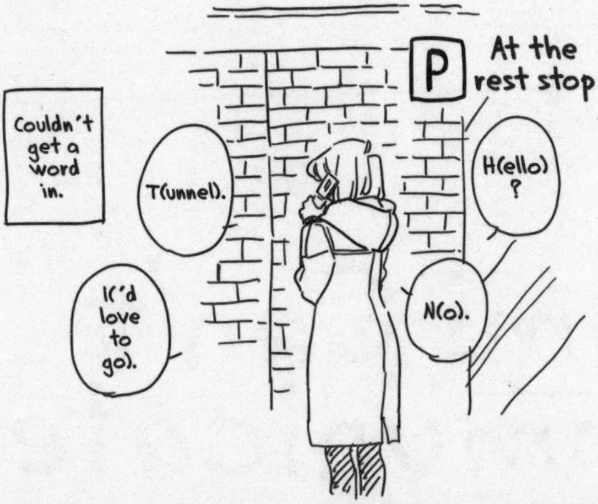
At the rest stop
H(ello)?
N(o).
T(unnel).
I('d love to go).
Couldn't get a word in.

Komi Can't
Communicate

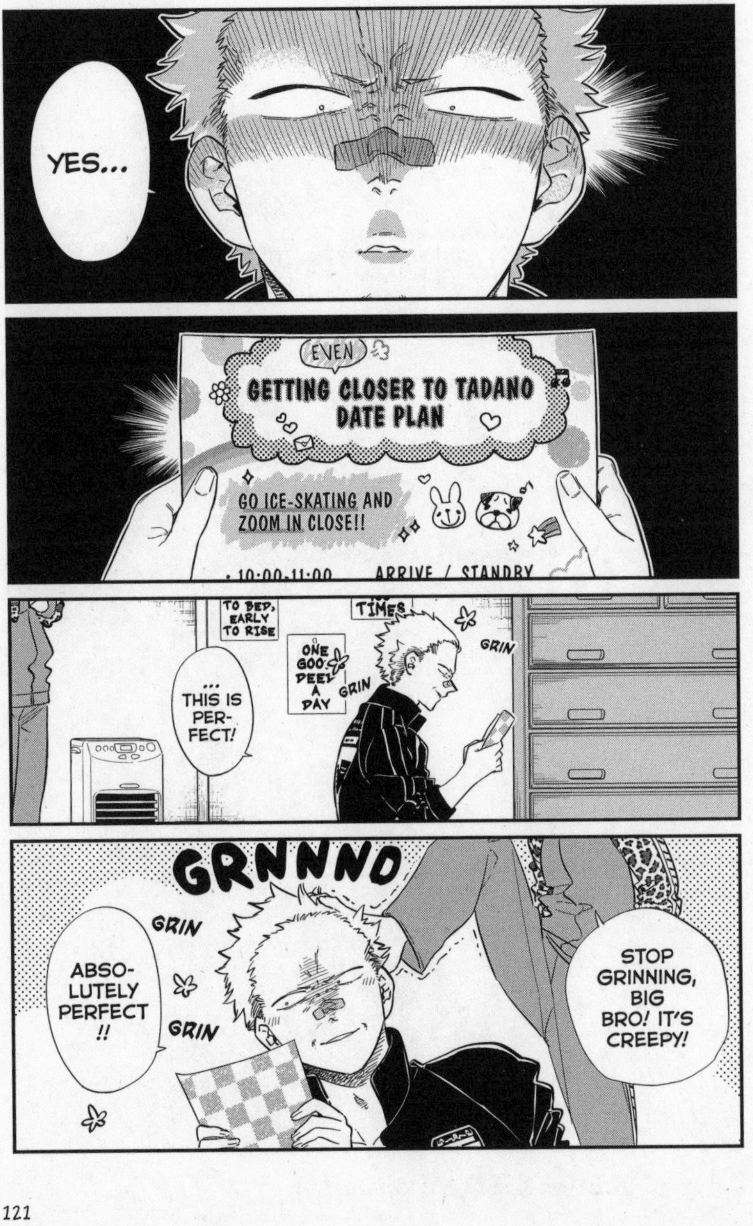
YES...
EVEN
GETTING CLOSER TO TADANO DATE PLAN
GO ICE-SKATING AND ZOOM IN CLOSE!!
10:00-11:00 ARRIVE / STANDBY
TIMES
GRIN
TO BED, EARLY TO RISE
ONE GOO DEEL A DAY
GRIN
... THIS IS PER-FECT!
GRNNND
STOP GRINNING, BIG BRO! IT'S CREEPY!
GRIN
ABSO-LUTELY PERFECT!!
GRIN

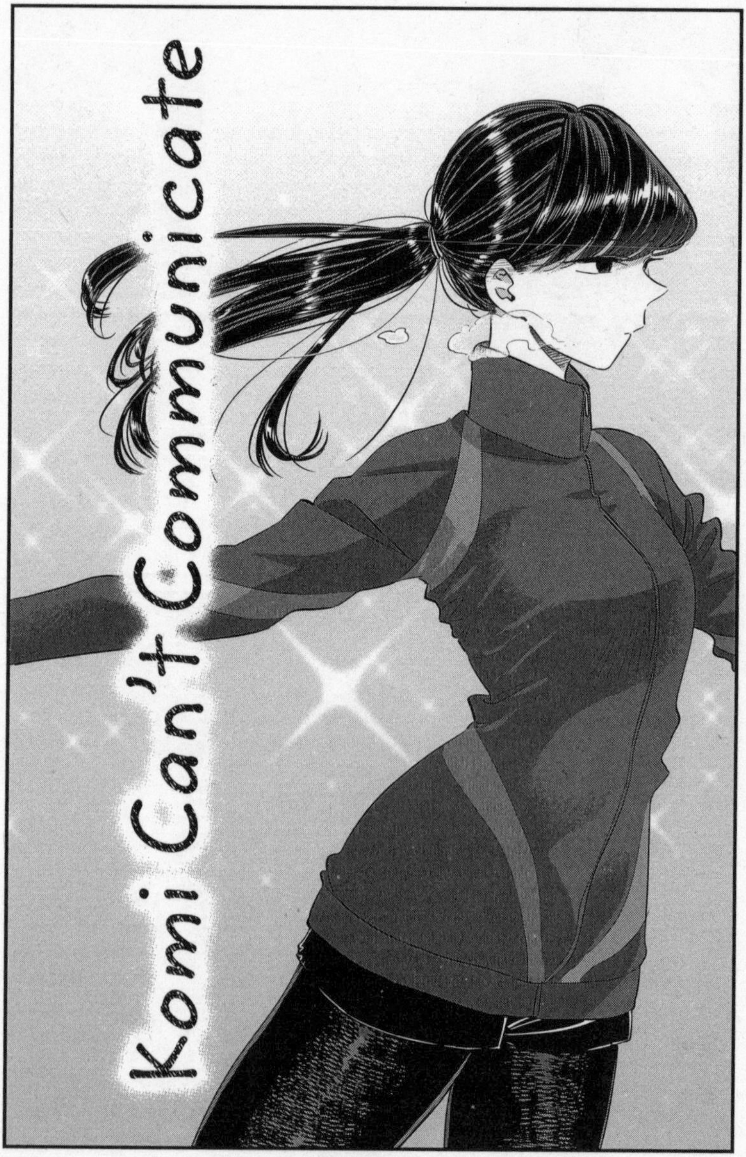
Komi Can't Communicate

Communication 95: Ice-Skating

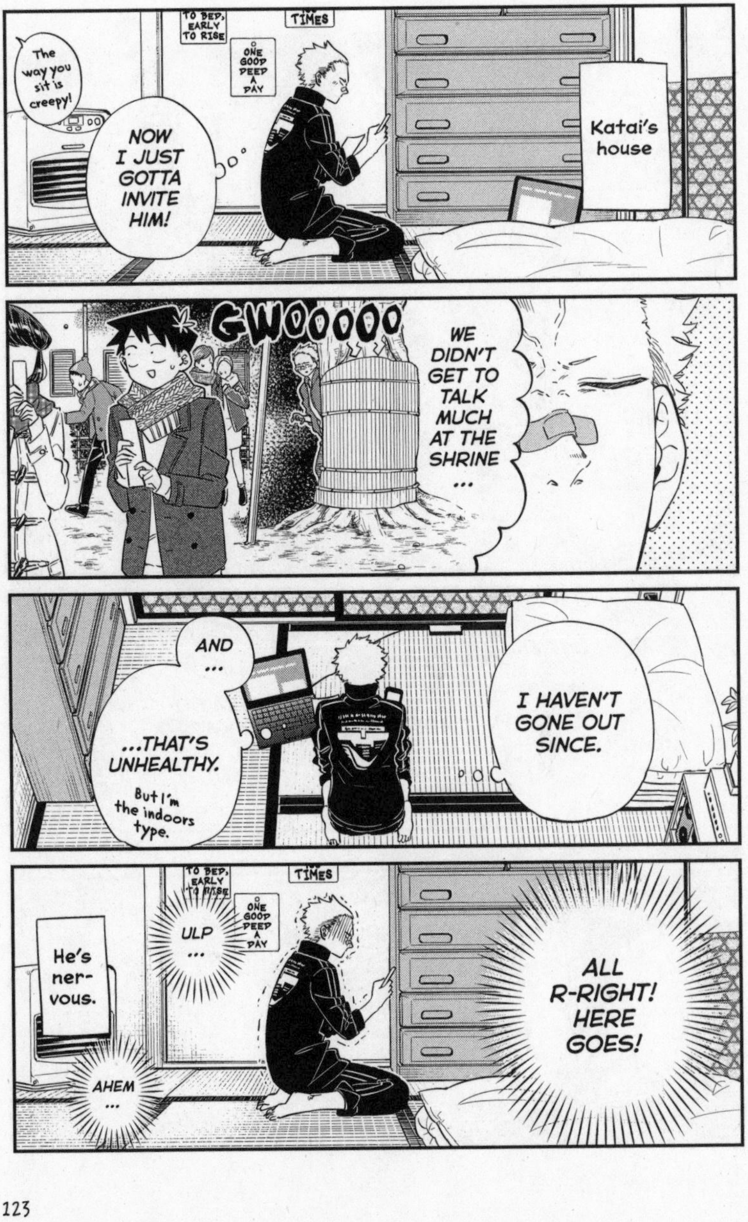
Katai's house
TIMES
ONE GOOD DEED A DAY
NOW I JUST GOTTA INVITE HIM!
TO BED, EARLY TO RISE
The way you sit is creepy!
WE DIDN'T GET TO TALK MUCH AT THE SHRINE ...
GWOOOOO
I HAVEN'T GONE OUT SINCE.
AND ...
...THAT'S UNHEALTHY.
But I'm the indoors type.
ALL R-RIGHT! HERE GOES!
TIMES
ONE GOOD DEED A DAY
ULP ...
TO BED, EARLY TO RISE
He's ner-vous.
AHEM ...

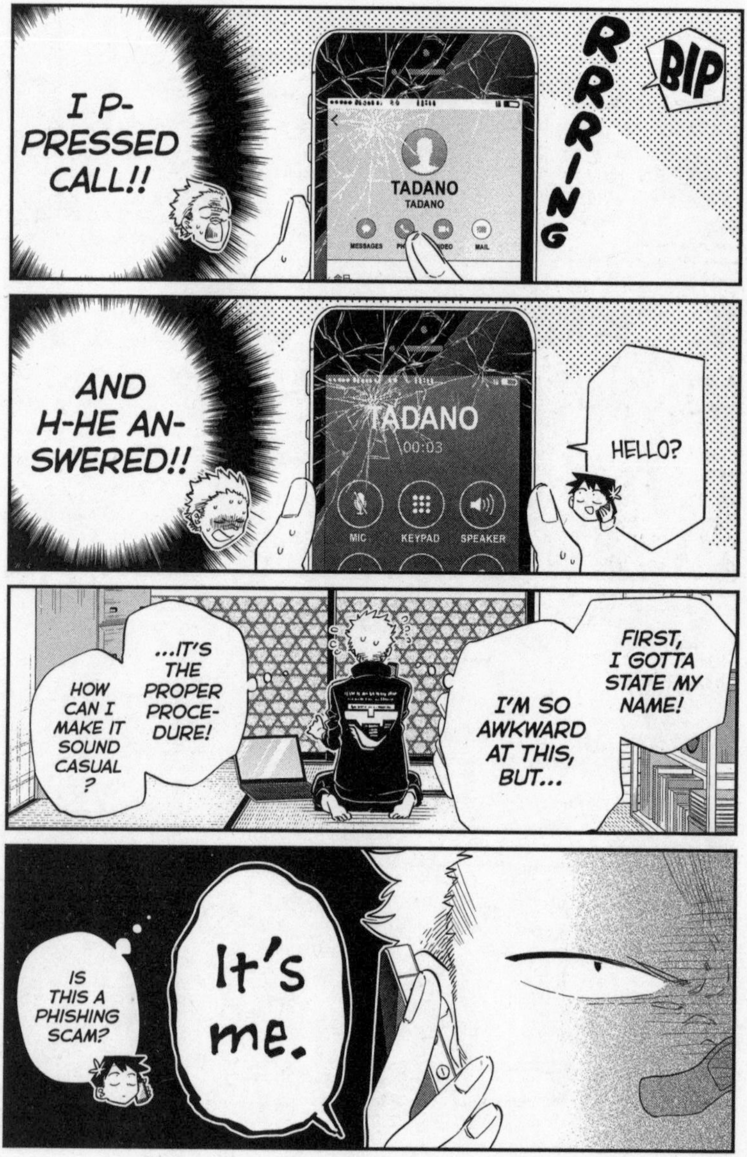
BIP
RRRING
TADANO
TADANO
MESSAGES
MAIL
I P-PRESSED CALL!!
HELLO?
TADANO
00:03
MIC
KEYPAD
SPEAKER
AND H-HE AN-SWERED!!
FIRST, I GOTTA STATE MY NAME!
I'M SO AWKWARD AT THIS, BUT...
...IT'S THE PROPER PROCEDURE!
HOW CAN I MAKE IT SOUND CASUAL?
It's me.
IS THIS A PHISHING SCAM?

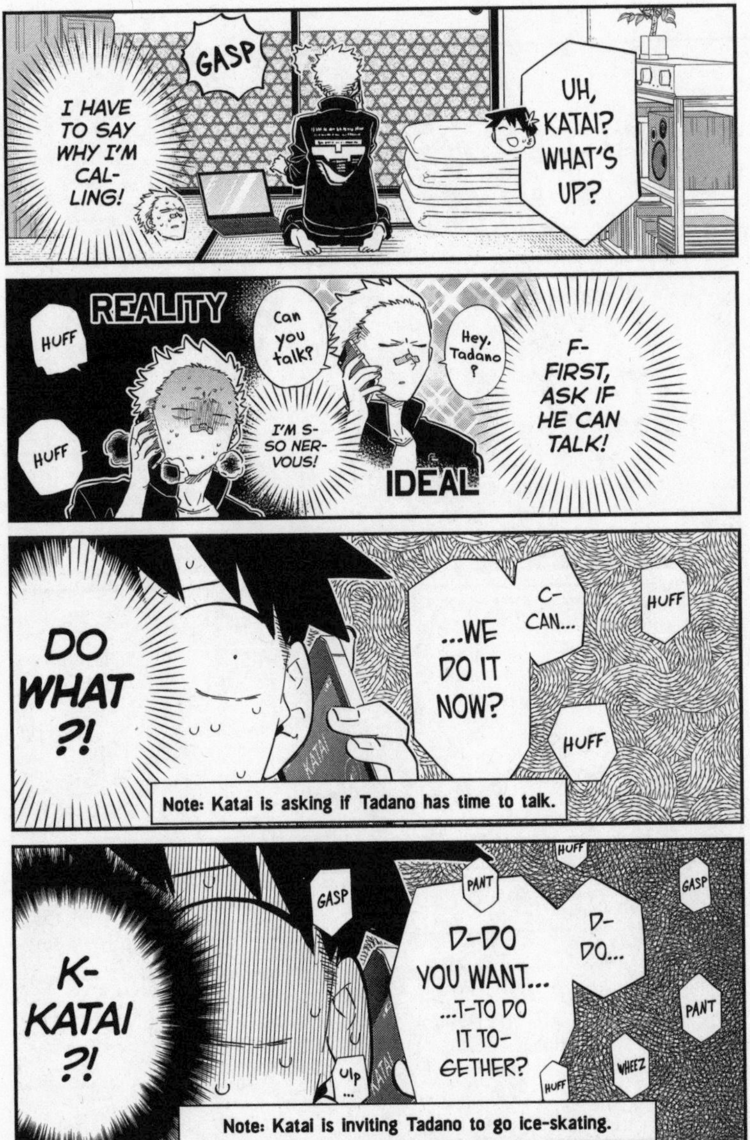
UH, KATAI? WHAT'S UP?
GASP
I HAVE TO SAY WHY I'M CAL-LING!
F-FIRST, ASK IF HE CAN TALK!
Hey, Tadano?
IDEAL
Can you talk?
I'M S-SO NER-VOUS!
REALITY
HUFF
HUFF
HUFF
C-CAN...
...WE DO IT NOW?
HUFF
DO WHAT?!
Note: Katai is asking if Tadano has time to talk.
HUFF
GASP
D-DO...
PANT
D-DO YOU WANT... ...T-TO DO IT TO-GETHER?
GASP
PANT
WHEEZ
HUFF
Ulp...
K-KATAI?!
Note: Katai is inviting Tadano to go ice-skating.

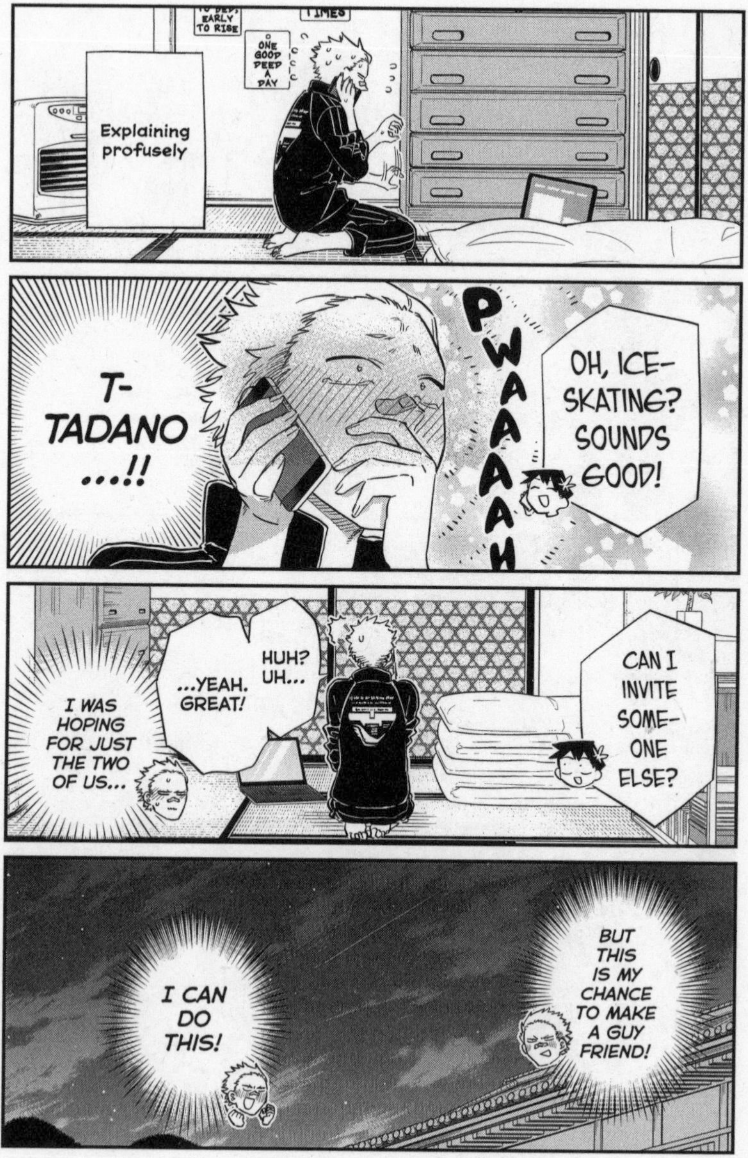
TIMES
ONE GOOD DEED A DAY
EARLY TO RISE
Explaining profusely
OH, ICE-SKATING? SOUNDS GOOD!
PWAAAAAH
T-TADANO ...!!
CAN I INVITE SOME-ONE ELSE?
HUH? UH...
...YEAH. GREAT!
I WAS HOPING FOR JUST THE TWO OF US...
BUT THIS IS MY CHANCE TO MAKE A GUY FRIEND!
I CAN DO THIS!

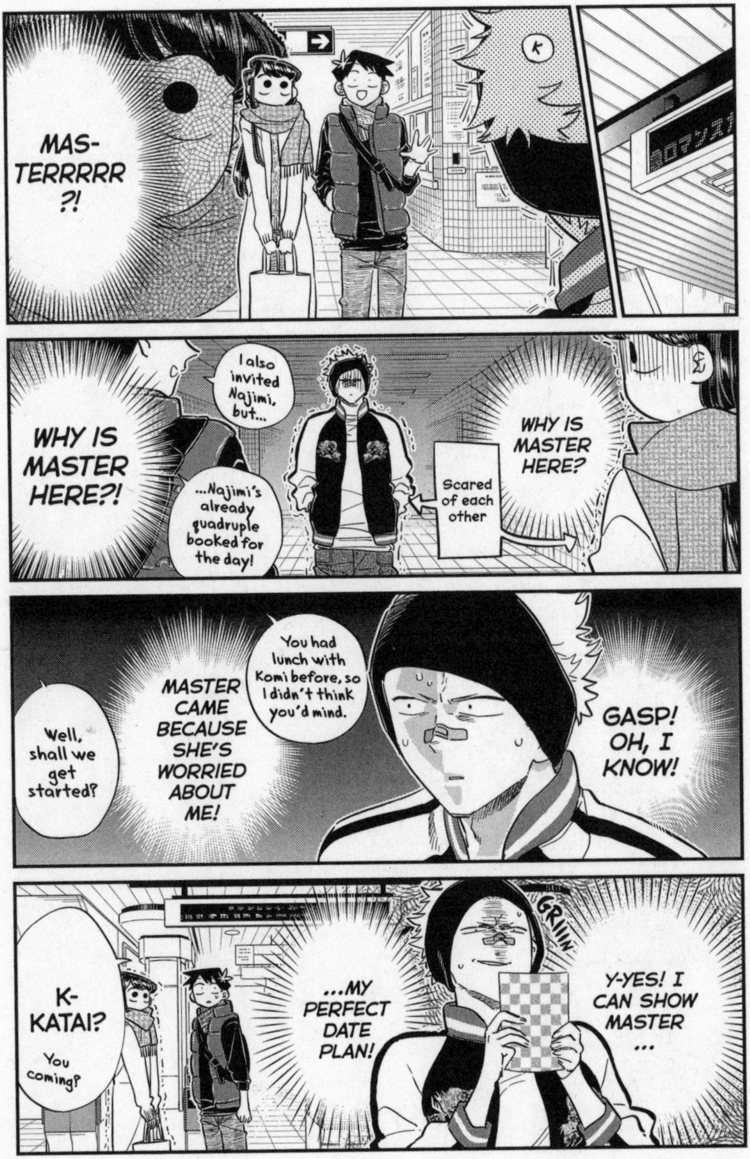
K
MAS-TERRRRR?!
WHY IS MASTER HERE?
Scared of each other
I also invited Najimi, but...
...Najimi's already quadruple booked for the day!
WHY IS MASTER HERE?!
GASP! OH, I KNOW!
You had lunch with Komi before, so I didn't think you'd mind.
MASTER CAME BECAUSE SHE'S WORRIED ABOUT ME!
Well, shall we get started?
GRIIIN
Y-YES! I CAN SHOW MASTER ...
...MY PERFECT DATE PLAN!
K-KATAI?
You coming?

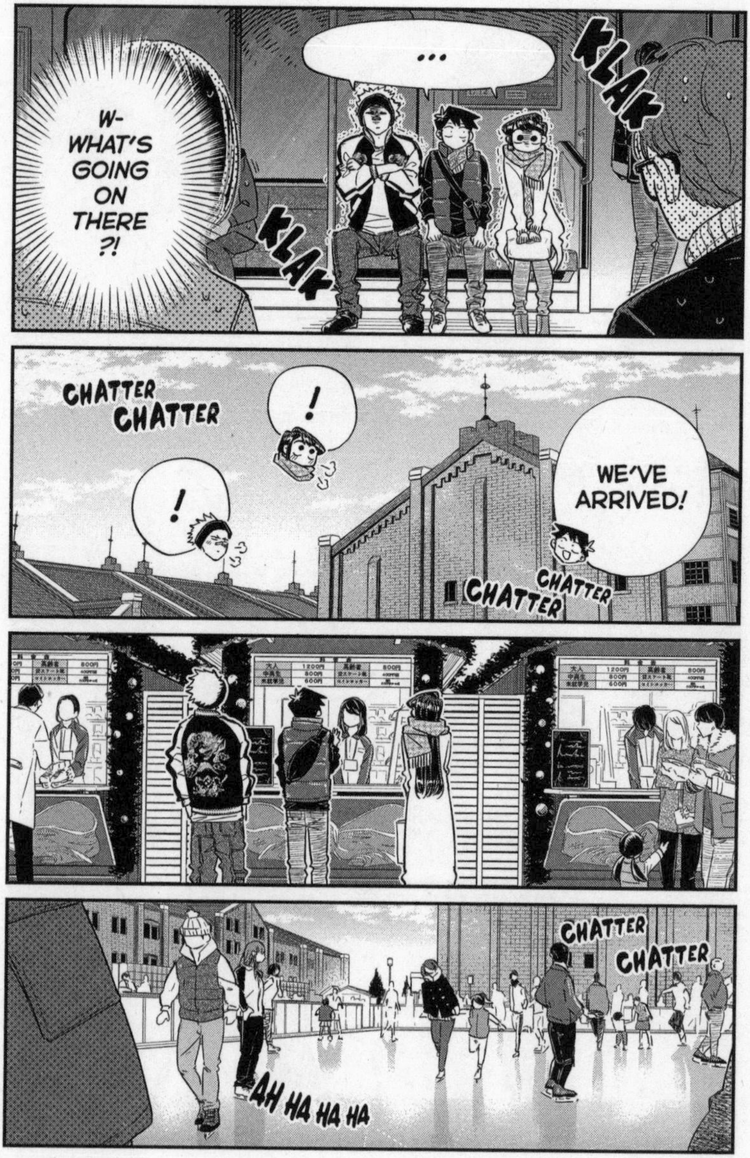
KLAK
...
W-WHAT'S GOING ON THERE?!
KLAK
WE'VE ARRIVED!
CHATTER CHATTER
!
!
CHATTER CHATTER
CHATTER CHATTER
AH HA HA HA

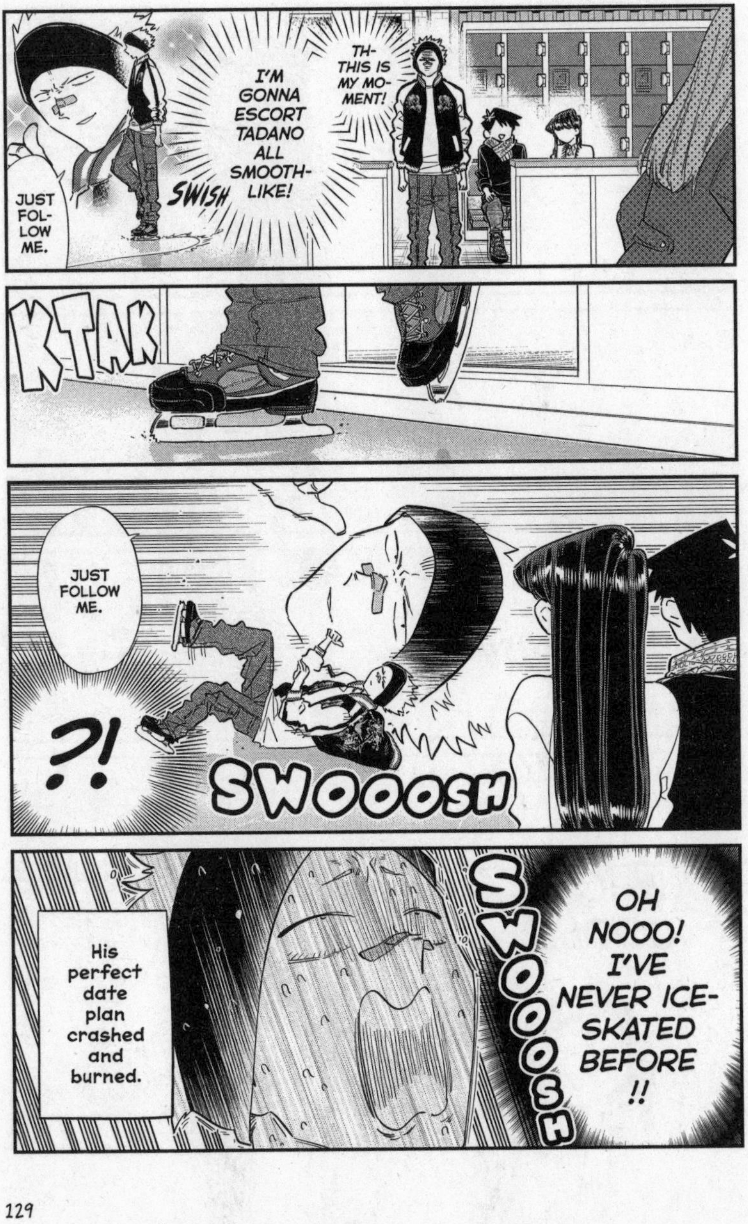
TH- THIS IS MY MO- MENT!
I'M GONNA ESCORT TADANO ALL SMOOTH-LIKE!
SWISH
JUST FOL- LOW ME.
KTAK
JUST FOLLOW ME.
SWOOOSH
?!
OH NOOO! I'VE NEVER ICE-SKATED BEFORE !!
SWOOOOSH
His perfect date plan crashed and burned.

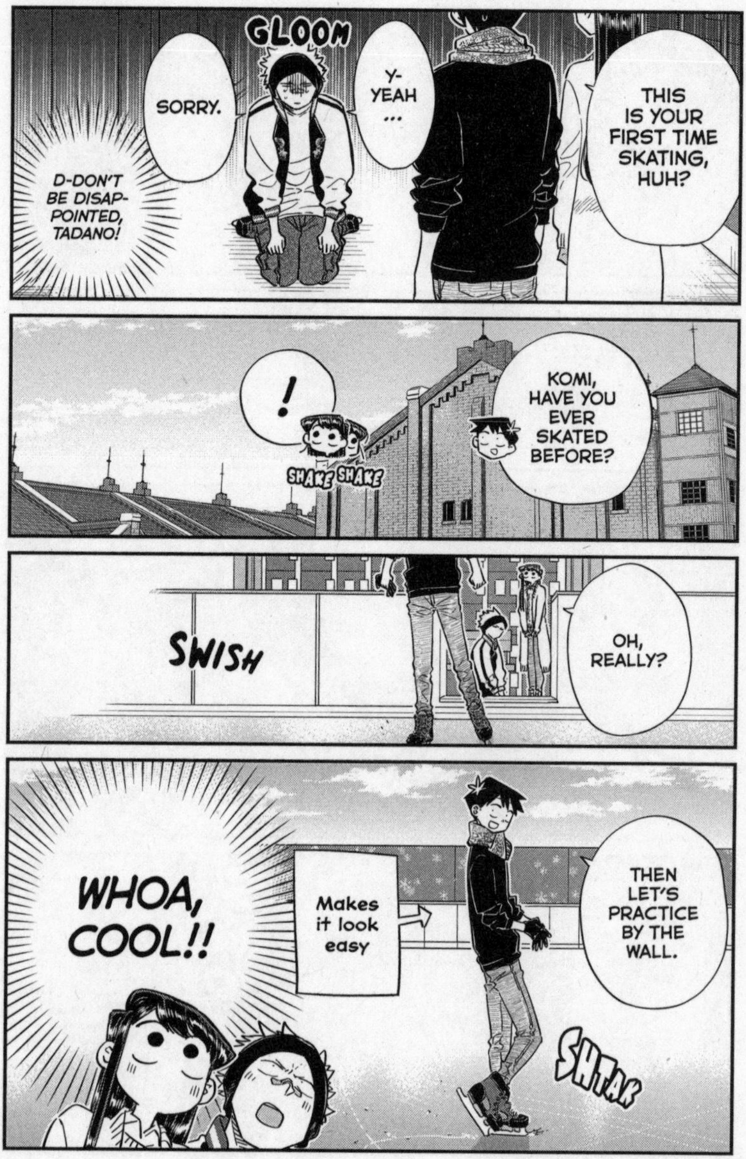
THIS IS YOUR FIRST TIME SKATING, HUH?
Y-YEAH ...
GLOOM
SORRY.
D-DON'T BE DISAP-POINTED, TADANO!
KOMI, HAVE YOU EVER SKATED BEFORE?
!
SHAKE SHAKE
OH, REALLY?
SWISH
THEN LET'S PRACTICE BY THE WALL.
SHTAK
Makes it look easy
WHOA, COOL!!

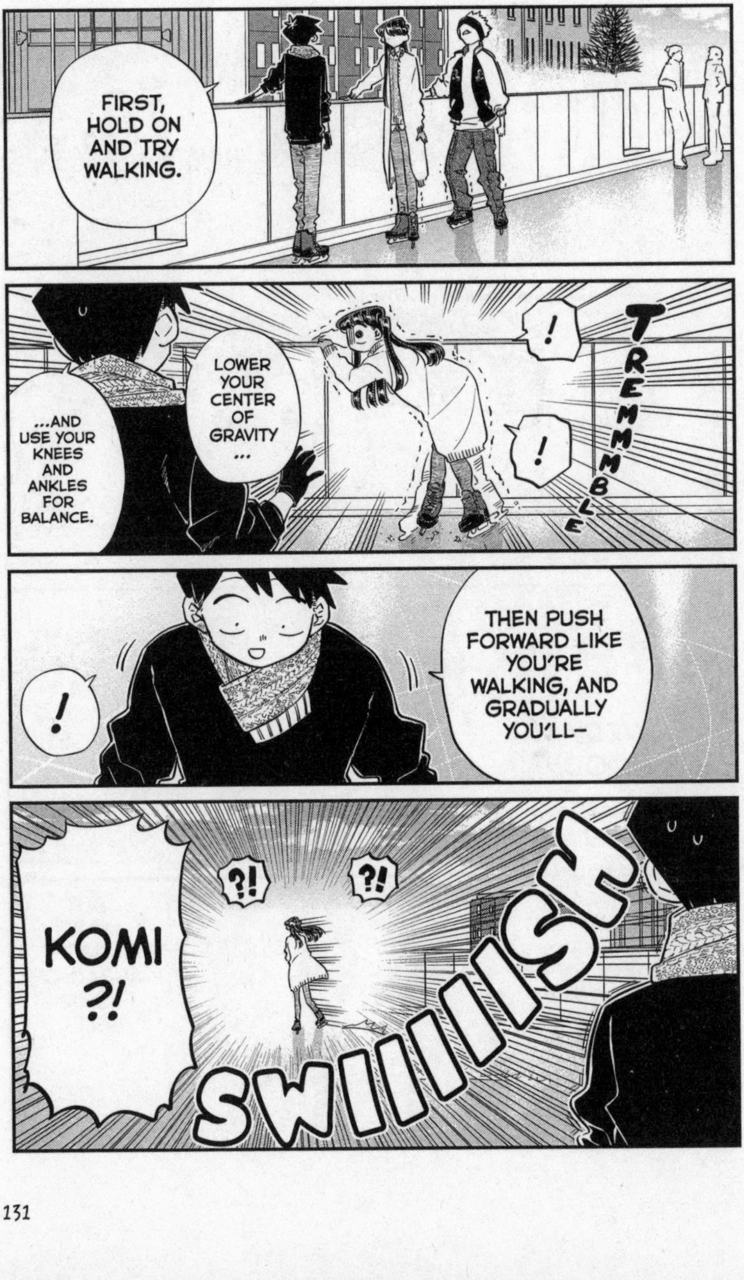
FIRST, HOLD ON AND TRY WALKING.
TREMMMBLE
!
!
LOWER YOUR CENTER OF GRAVITY ...
...AND USE YOUR KNEES AND ANKLES FOR BALANCE.
THEN PUSH FORWARD LIKE YOU'RE WALKING, AND GRADUALLY YOU'LL—
!
SWIIIIISH
?!
?!
KOMI ?!

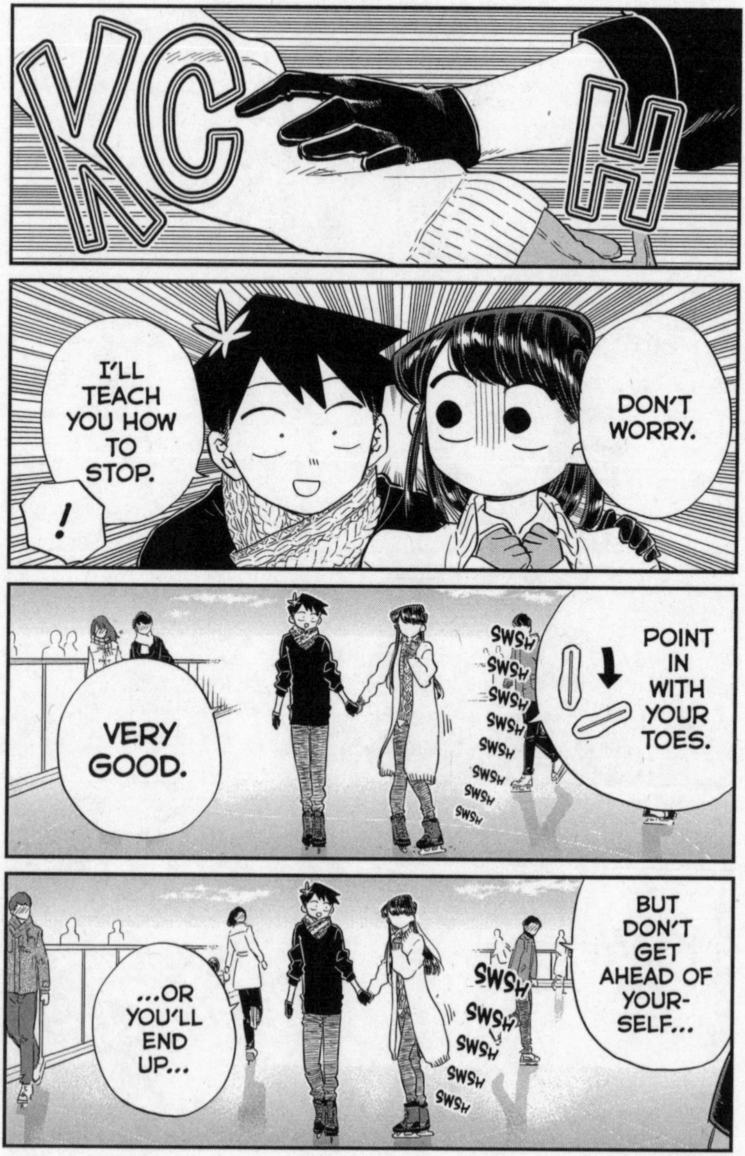
KCH
DON'T WORRY.
I'LL TEACH YOU HOW TO STOP.
!
POINT IN WITH YOUR TOES.
SWSH SWSH SWSH SWSH SWSH SWSH SWSH SWSH
VERY GOOD.
BUT DON'T GET AHEAD OF YOUR-SELF...
SWSH SWSH SWSH SWSH SWSH
...OR YOU'LL END UP...

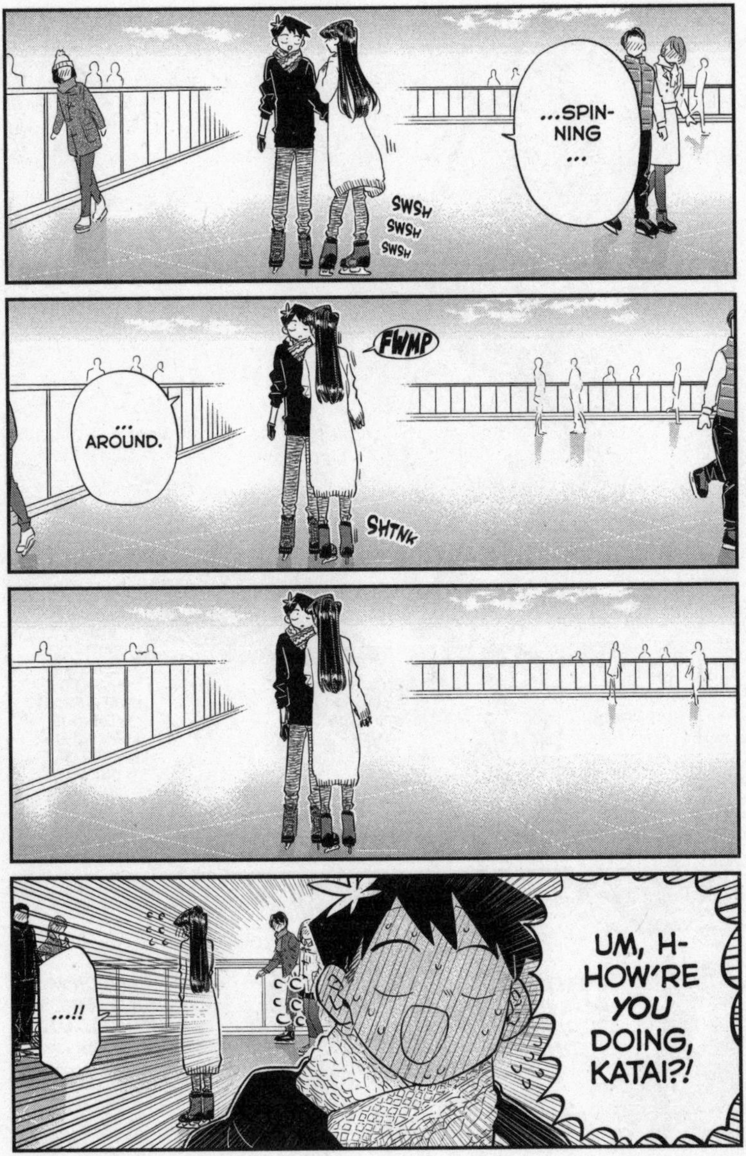

...SPIN-NING ...
SWSH SWSH SWSH
FWMP
... AROUND.
SHTNK
UM, H-HOW'RE *YOU* DOING, KATAI?!
...!!

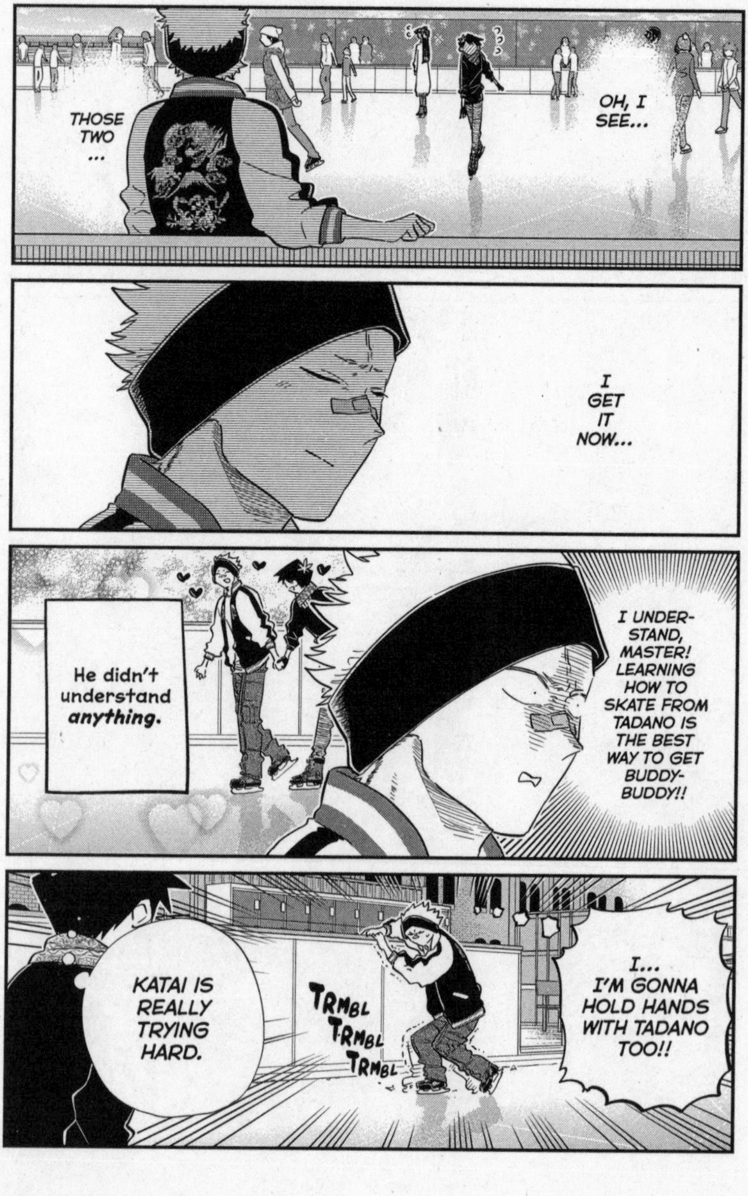
OH, I SEE...
THOSE TWO ...
I GET IT NOW...
I UNDERSTAND, MASTER! LEARNING HOW TO SKATE FROM TADANO IS THE BEST WAY TO GET BUDDY-BUDDY!!
He didn't understand *anything.*
I... I'M GONNA HOLD HANDS WITH TADANO TOO!!
TRMBL TRMBL TRMBL
KATAI IS REALLY TRYING HARD.

HUFF!
HUFF!
SHAK
SHAK
WHOA!
WAH!
WOBBLE
WHOOPS!
SHTAK

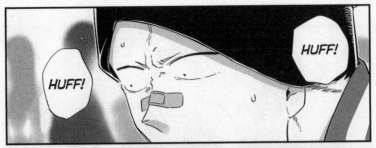

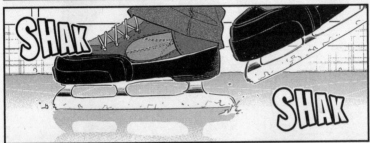

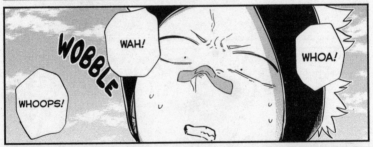

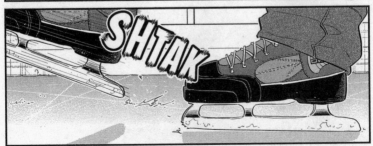

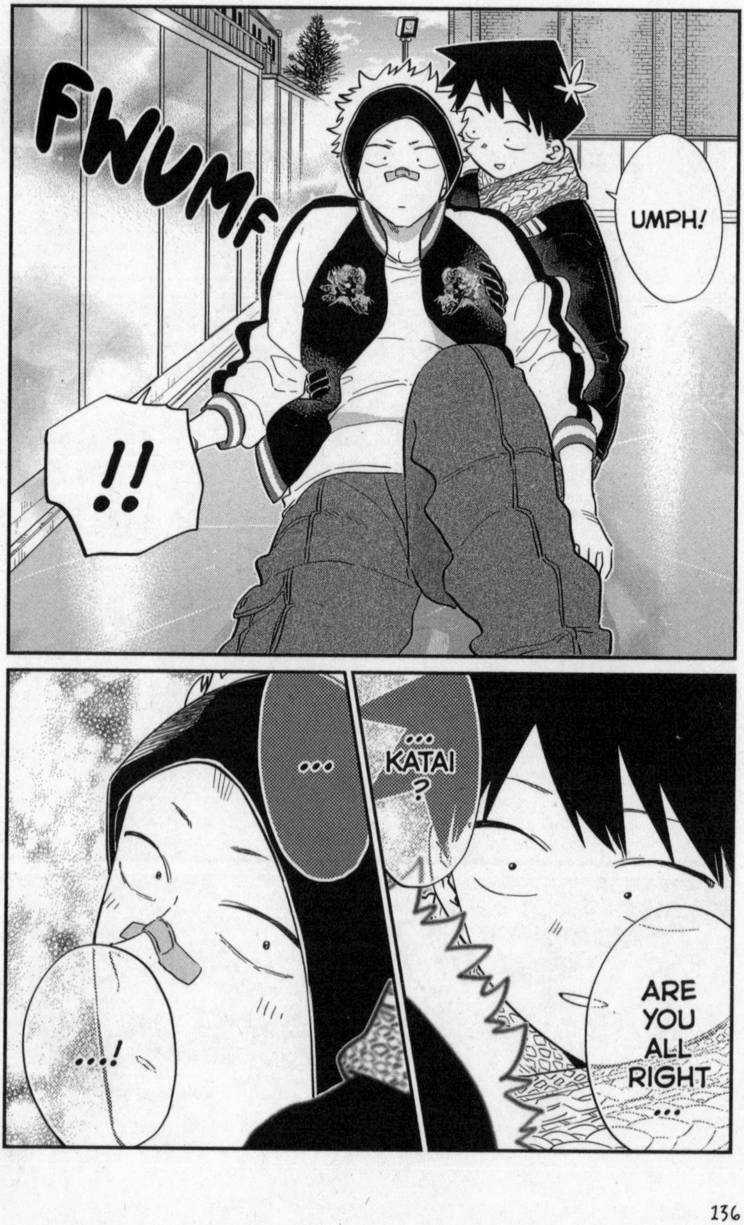
UMPH!
FWUMF
!!
...KATAI?
ARE YOU ALL RIGHT...
...
...!

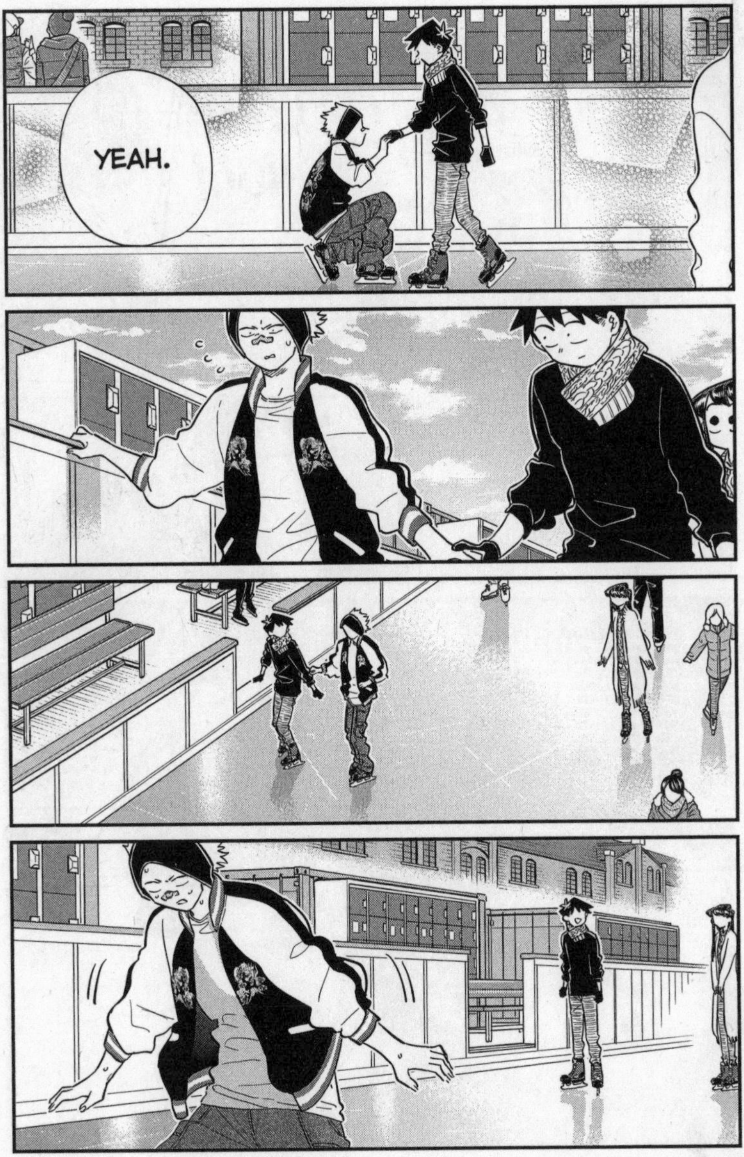
YEAH.

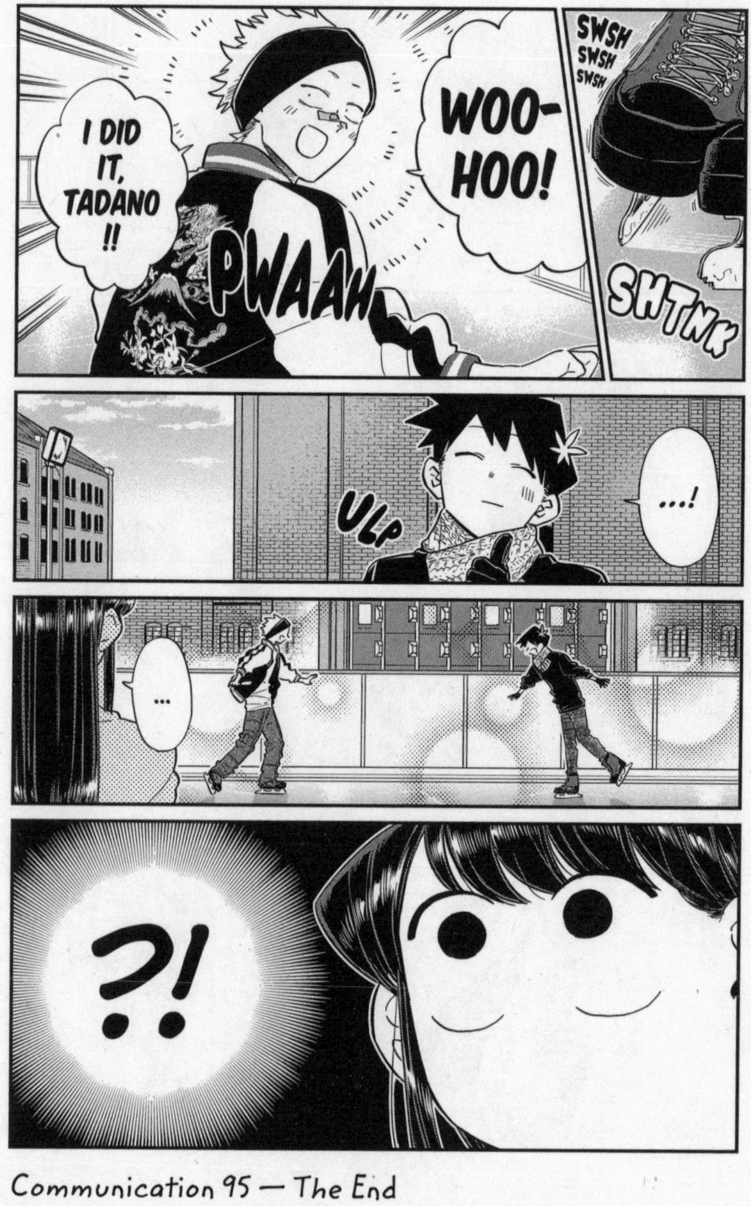
SWSH
SWSH
SWSH
SHTNK
WOO-HOO!
I DID IT, TADANO!!
PWAAH
...!
ULP
...
?!

Communication 95 — The End

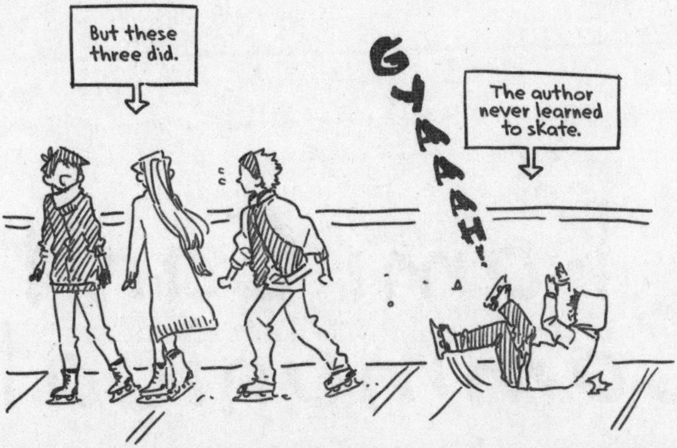
The author never learned to skate.
GYAAAH!
But these three did.

Komi Can't
Communicate

Komi Can't Communicate

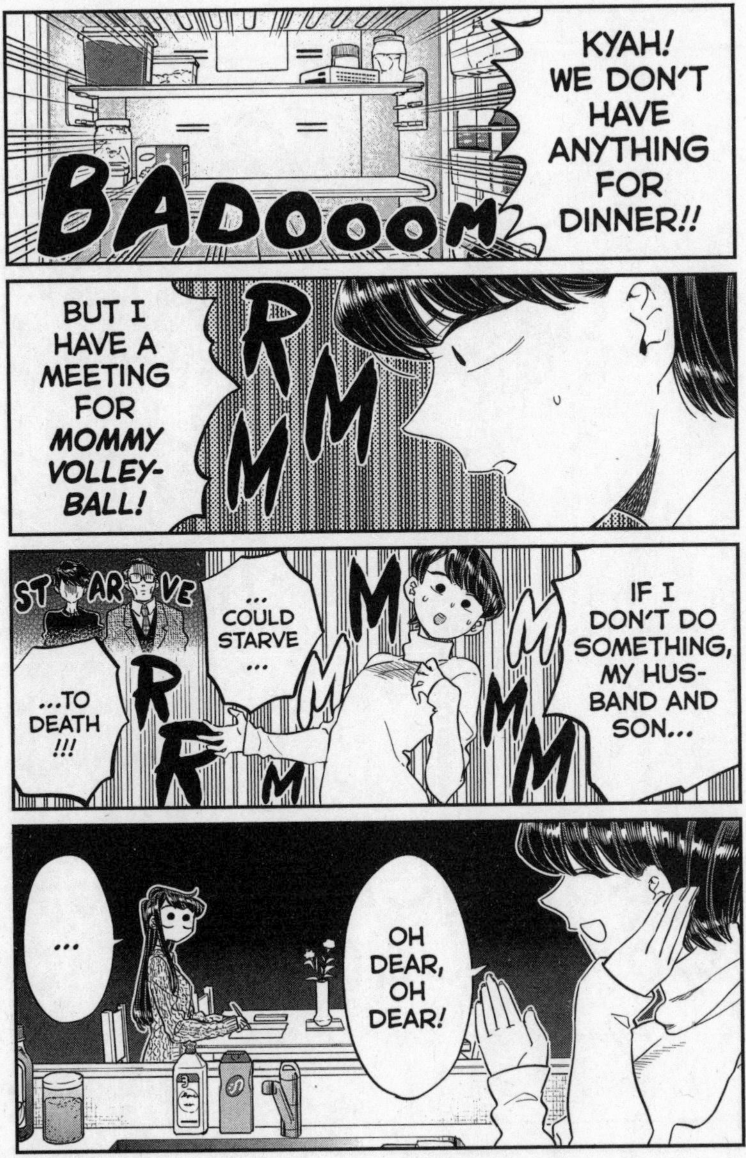
KYAH! WE DON'T HAVE ANYTHING FOR DINNER!!
BADOOOM
RMMM
BUT I HAVE A MEETING FOR *MOMMY VOLLEY-BALL!*
IF I DON'T DO SOMETHING, MY HUS-BAND AND SON...
MMMMMMMM
... COULD STARVE ...
STARVE
...TO DEATH !!!
RR
OH DEAR, OH DEAR!
...

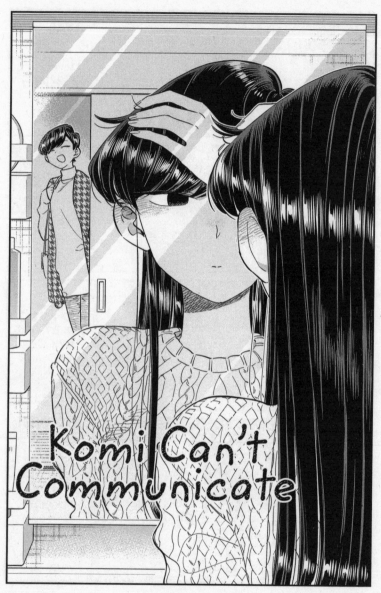

Communication 96: Shopping for Dinner

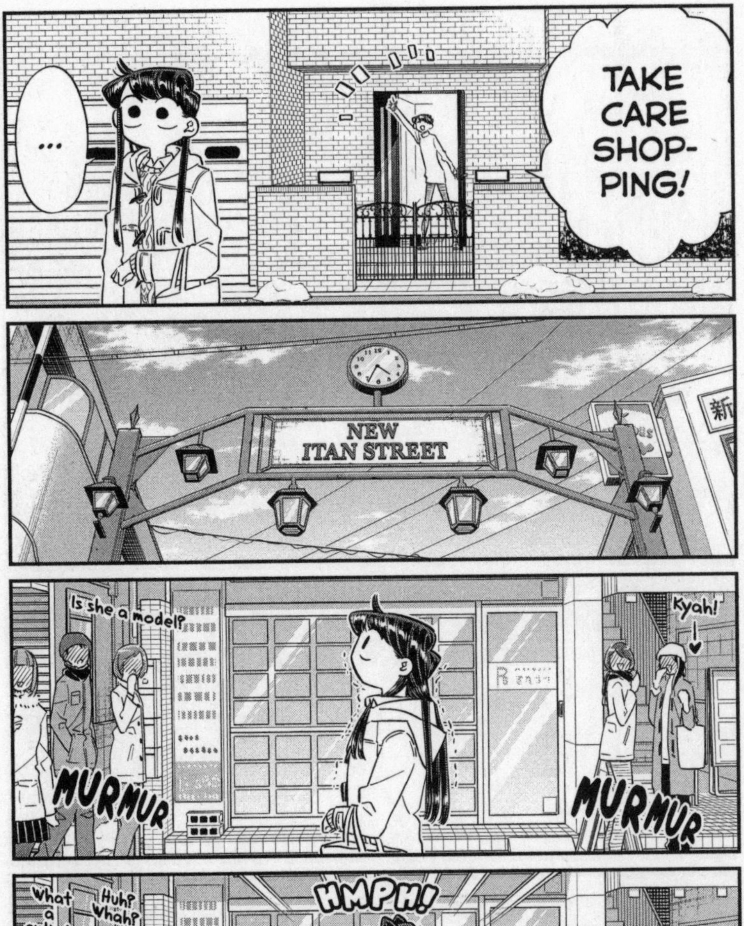
TAKE CARE SHOP-PING!
...
NEW ITAN STREET
Kyah!
Is she a model?
MURMUR
MURMUR
HMPH!
Huh? Whah?
What a cutie!
Steel-ing her nerves
CHATTER
CHATTER
CHATTER
CHATTER

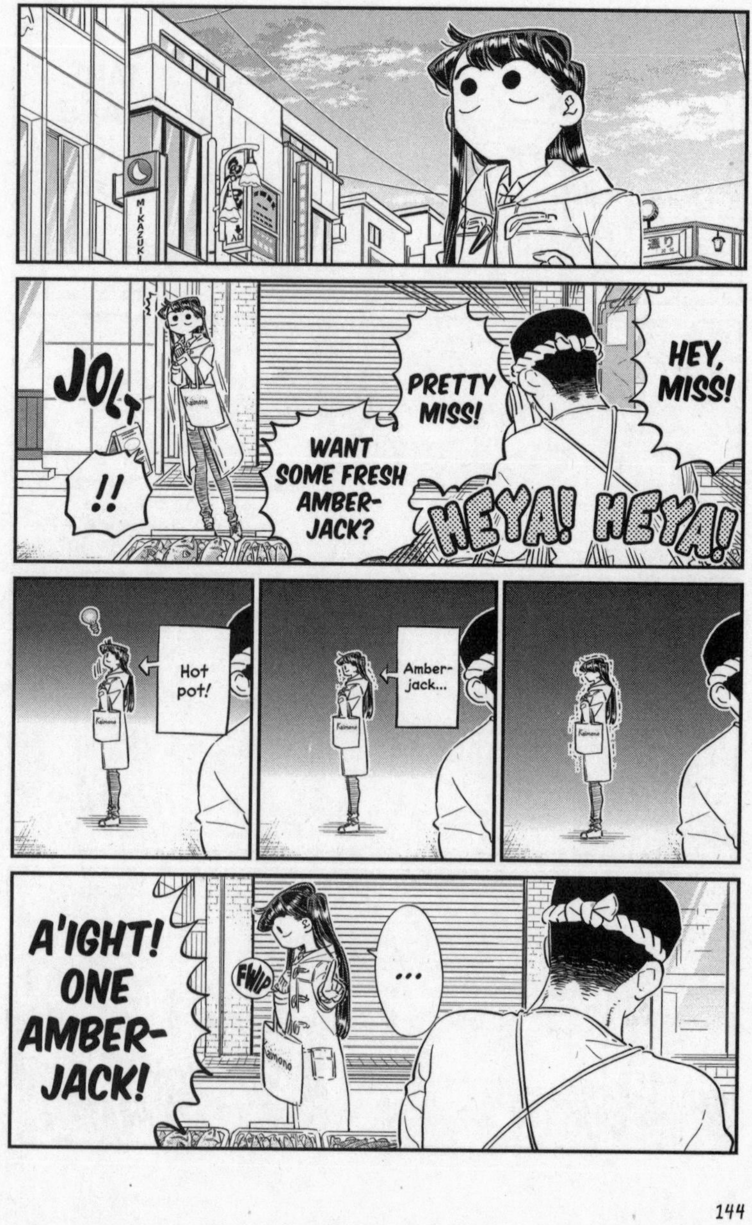
MIKAZUKI
HEY, MISS!
PRETTY MISS!
WANT SOME FRESH AMBER-JACK?
HEYA! HEYA!
JOLT
!!
Amber-jack...
Hot pot!
...
FWIP
A'IGHT! ONE AMBER-JACK!

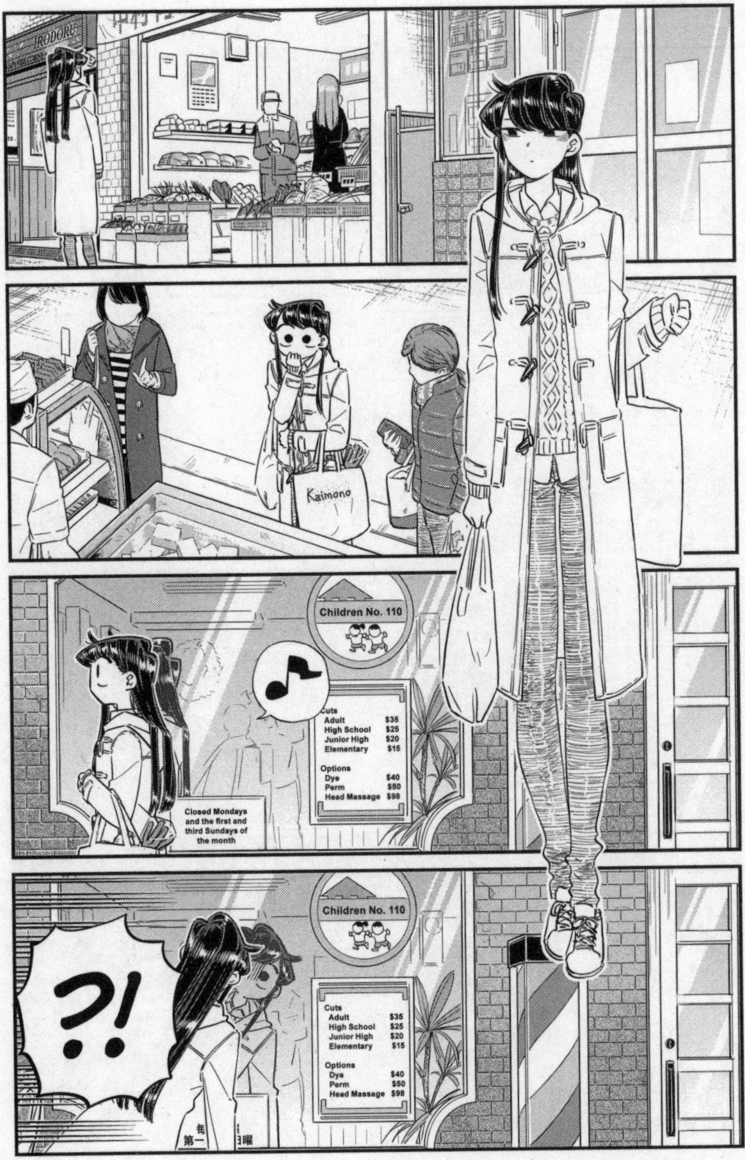
IRODORU
Kaimono
Children No. 110
♪
Cuts
Adult $35
High School $25
Junior High $20
Elementary $15
Options
Dye $40
Perm $50
Head Massage $98
Closed Mondays and the first and third Sundays of the month
?!
Children No. 110
Cuts
Adult $35
High School $25
Junior High $20
Elementary $15
Options
Dye $40
Perm $50
Head Massage $98

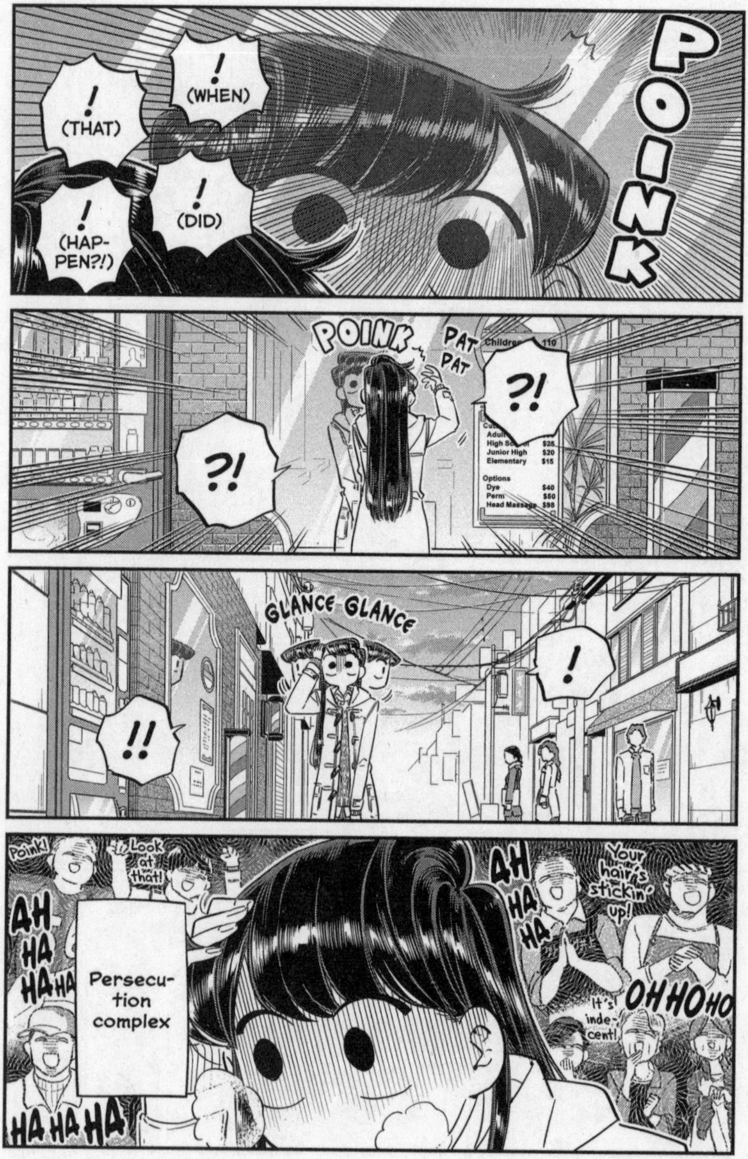
POINK
! (WHEN)
! (DID)
! (THAT)
! (HAP-PEN?!)
POINK
PAT PAT
Junior High $20
Elementary $15
Options
Dye $40
Perm $50
Head Massage $98
?!
?!
GLANCE GLANCE
!
!!
Your hair's stickin' up!
AH HA HA
OHHOHOHO
It's inde-cent!
Persecu-tion complex
Look at that!
Poink!
AH HA HA HA
HA HA HA

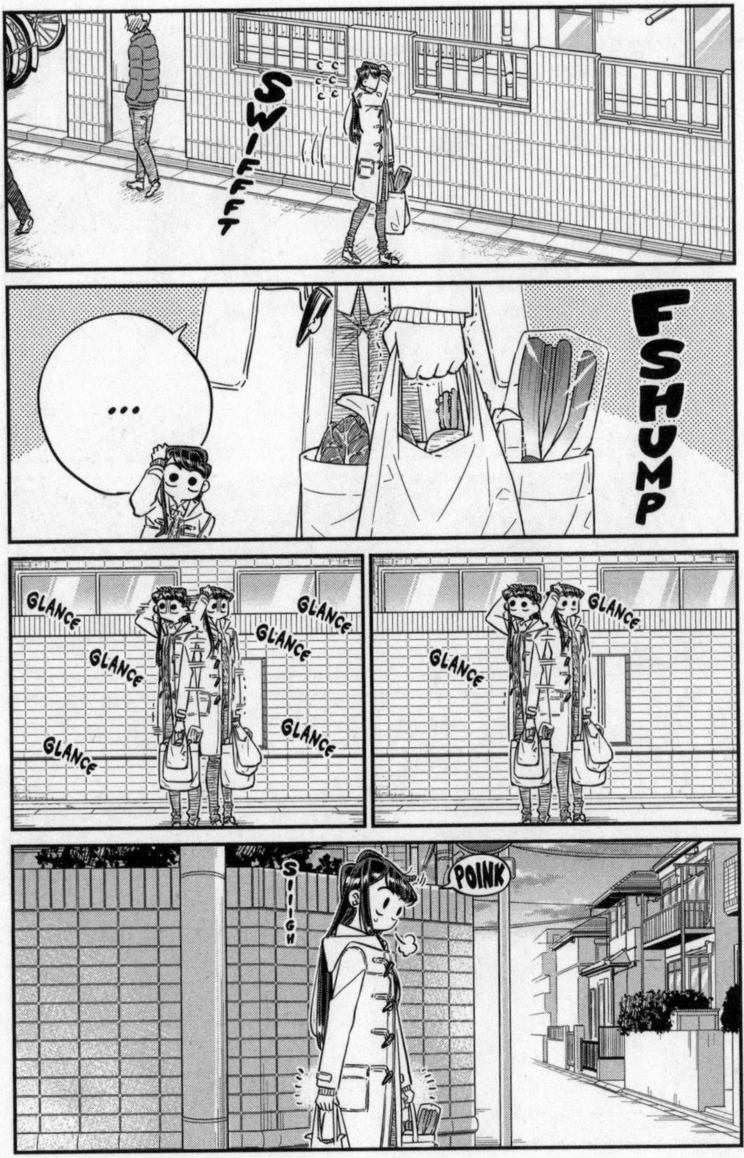
SWIFFFT
FSHUMP
...
GLANCE
GLANCE
GLANCE
GLANCE
GLANCE
GLANCE
GLANCE
POINK
SIIIGH

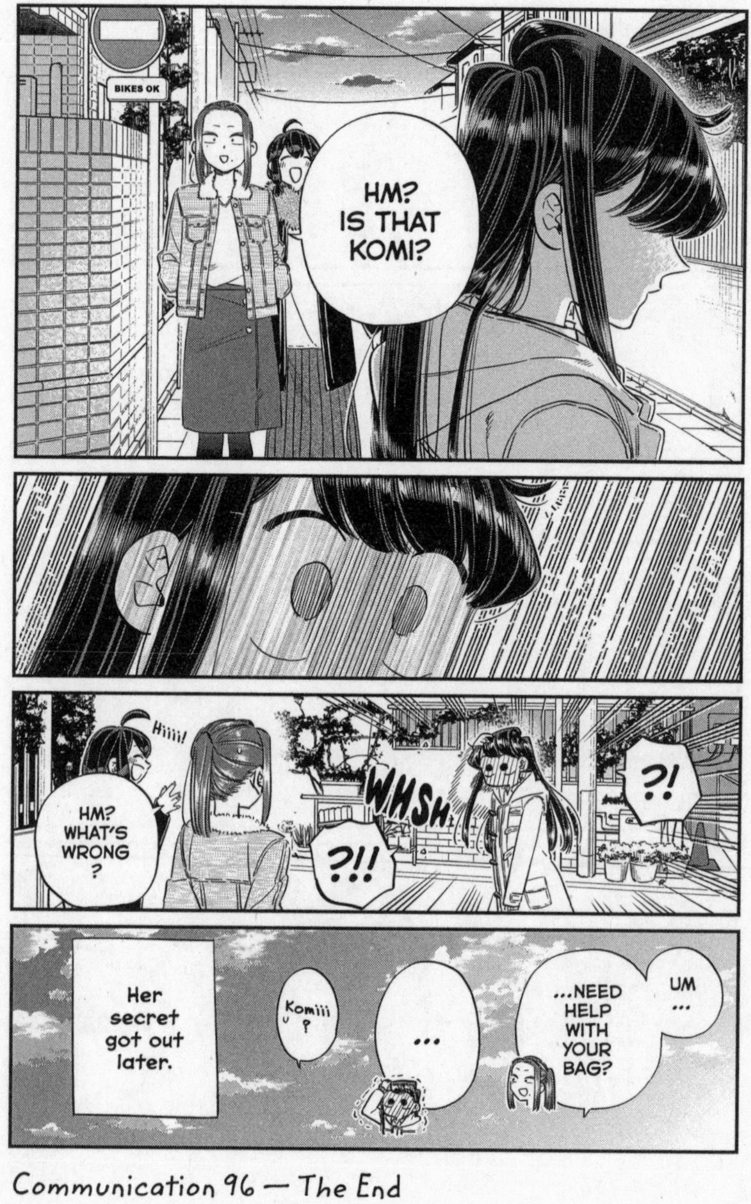
HM? IS THAT KOMI?
BIKES OK
?!
WHSH
?!!
HM? WHAT'S WRONG ?
Hiiii!
UM ...
...NEED HELP WITH YOUR BAG?
...
Komiii ?
Her secret got out later.

Communication 96 — The End

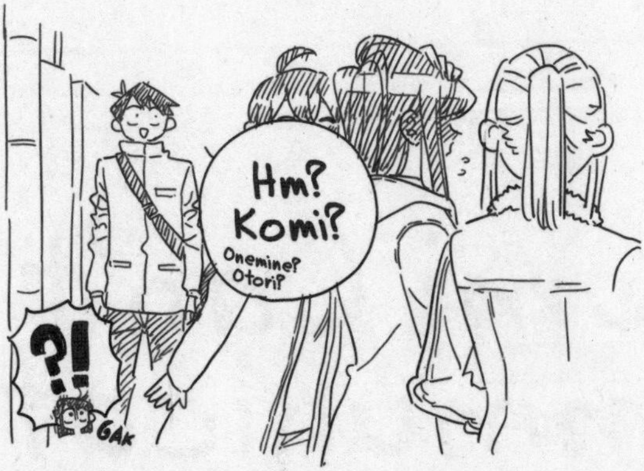
Hm? Komi?
Onemine? Otori?
?!
GAK

Komi Can't
Communicate

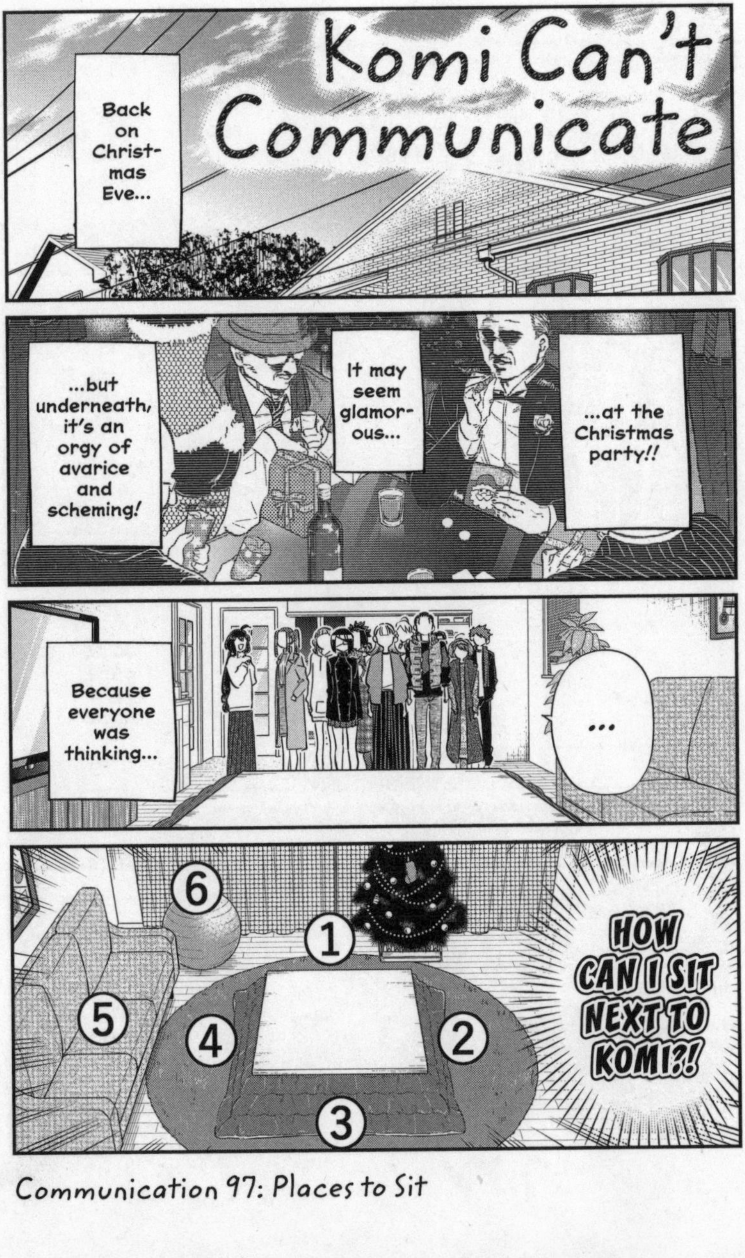
Komi Can't Communicate
Back on Christmas Eve...
...at the Christmas party!!
It may seem glamorous...
...but underneath, it's an orgy of avarice and scheming!
...
Because everyone was thinking...
HOW CAN I SIT NEXT TO KOMI?!
1
6
2
4
5
3

Communication 97: Places to Sit

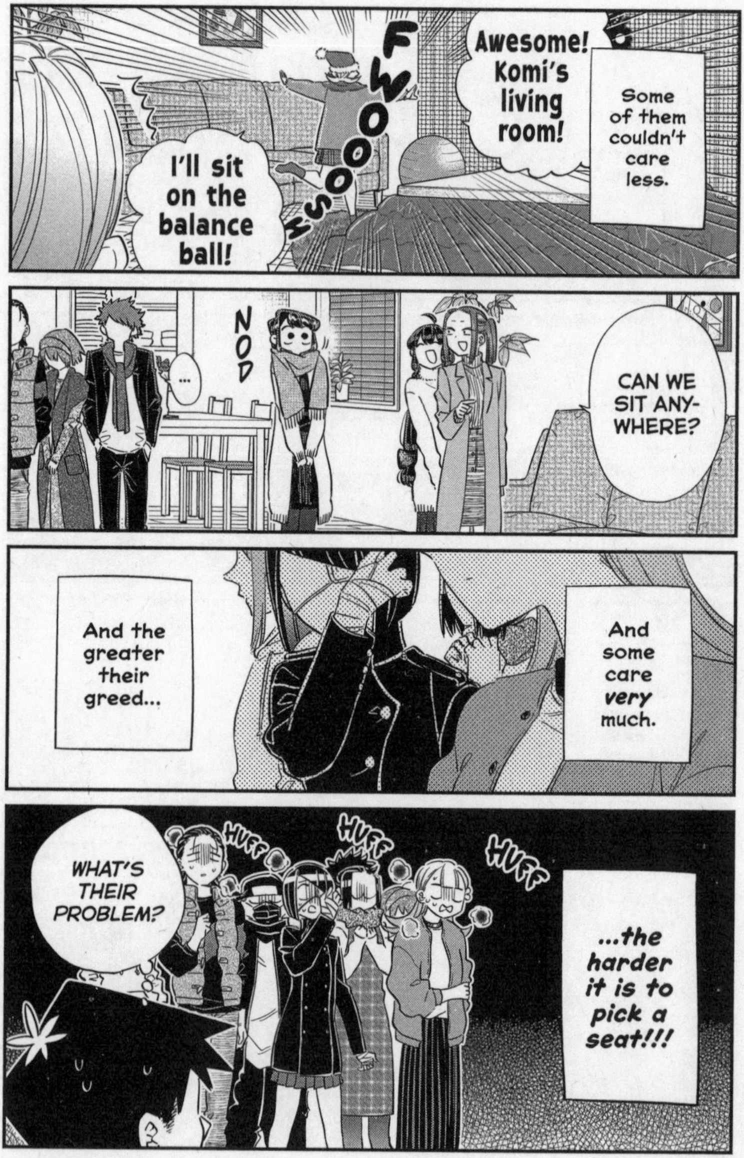
Some of them couldn't care less.
Awesome! Komi's living room!
FWOOOOSH
I'll sit on the balance ball!
CAN WE SIT ANYWHERE?
NOD
...
And some care *very* much.
And the greater their greed...
...the harder it is to pick a seat!!!
HUFF
HUFF
HUFF
WHAT'S THEIR PROBLEM?

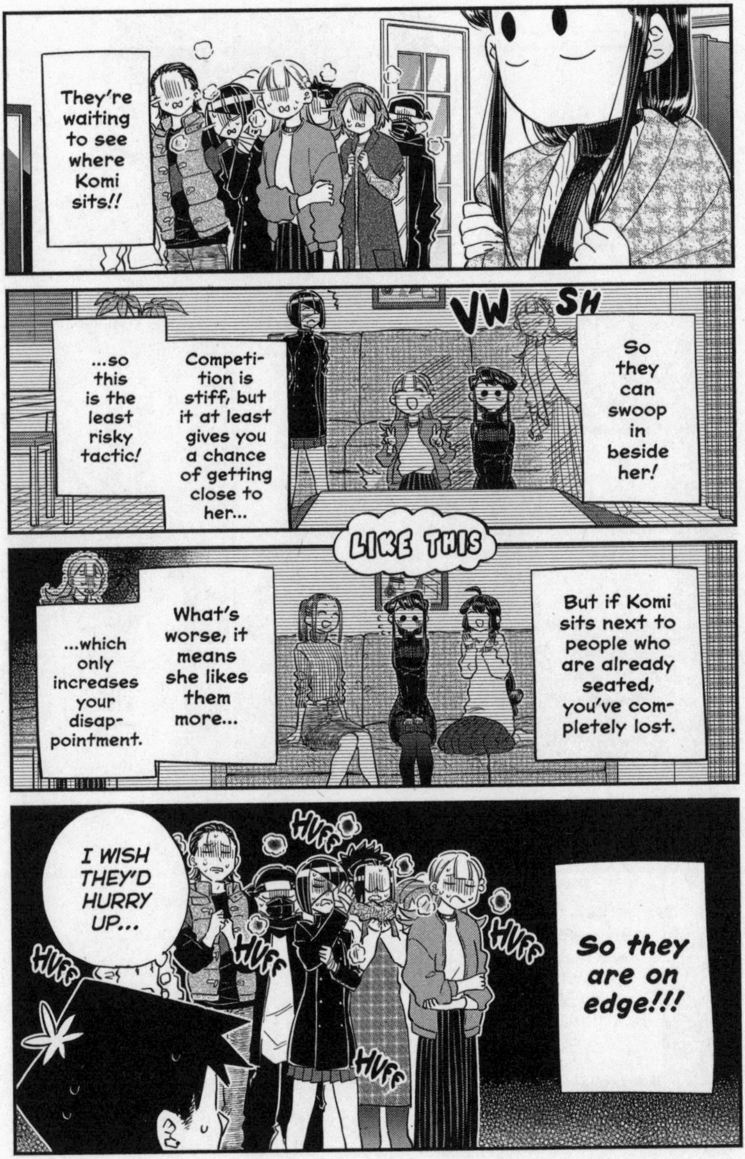
They're waiting to see where Komi sits!!
VWSH
So they can swoop in beside her!
Competition is stiff, but it at least gives you a chance of getting close to her...
...so this is the least risky tactic!
LIKE THIS
But if Komi sits next to people who are already seated, you've completely lost.
What's worse, it means she likes them more...
...which only increases your disappointment.
So they are on edge!!!
HUFF
HUFF
HUFF
I WISH THEY'D HURRY UP...
HUFF
HUFF

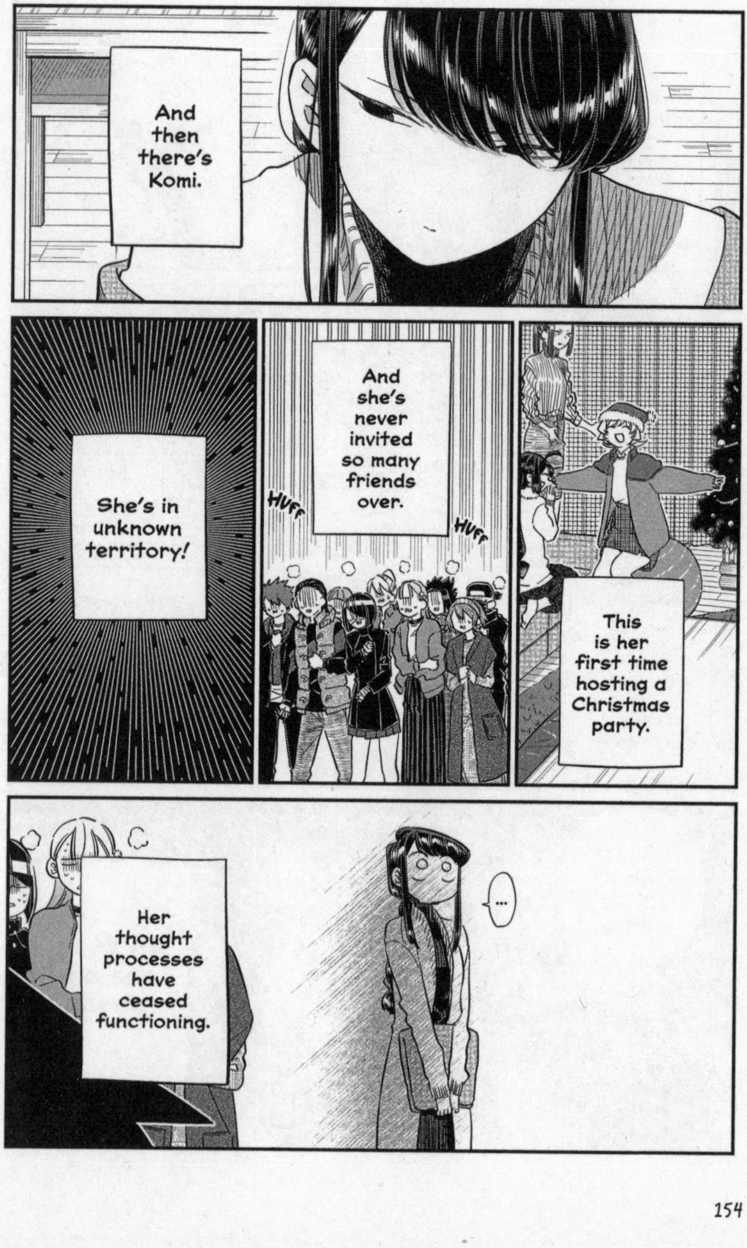
And then there's Komi.
This is her first time hosting a Christmas party.
And she's never invited so many friends over.
HUFF
HUFF
She's in unknown territory!
...
Her thought processes have ceased functioning.

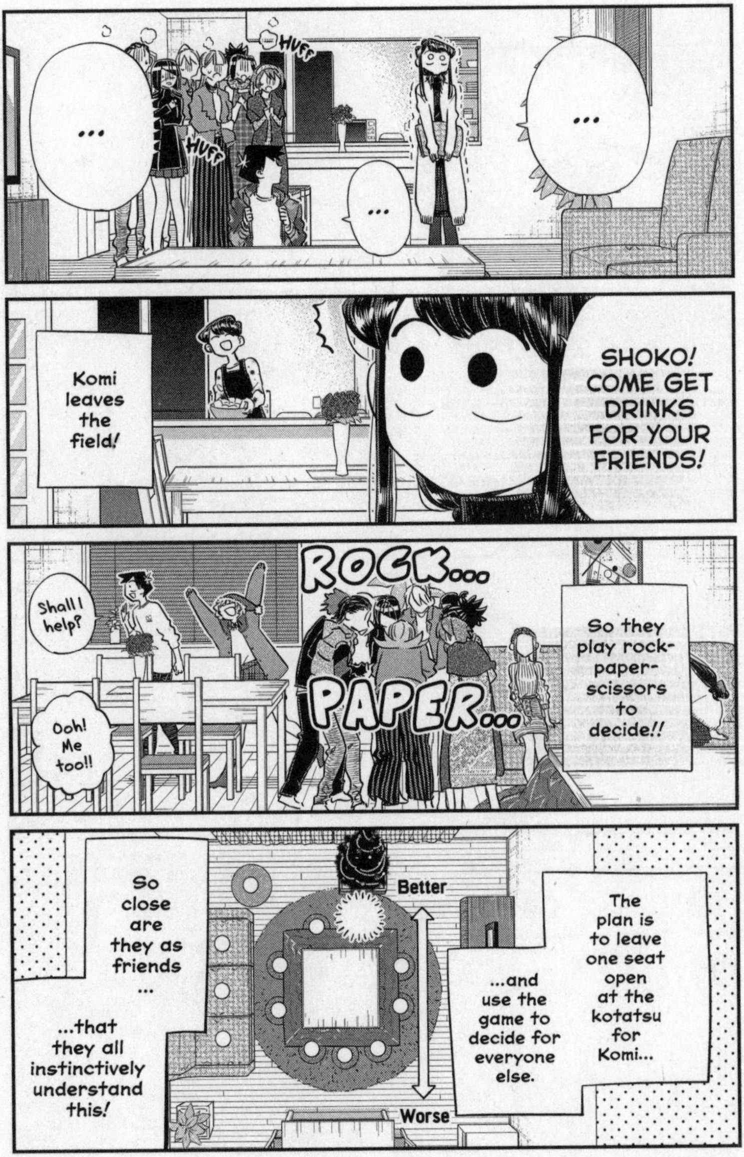
...
...
HUFF
...
HUFF
SHOKO! COME GET DRINKS FOR YOUR FRIENDS!
Komi leaves the field!
So they play rock-paper-scissors to decide!!
ROCK...
PAPER...
Shall I help?
Ooh! Me too!!
The plan is to leave one seat open at the kotatsu for Komi...
...and use the game to decide for everyone else.
Better
Worse
So close are they as friends...
...that they all instinctively understand this!

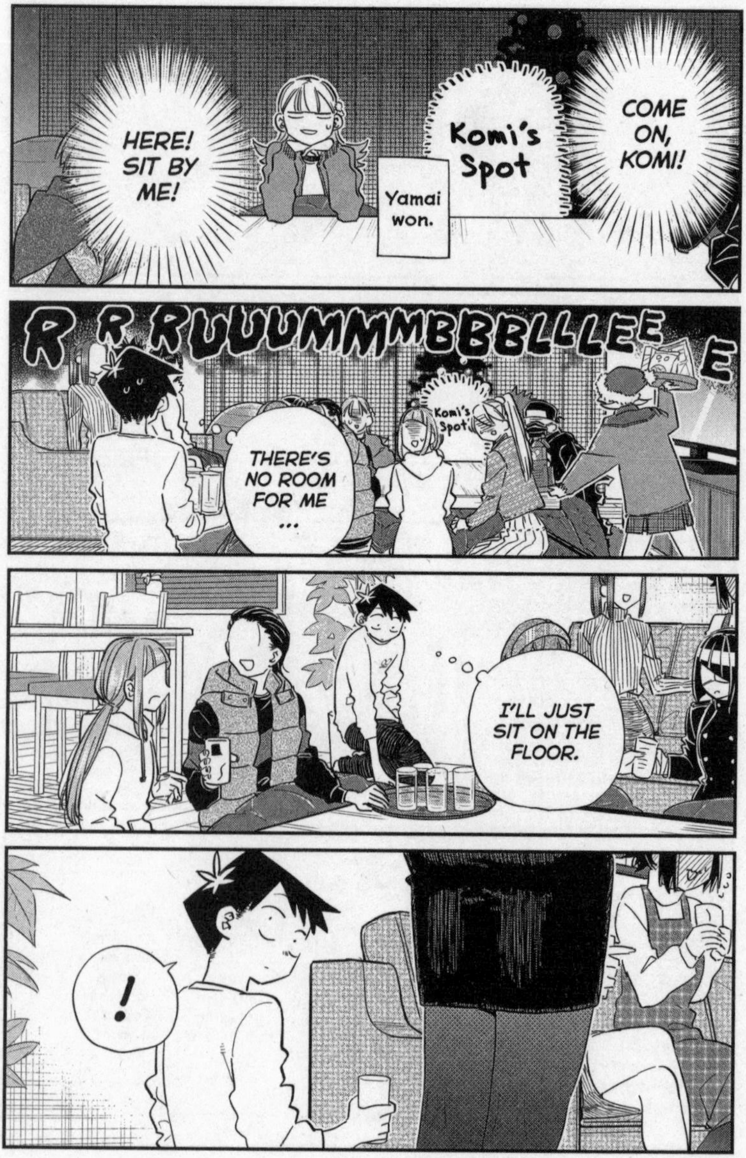
COME ON, KOMI!
Komi's Spot
Yamai won.
HERE! SIT BY ME!
RRRUUUMMMMBBBLLLEEE E
Komi's Spot
THERE'S NO ROOM FOR ME ...
I'LL JUST SIT ON THE FLOOR.
!

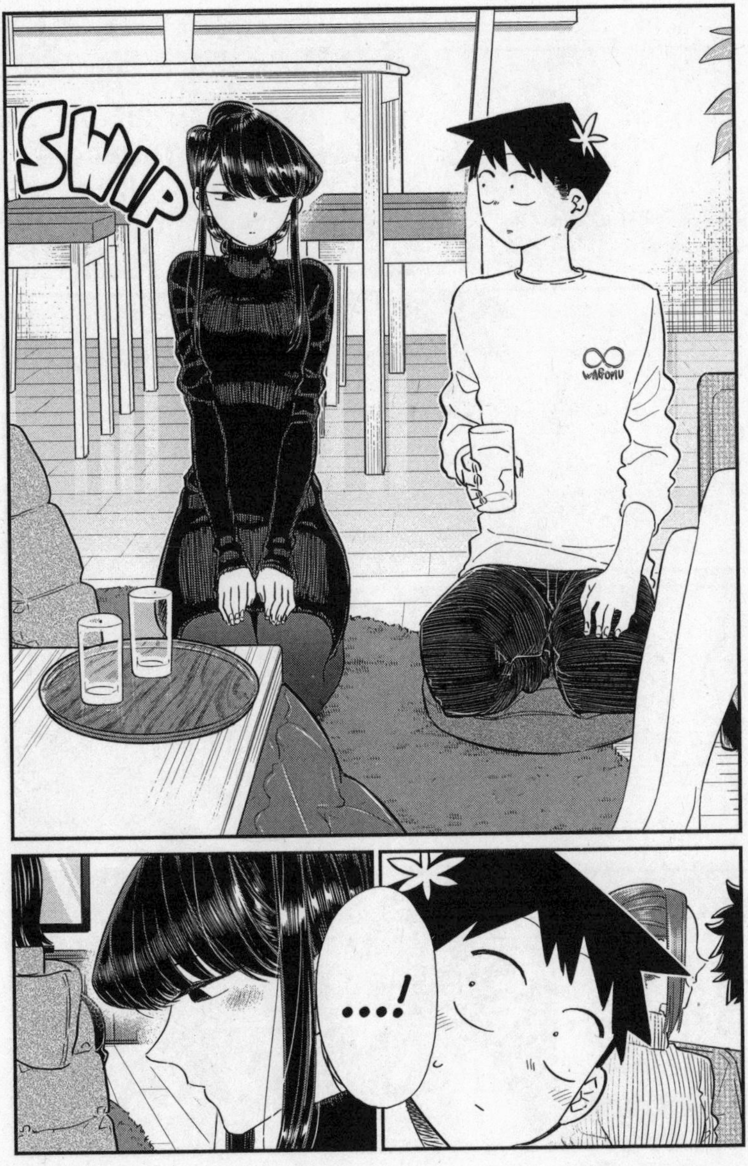
SWIP
WAGOMU
...!

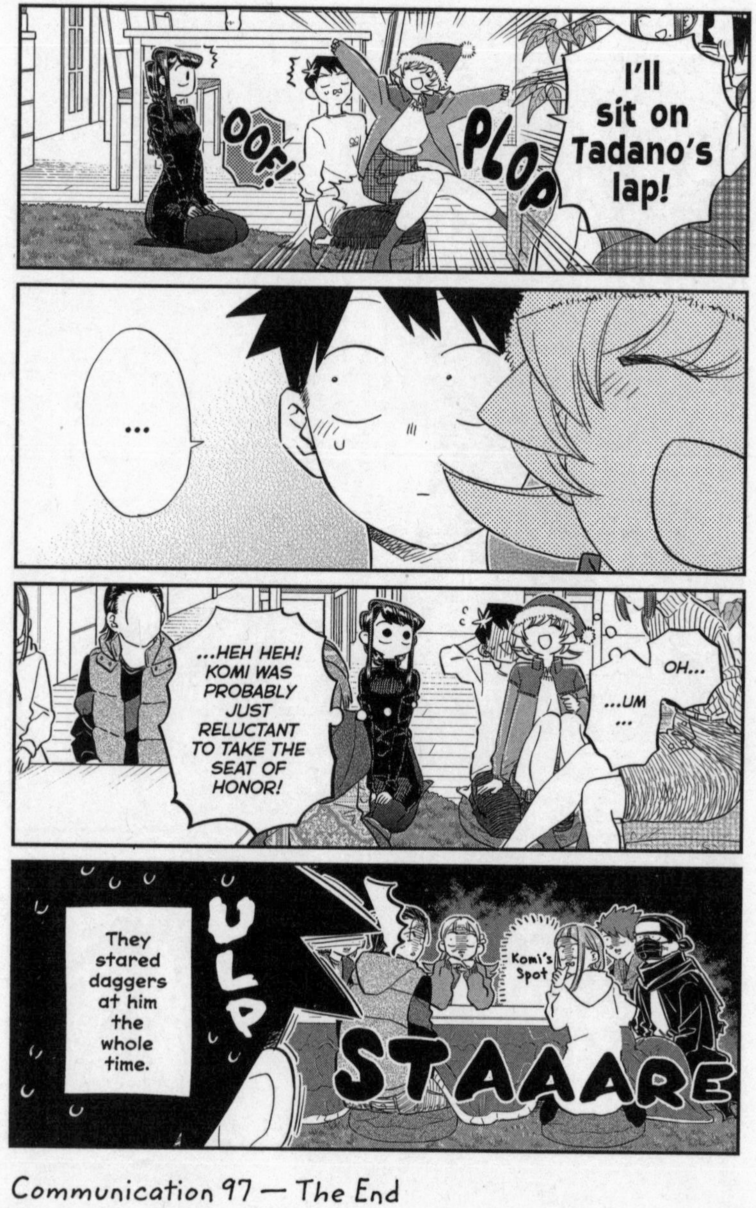
I'll sit on Tadano's lap!
PLOP
OOF!
...
OH...
...UM ...
...HEH HEH! KOMI WAS PROBABLY JUST RELUCTANT TO TAKE THE SEAT OF HONOR!
Komi's Spot
ULP
They stared daggers at him the whole time.
STAAARE

Communication 97 — The End

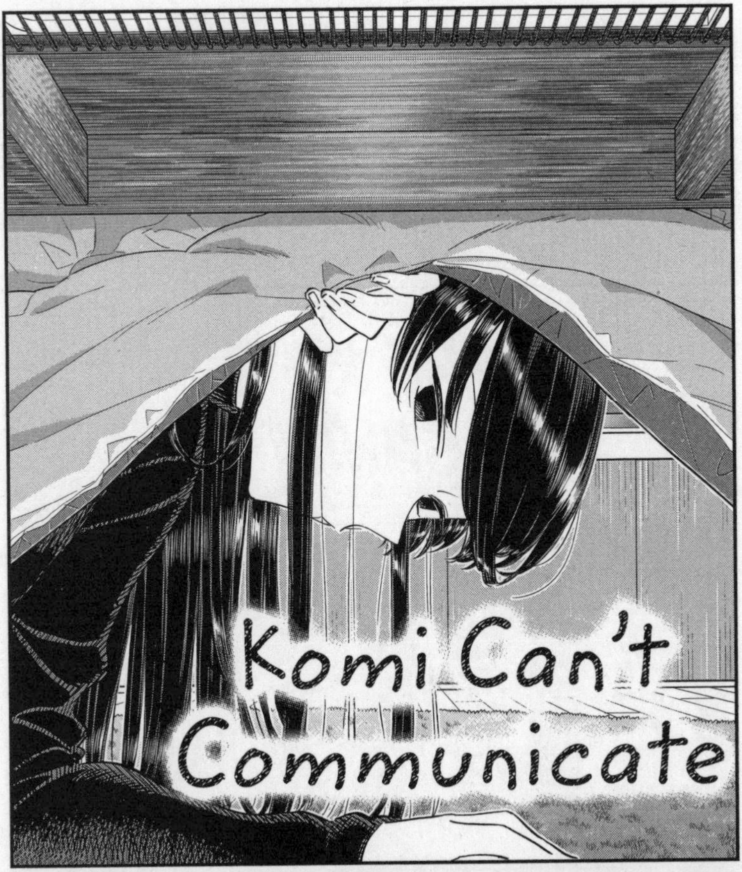
Komi Can't Communicate

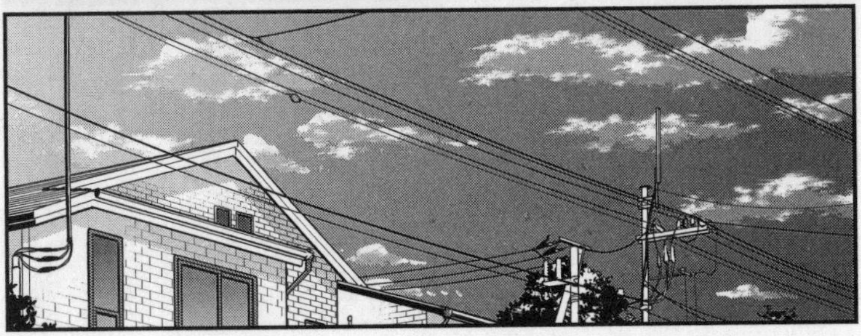

Communication 98: The King

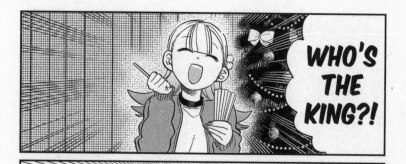

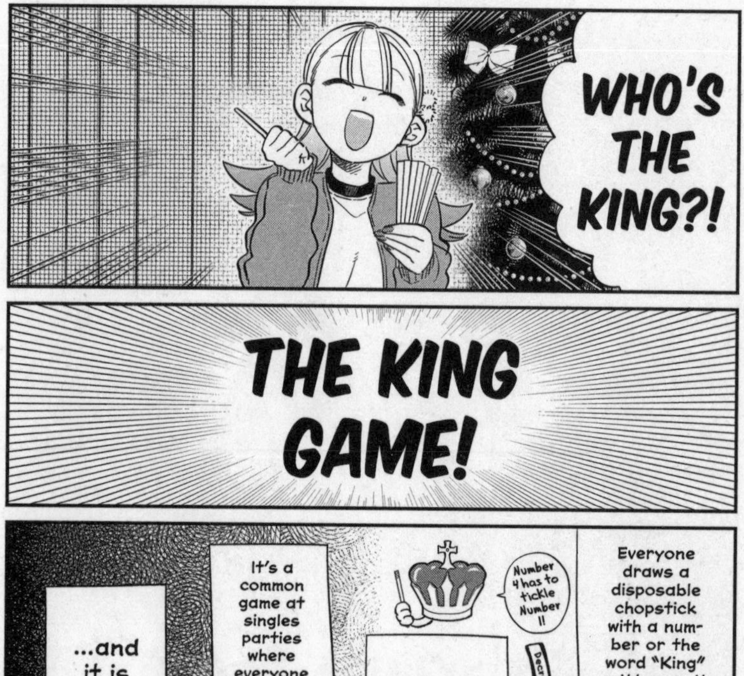

WHO'S THE KING?!
THE KING GAME!
Everyone draws a disposable chopstick with a number or the word "King" written on it.
Number 4 has to tickle Number 1!
Decree
1
2
3
4
Then the King issues a decree to the others.
It's a common game at singles parties where everyone is maneuvering for gain...
...and it is *pure evil.*
And Yamai was stoked!!
I'M THE KING!!
King
SHE'S BEEN HOLDING THAT THE WHOLE TIME!

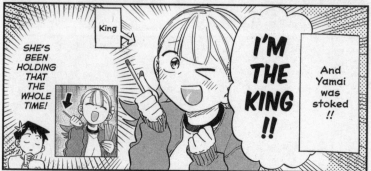

According to Plan!

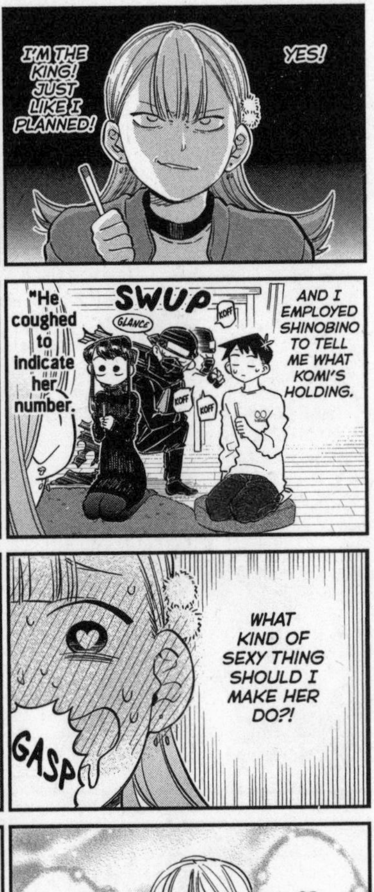
YES!
I'M THE KING! JUST LIKE I PLANNED!
AND I EMPLOYED SHINOBINO TO TELL ME WHAT KOMI'S HOLDING.
KOFF
SWUP
GLANCE
"He coughed to indicate her number.
KOFF
KOFF
WHAT KIND OF SEXY THING SHOULD I MAKE HER DO?!
GASP
OR SHOULD I...
...JUST ASK TO EXCHANGE ADDRESSES?

Desperation

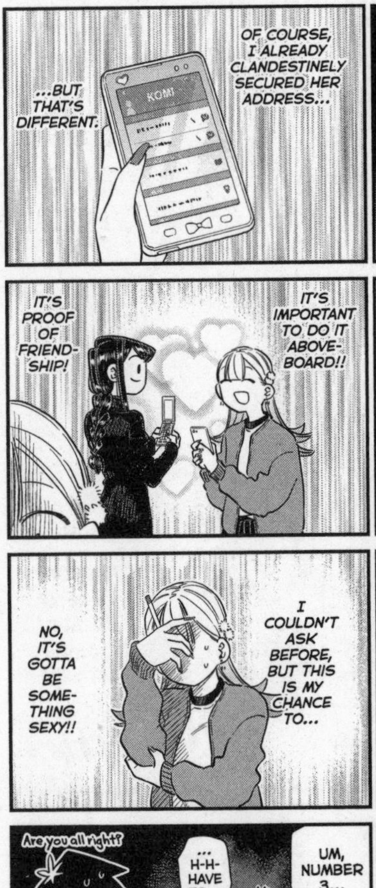
OF COURSE, I ALREADY CLANDESTINELY SECURED HER ADDRESS...
...BUT THAT'S DIFFERENT.
KOMI
IT'S IMPORTANT TO DO IT ABOVE-BOARD!!
IT'S PROOF OF FRIEND-SHIP!
I COULDN'T ASK BEFORE, BUT THIS IS MY CHANCE TO...
NO, IT'S GOTTA BE SOME-THING SEXY!!
UM, NUMBER 3...
...H-H-HAVE TO...
HUFF
HUFF
HUFF
Are you all right?
...AND I...
...EX-EX-EX-EX-EX-CHANGE...
WHY'S SHE PANT-ING?

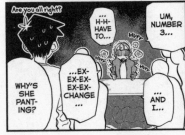

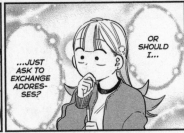

Psychic

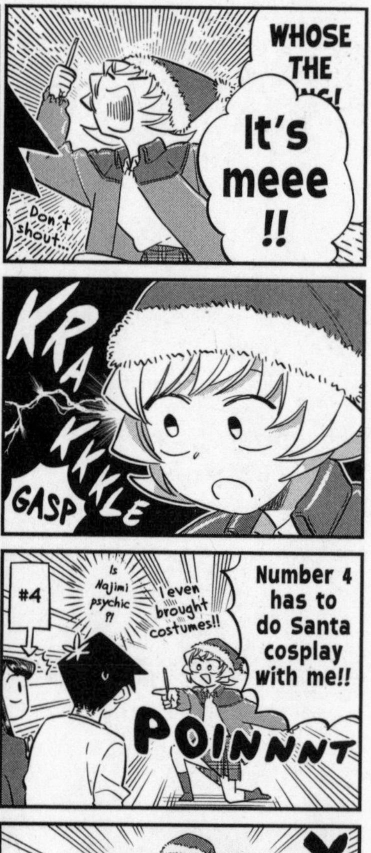
WHOSE THE
It's meee !!
Don't shout...
KRAKKKKLE
GASP
Number 4 has to do Santa cosplay with me!!
I even brought costumes!!
Is Najimi psychic ?!
#4
POINNNT
YAHOOOOOOO
The high point of the day

Killing the Mood

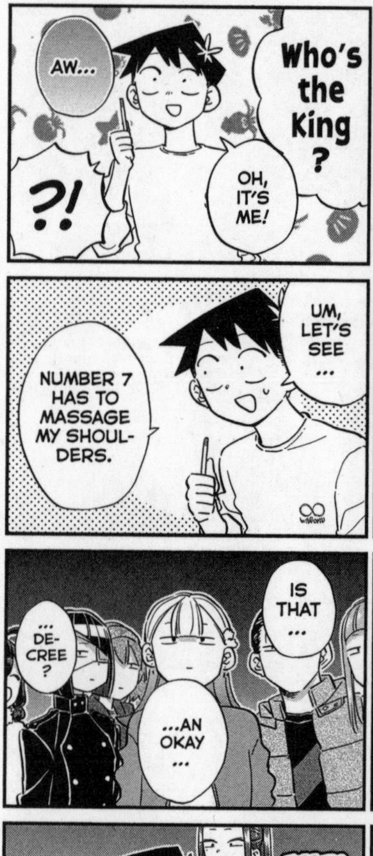
Who's the King ?
OH, IT'S ME!
AW...
?!
UM, LET'S SEE ...
NUMBER 7 HAS TO MASSAGE MY SHOUL-DERS.
IS THAT ...
...AN OKAY ...
... DE-CREE ?
The low point of the day
THAT'S SO NORMAL.

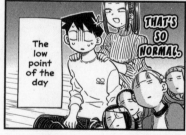

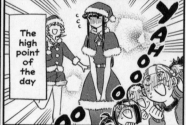

Total Time: Ten Minutes

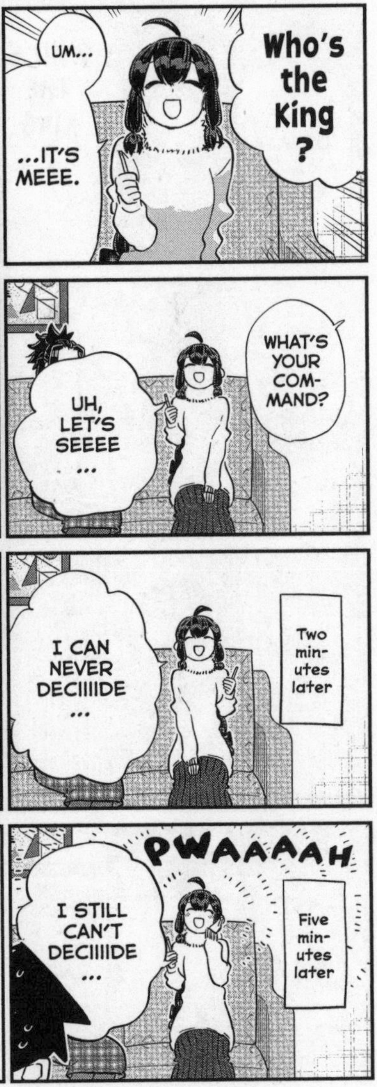
Who's the King?
UM...
...IT'S MEEE.
WHAT'S YOUR COM-MAND?
UH, LET'S SEEEE ...
Two min-utes later
I CAN NEVER DECIIIIDE ...
Five min-utes later
PWAAAAH
I STILL CAN'T DECIIIIDE ...

The Fan Club's Model

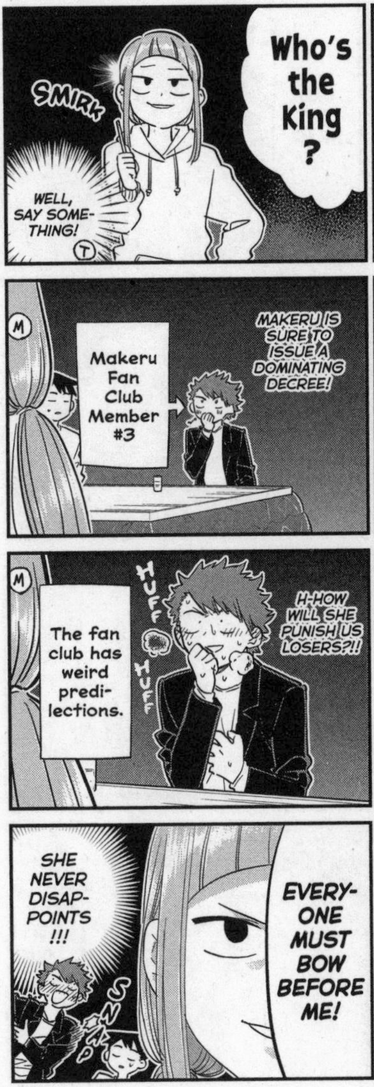
Who's the King?
SMIRK
WELL, SAY SOME-THING!
MAKERU IS SURE TO ISSUE A DOMINATING DECREE!
Makeru Fan Club Member #3
H-HOW WILL SHE PUNISH US LOSERS?!!
HUFF HUFF
The fan club has weird predi-lections.
EVERY-ONE MUST BOW BEFORE ME!
SHE NEVER DISAP-POINTS!!!
SNAP

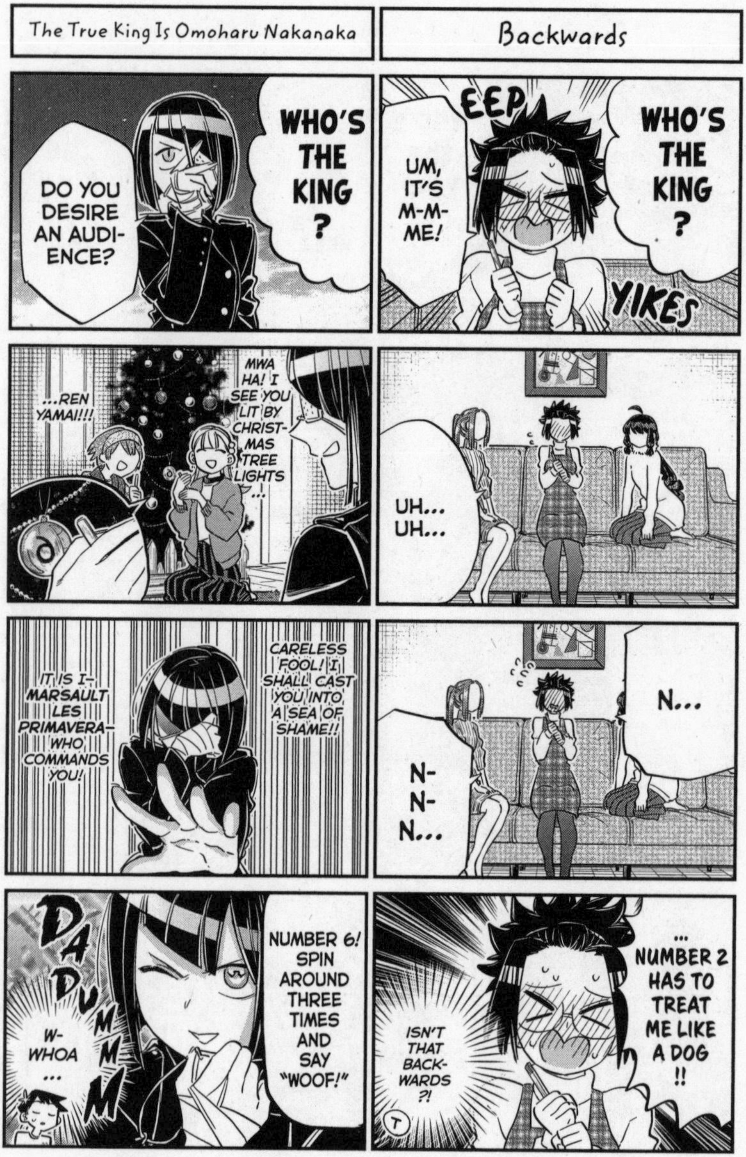
Backwards
WHO'S THE KING?
EEP
UM, IT'S M-M-ME!
YIKES
UH... UH...
N...
N-N-N...
... NUMBER 2 HAS TO TREAT ME LIKE A DOG!!
ISN'T THAT BACKWARDS?!
The True King Is Omoharu Nakanaka
WHO'S THE KING?
DO YOU DESIRE AN AUDIENCE?
MWA HA! I SEE YOU LIT BY CHRISTMAS TREE LIGHTS...
...REN YAMAI!!!
CARELESS FOOL! I SHALL CAST YOU INTO A SEA OF SHAME!!
IT IS I—MARSAULT LES PRIMAVERA—WHO COMMANDS YOU!
NUMBER 6! SPIN AROUND THREE TIMES AND SAY "WOOF!"
DADUMMMM
W-WHOA...

Yamai Strikes Back

BWA HA...
...HA HA HA!
TOO BAD, SO SAD, NAKA-NAKA!!
What?!
9
SHE WAS HOLDING HER STICK UPSIDE-DOWN!!
6 9
Contacts
IT WAS A TRAP!!
TEE HEE HEE HEE HEE HEE
#6

Kiss

WHO'S THE KING?
ME!
?!
WHEN DID *YOU* START PLAYING?
I SNUCK IN! ♡
CAN I MAKE A DECREE?
Uh, sure.
NUMBER 4 MUST KISS NUMBER 9.
SHE GOES STRAIGHT FOR THE JUGULAR.
Huh?
UM...
NOW.
...

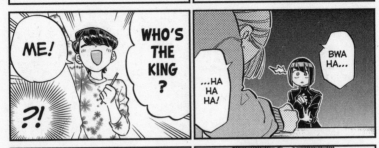

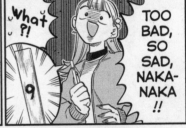

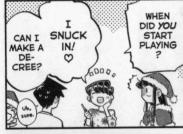

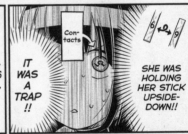

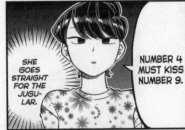

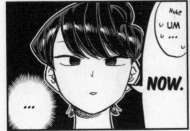

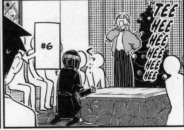

Kiss Decree

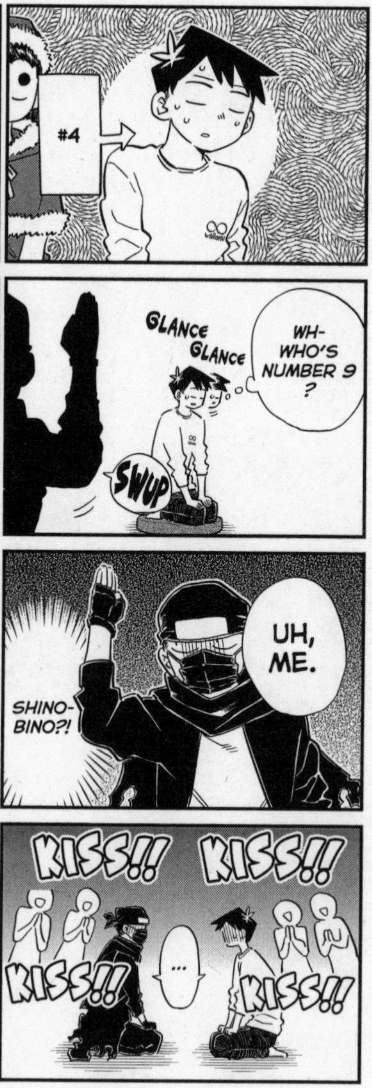
#4
WH- WHO'S NUMBER 9 ?
GLANCE GLANCE
SWUP
UH, ME.
SHINO-BINO?!
KISS!! KISS!!
KISS!!
...
KISS!!

Not So Bad

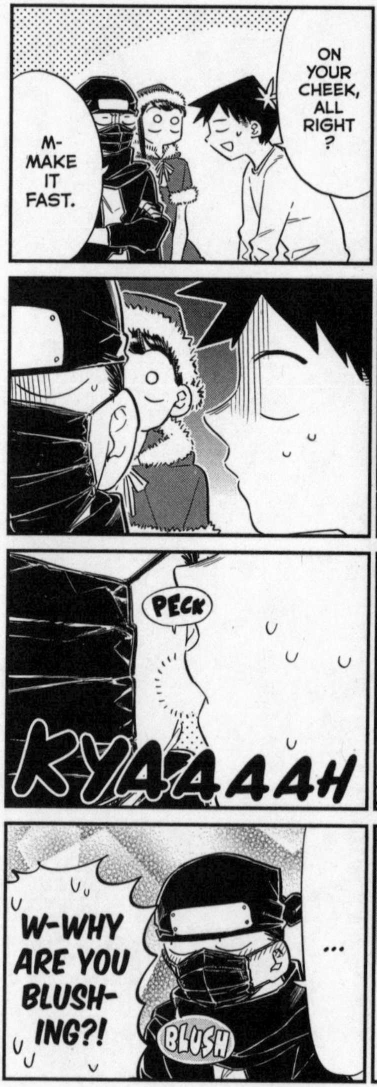
ON YOUR CHEEK, ALL RIGHT?
M- MAKE IT FAST.
PECK
KYAAAAH
...
W-WHY ARE YOU BLUSHING?!
BLUSH

The King's Responsibility

WHO'S THE KING?
HUH?
AH HA HA!
MURMUR
WELL, WHO IS IT?
MURMUR
HM?
SERI-OUSLY?
CHATTER
THAT'S WEIRD.
CHATTER
TREMBLE
SWIP
IT'S KOMI!!

C-Can I Issue a Decree?

W-WHAT'S HER DECREE?
...
...
...
...
...
W-WHAT'S IT SAY?!

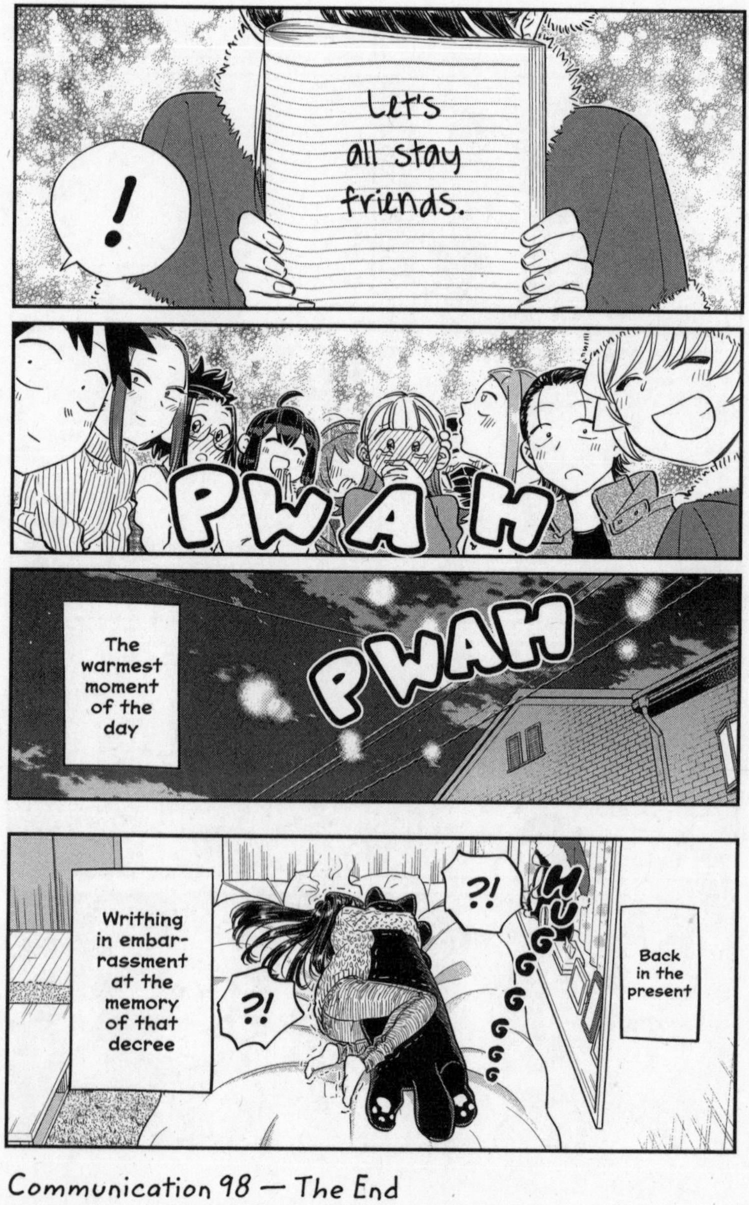
Let's all stay friends.
!
PWAH
PWAH
The warmest moment of the day
Back in the present
HUGGGGGG
?!
Writhing in embarrassment at the memory of that decree
?!

Communication 98 — The End

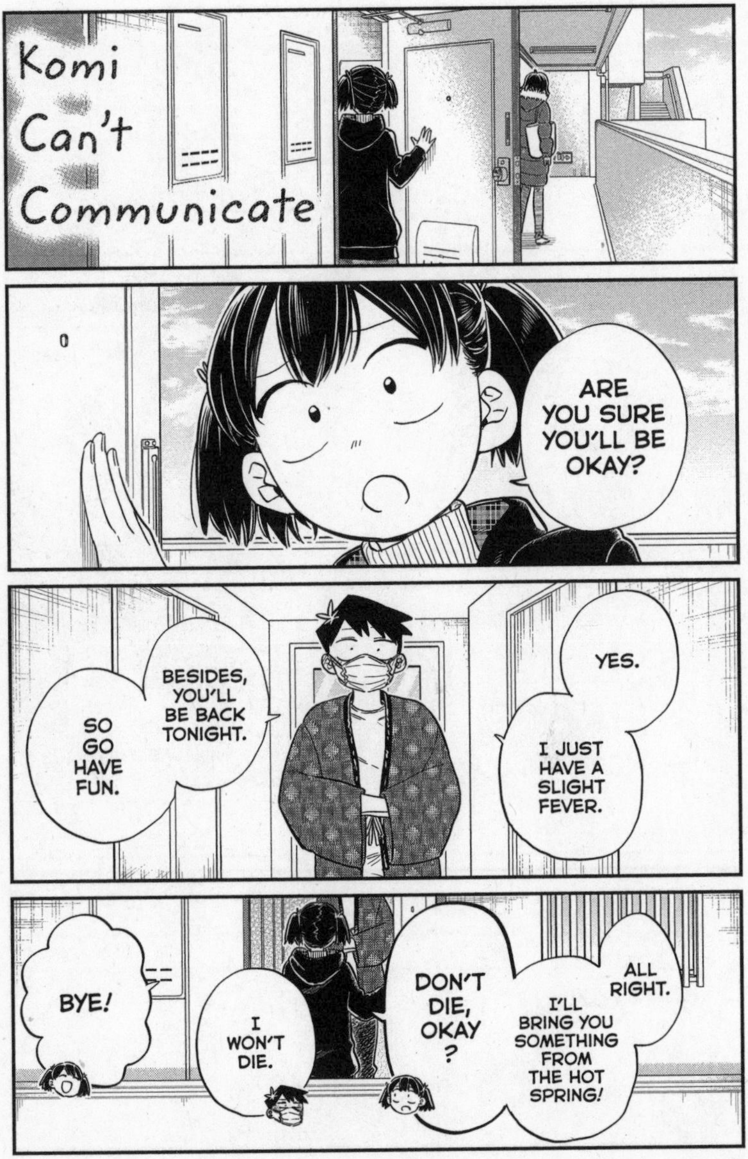
Komi Can't Communicate
ARE YOU SURE YOU'LL BE OKAY?
YES.
I JUST HAVE A SLIGHT FEVER.
BESIDES, YOU'LL BE BACK TONIGHT.
SO GO HAVE FUN.
ALL RIGHT.
I'LL BRING YOU SOMETHING FROM THE HOT SPRING!
DON'T DIE, OKAY?
I WON'T DIE.
BYE!

Communication 99: Having a Cold

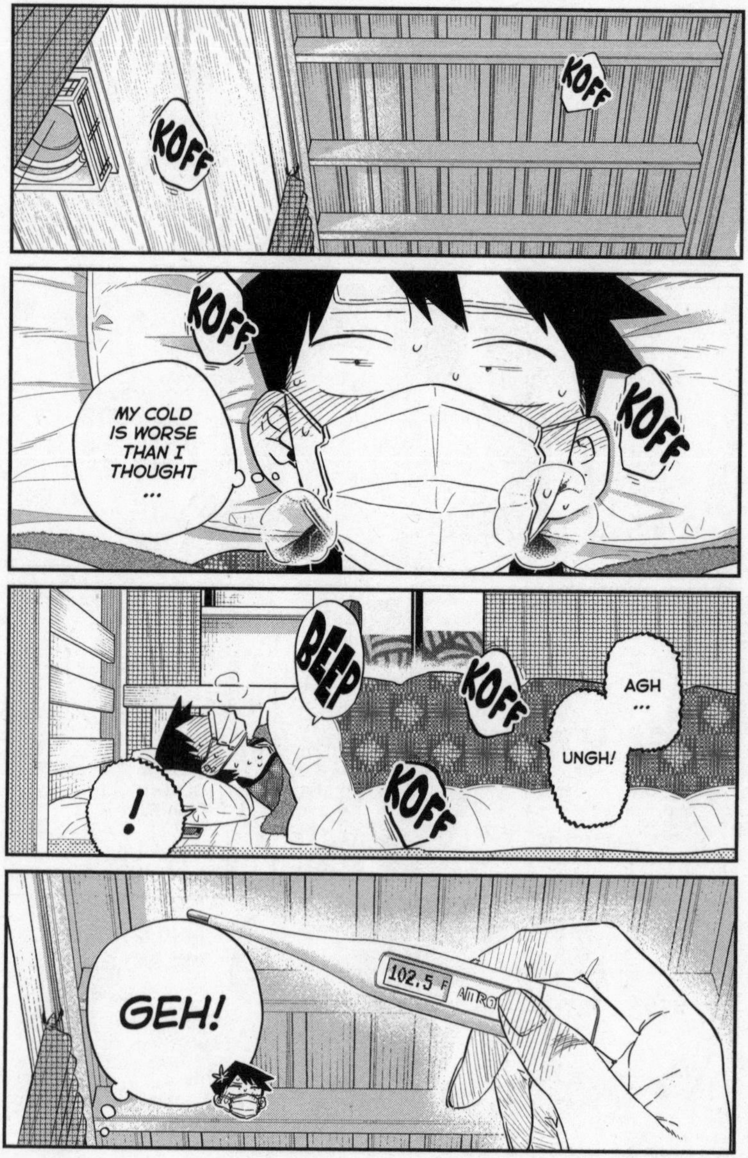
KOFF
KOFF
KOFF
KOFF
MY COLD IS WORSE THAN I THOUGHT ...
AGH ... UNGH!
KOFF
BEEP
KOFF
!
102.5 F
GEH!

...
KOFF
KOFF
...
OH NO! I MIGHT ACTUALLY DIE!!
Don't die, okay?
Nearly crying
Halluci-nation
okay? Don't die, Don't die, okay?

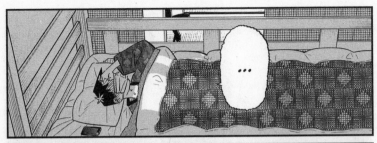

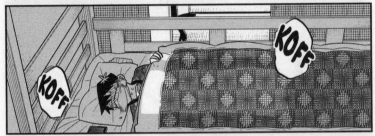

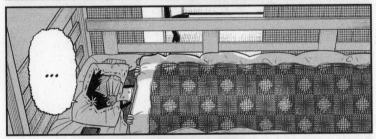

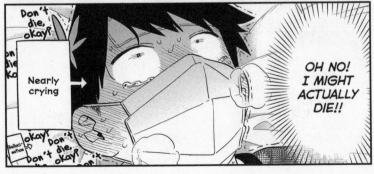

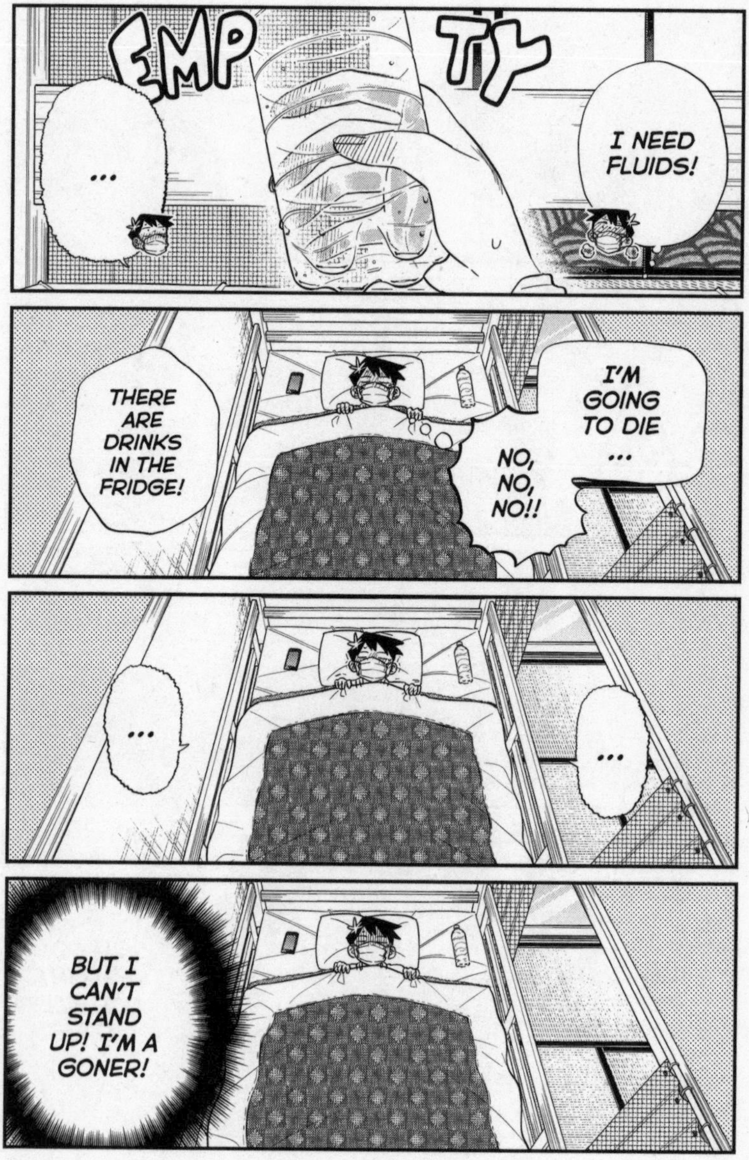
I NEED FLUIDS!
EMPTY
...
I'M GOING TO DIE ...
NO, NO, NO!!
THERE ARE DRINKS IN THE FRIDGE!
...
...
BUT I CAN'T STAND UP! I'M A GONER!

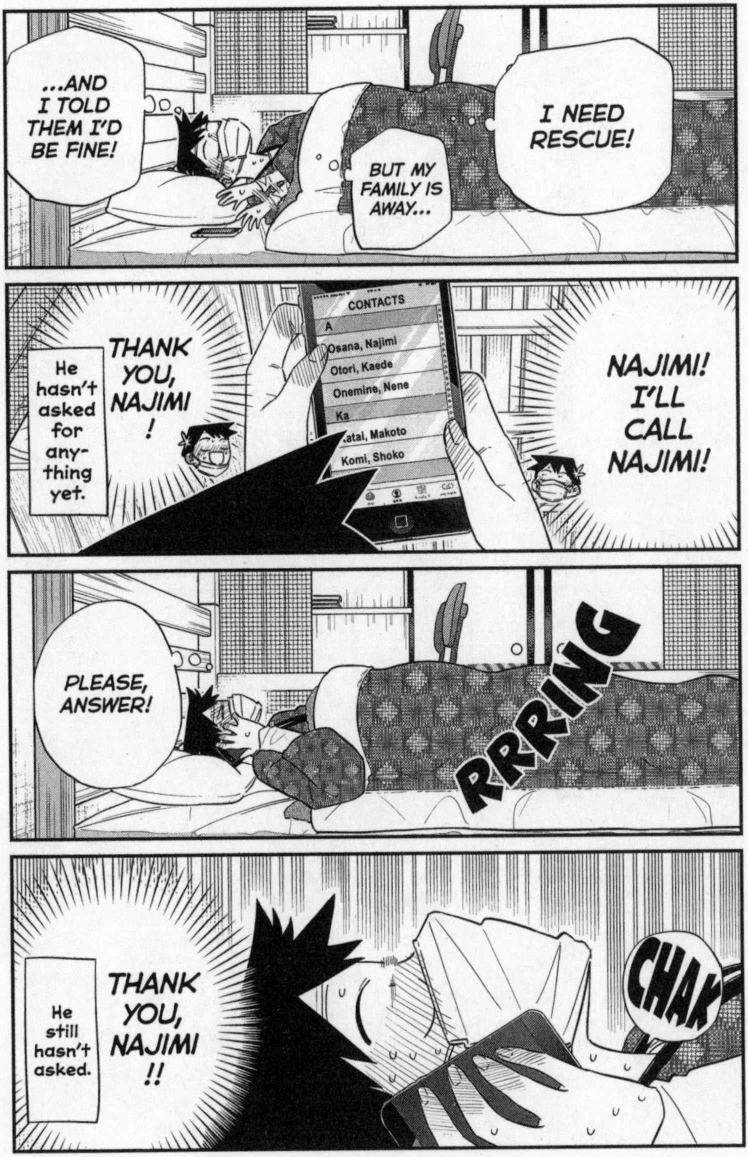
I NEED RESCUE!
BUT MY FAMILY IS AWAY...
...AND I TOLD THEM I'D BE FINE!
NAJIMI! I'LL CALL NAJIMI!
CONTACTS
A
Osana, Najimi
Otori, Kaede
Onemine, Nene
Ka
atai, Makoto
Komi, Shoko
THANK YOU, NAJIMI!
He hasn't asked for anything yet.
RRRING
PLEASE, ANSWER!
CHAK
THANK YOU, NAJIMI!!
He still hasn't asked.

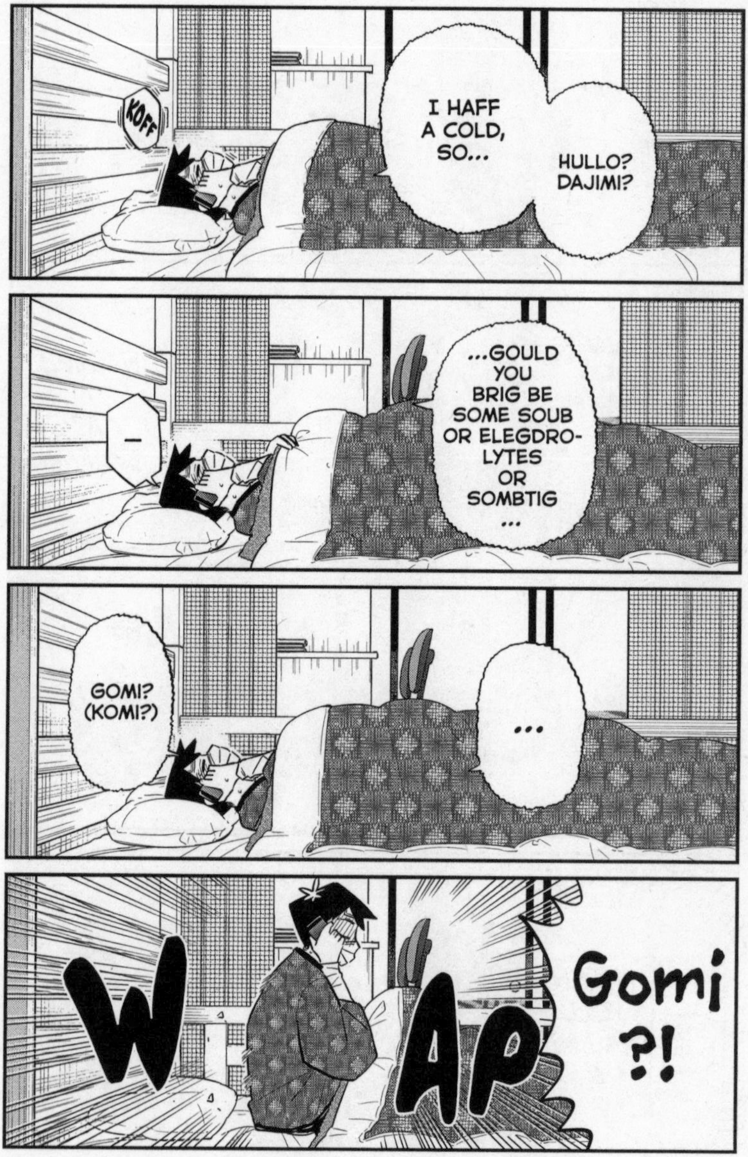
HULLO? DAJIMI?
I HAFF A COLD, SO...
KOFF
...GOULD YOU BRIG BE SOME SOUB OR ELEGDRO-LYTES OR SOMBTIG ...
—
...
GOMI? (KOMI?)
Gomi ?!
WAP

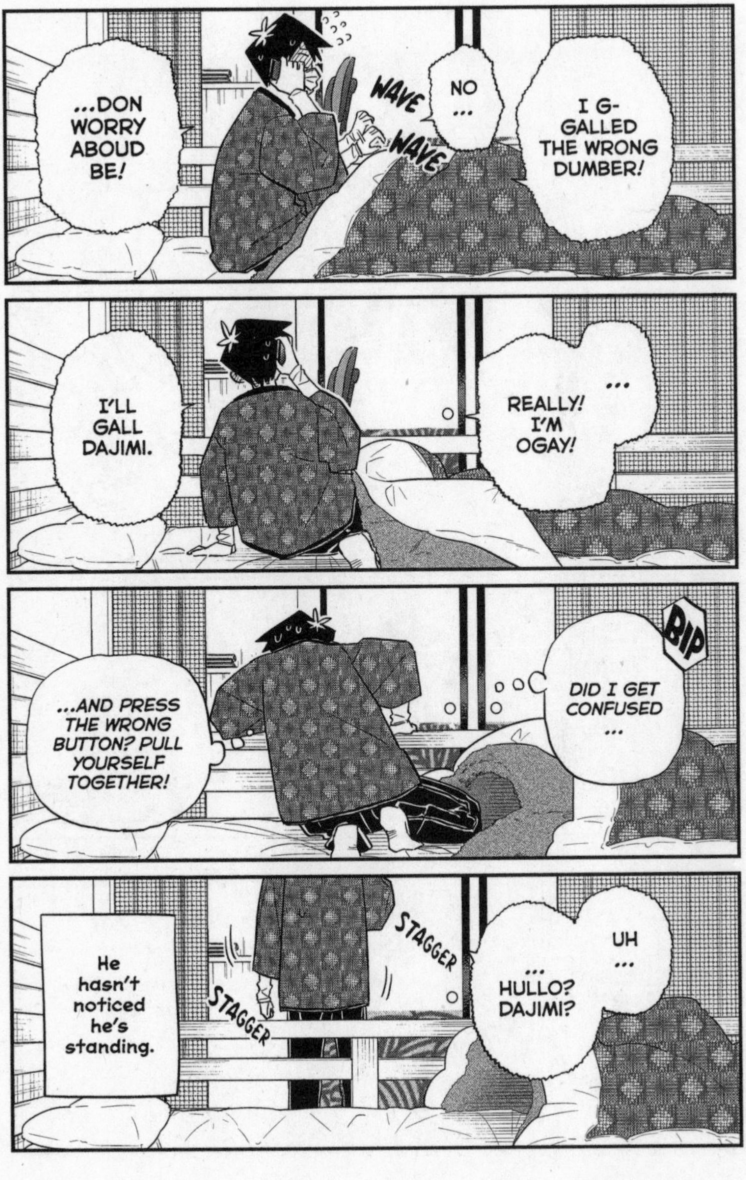
I G-GALLED THE WRONG DUMBER!
NO ...
WAVE
WAVE
...DON WORRY ABOUD BE!
... REALLY! I'M OGAY!
I'LL GALL DAJIMI.
BIP
DID I GET CONFUSED ...
...AND PRESS THE WRONG BUTTON? PULL YOURSELF TOGETHER!
UH ... ... HULLO? DAJIMI?
STAGGER
STAGGER
He hasn't noticed he's standing.

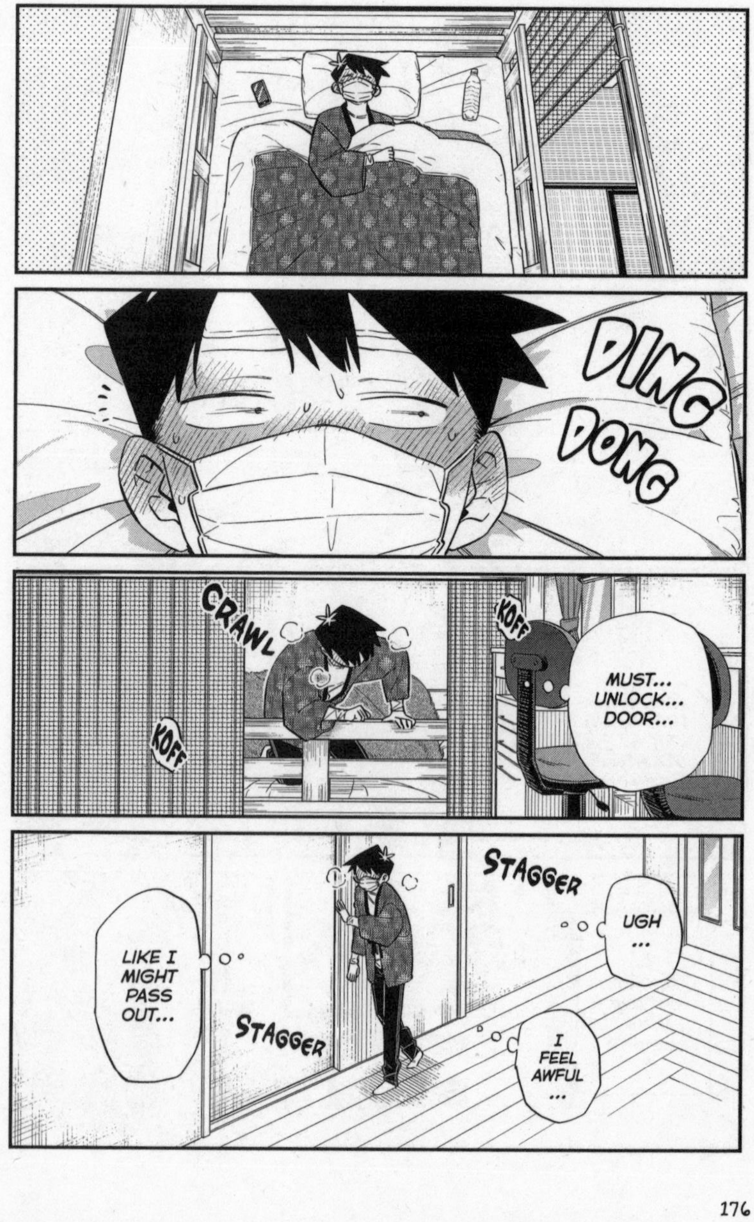
DING DONG
MUST... UNLOCK... DOOR...
KOFF
CRAWL
KOFF
STAGGER
UGH ...
I FEEL AWFUL ...
STAGGER
LIKE I MIGHT PASS OUT...

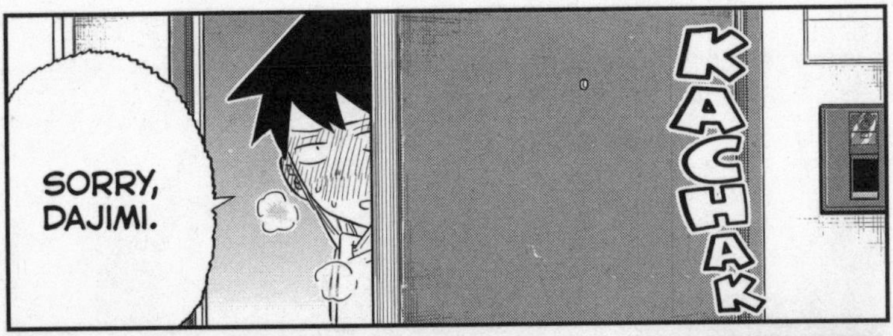
KACHAK
SORRY, DAJIMI.

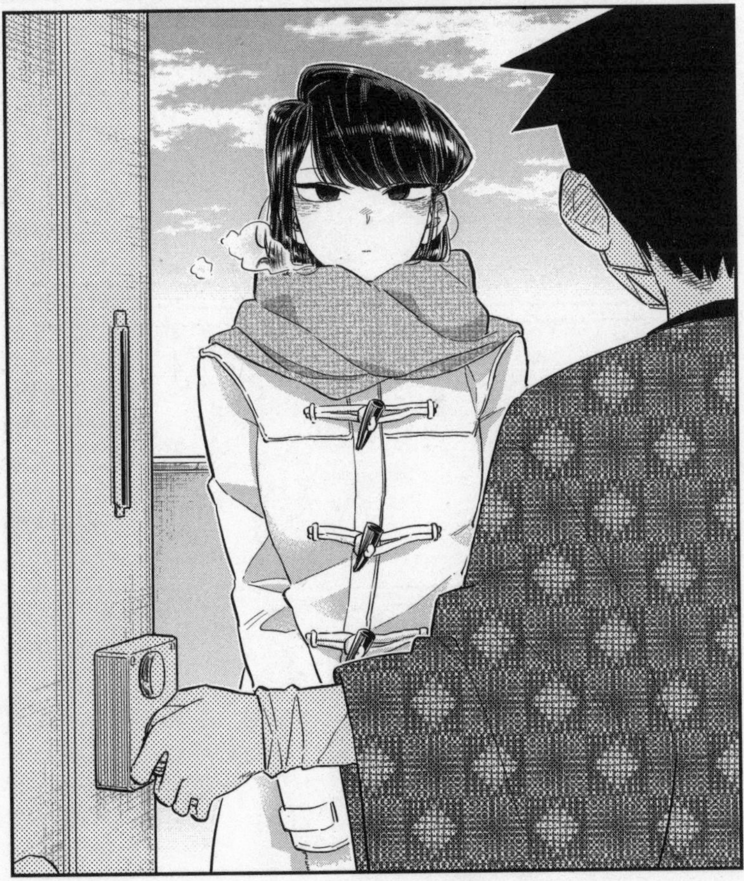

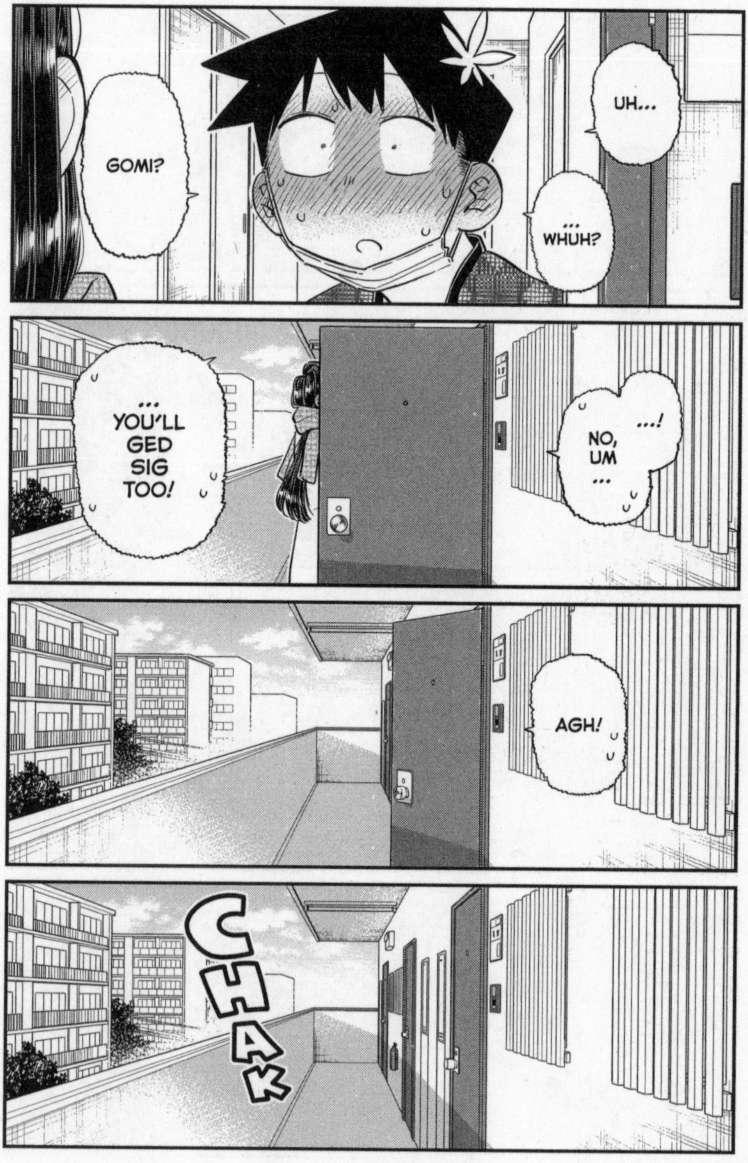
UH...
... WHUH?
GOMI?
...! NO, UM ...
... YOU'LL GED SIG TOO!
AGH!
CHAK

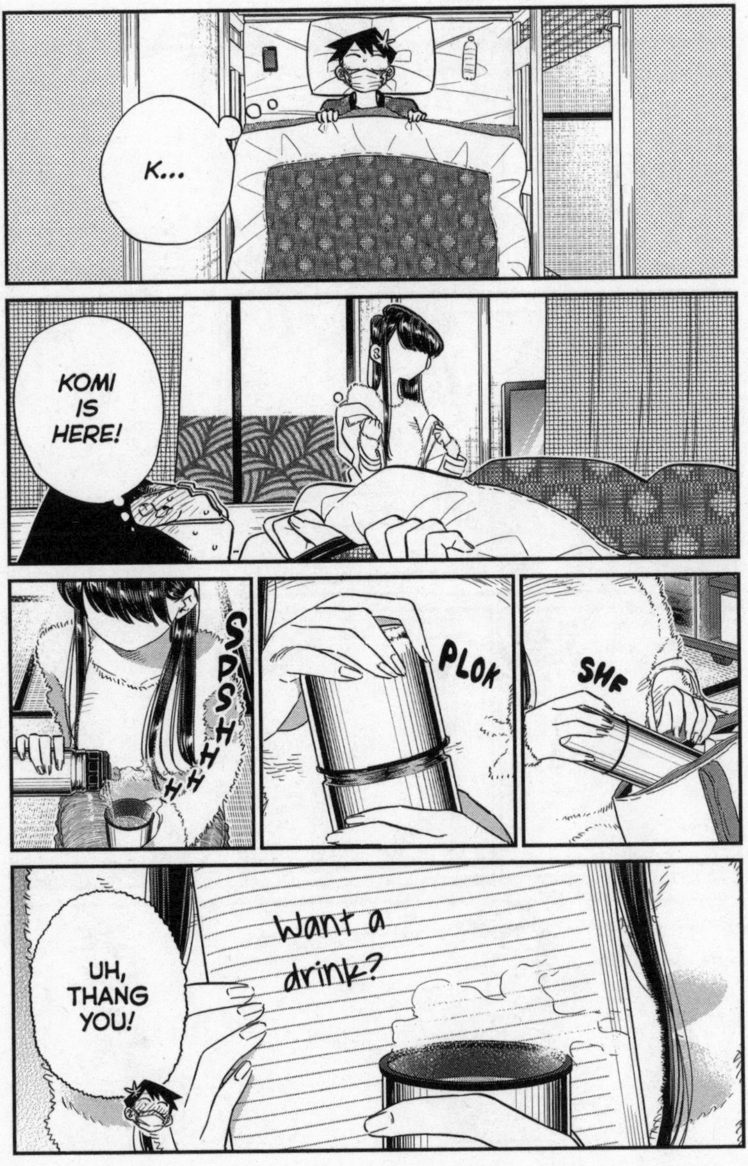
K...
KOMI IS HERE!
SHF
PLOK
SPSHHHH
Want a drink?
UH, THANG YOU!

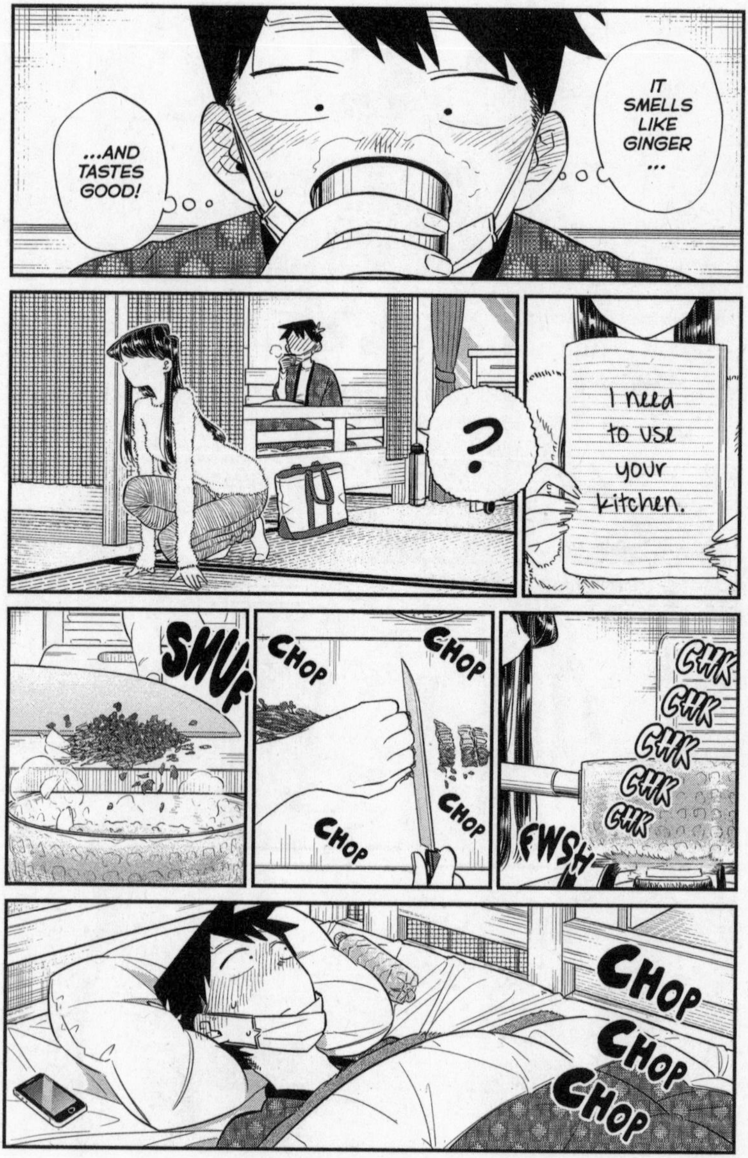
IT SMELLS LIKE GINGER ...
...AND TASTES GOOD!
I need to use your kitchen.
?
CHK CHK CHK CHK CHK
FWSH
CHOP
CHOP
CHOP
CHOP
SHUF
CHOP CHOP CHOP

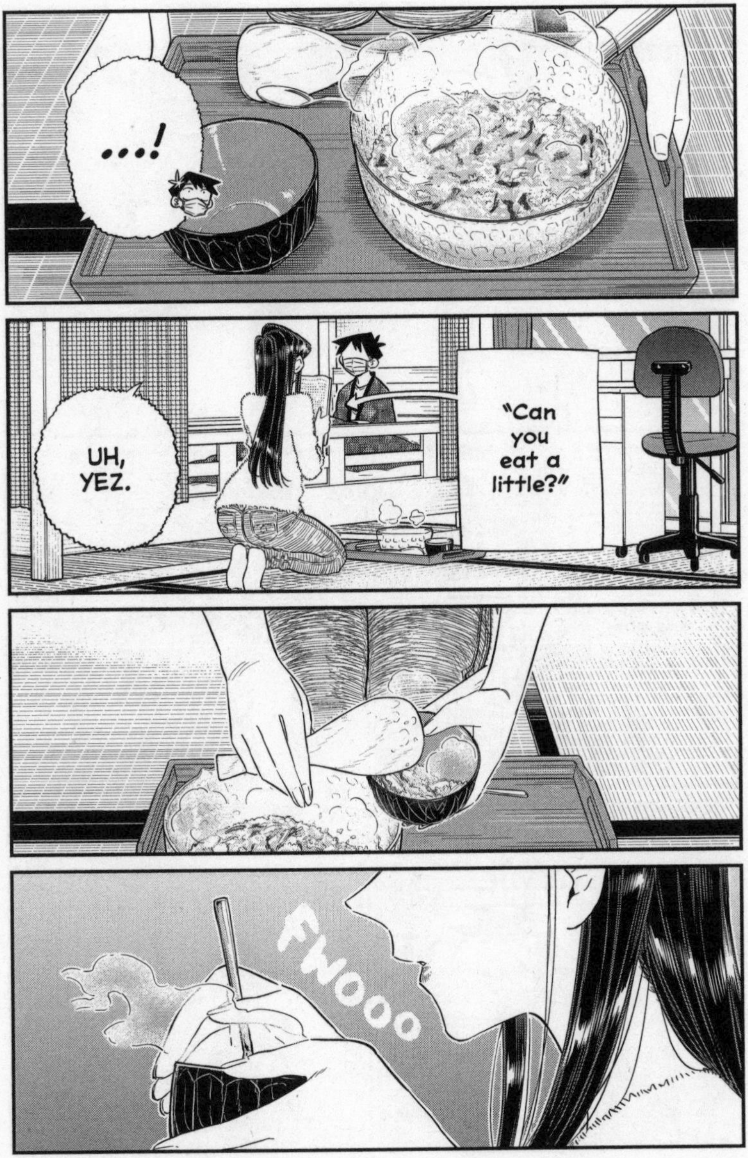
...!
"Can you eat a little?"
UH, YEZ.
FWOOO

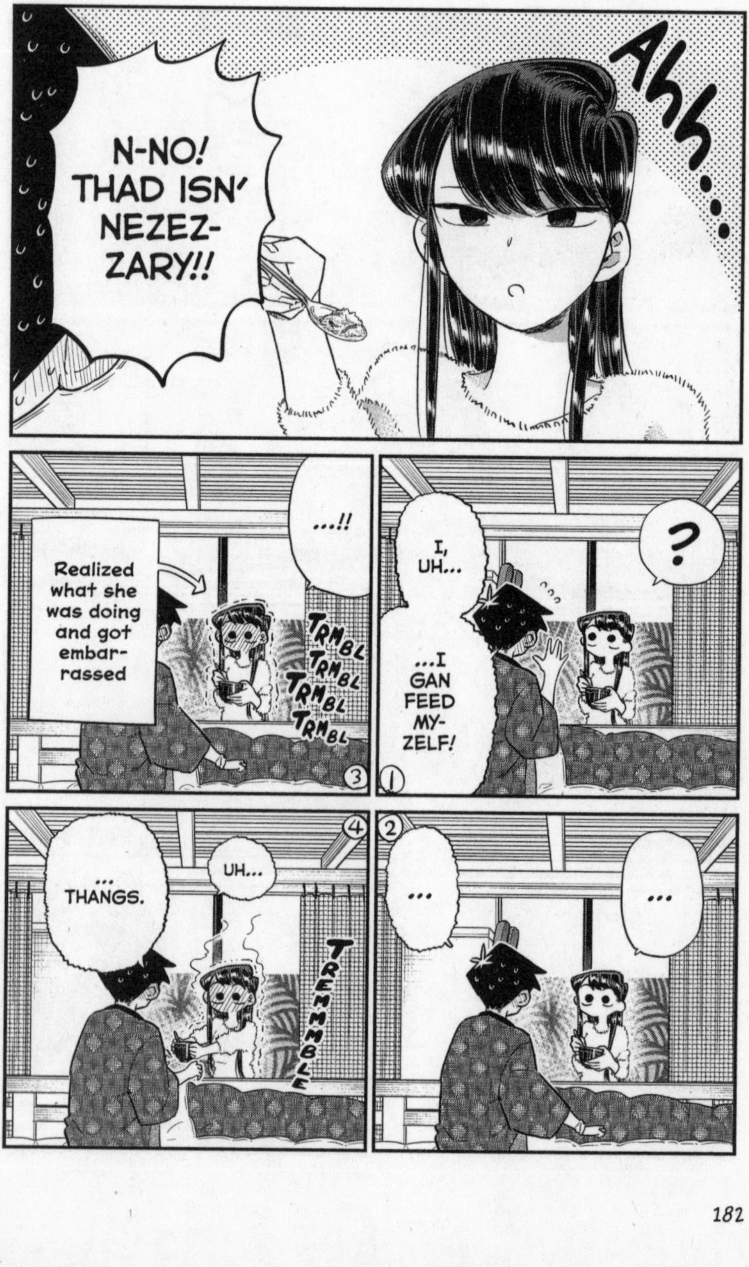
Ahh...
N-NO! THAD ISN' NEZEZ-ZARY!!
?
I, UH...
...I GAN FEED MY-ZELF!
...
...
...!!
TRMBL TRMBL TRMBL TRMBL
Realized what she was doing and got embar-rassed
UH...
TREMMMBLE
... THANGS.

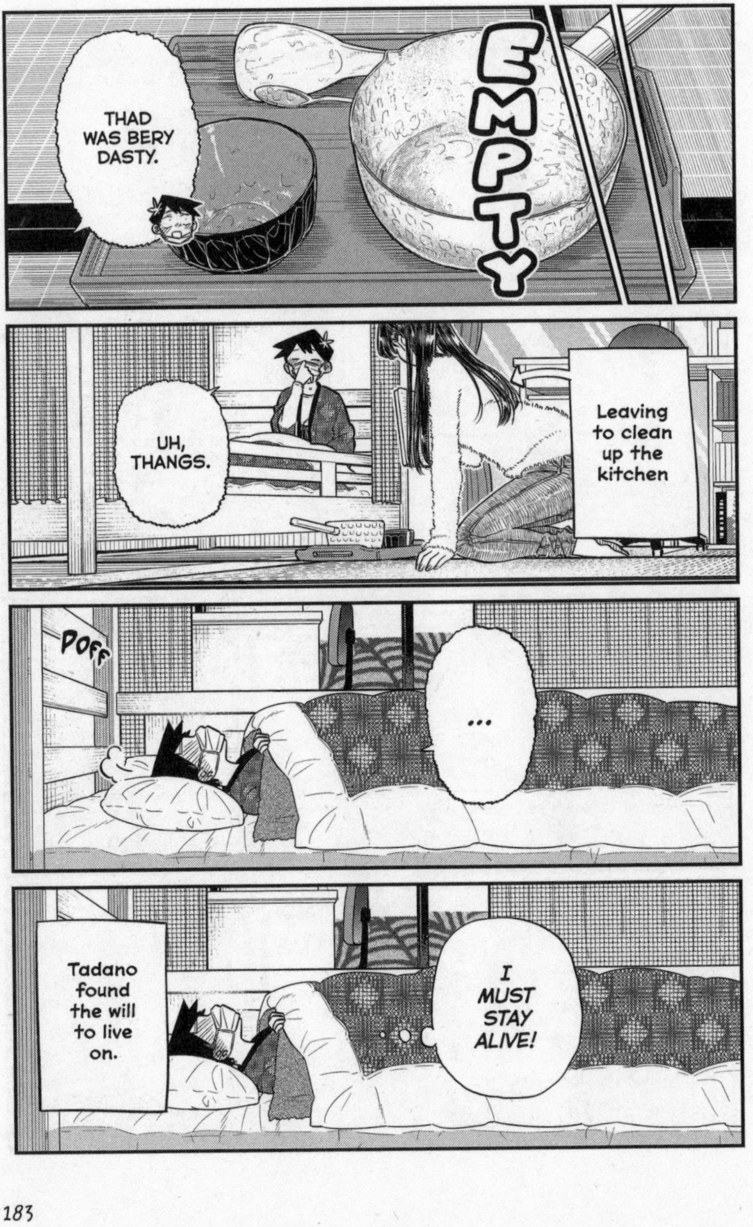
EMPTY
THAD WAS BERY DASTY.
Leaving to clean up the kitchen
UH, THANGS.
...
POFF
I MUST STAY ALIVE!
Tadano found the will to live on.

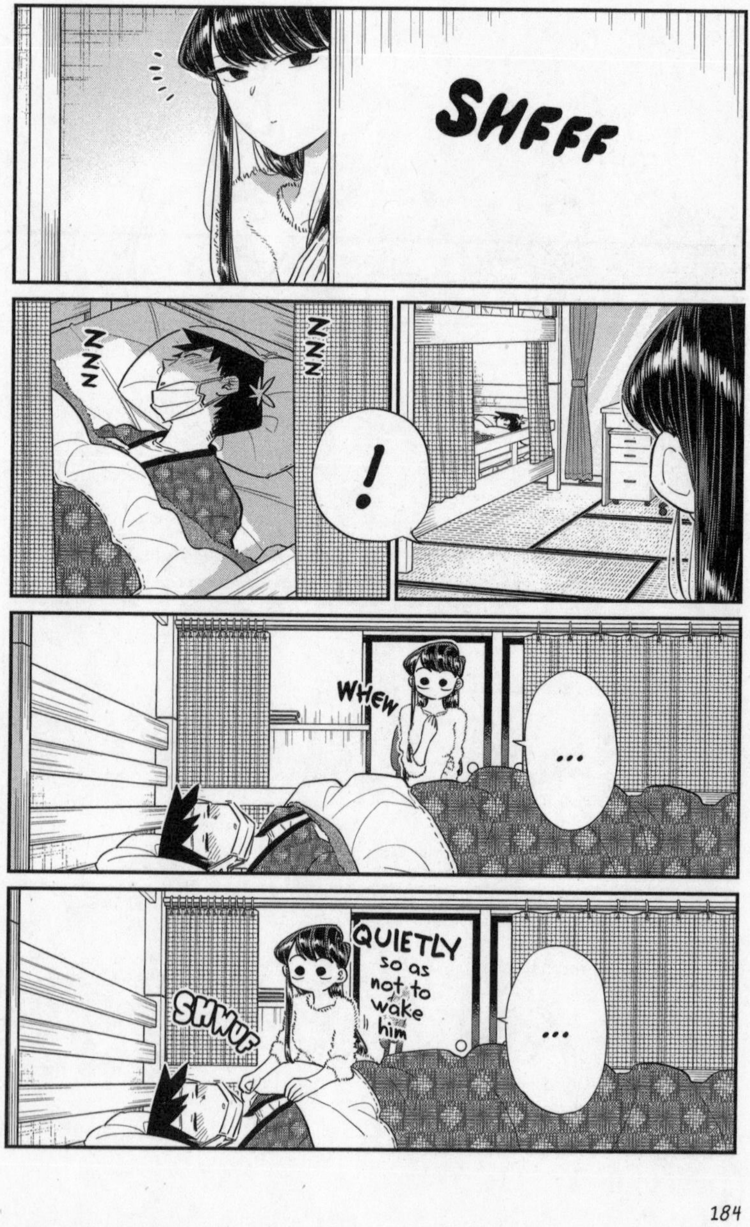
SHFFF
!
ZZZ
ZZZ
...
WHEW
...
QUIETLY so as not to wake him
SHWUF

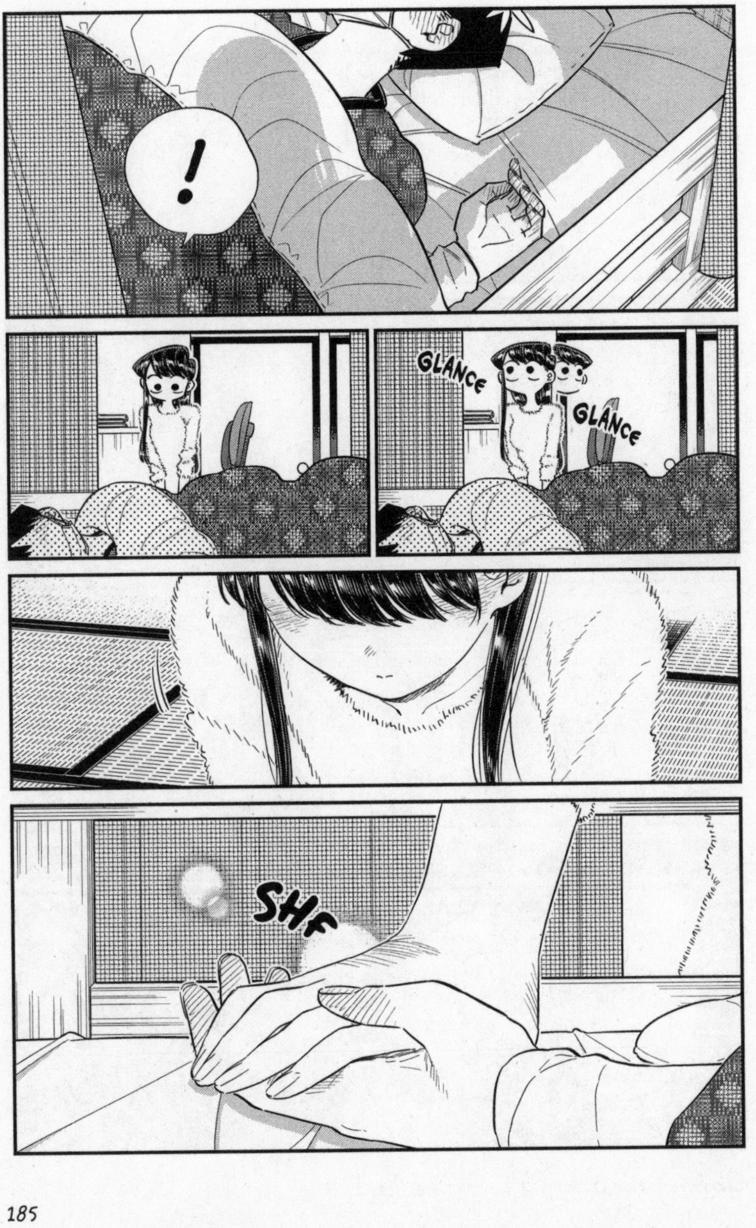
!
GLANCE
GLANCE
SHF

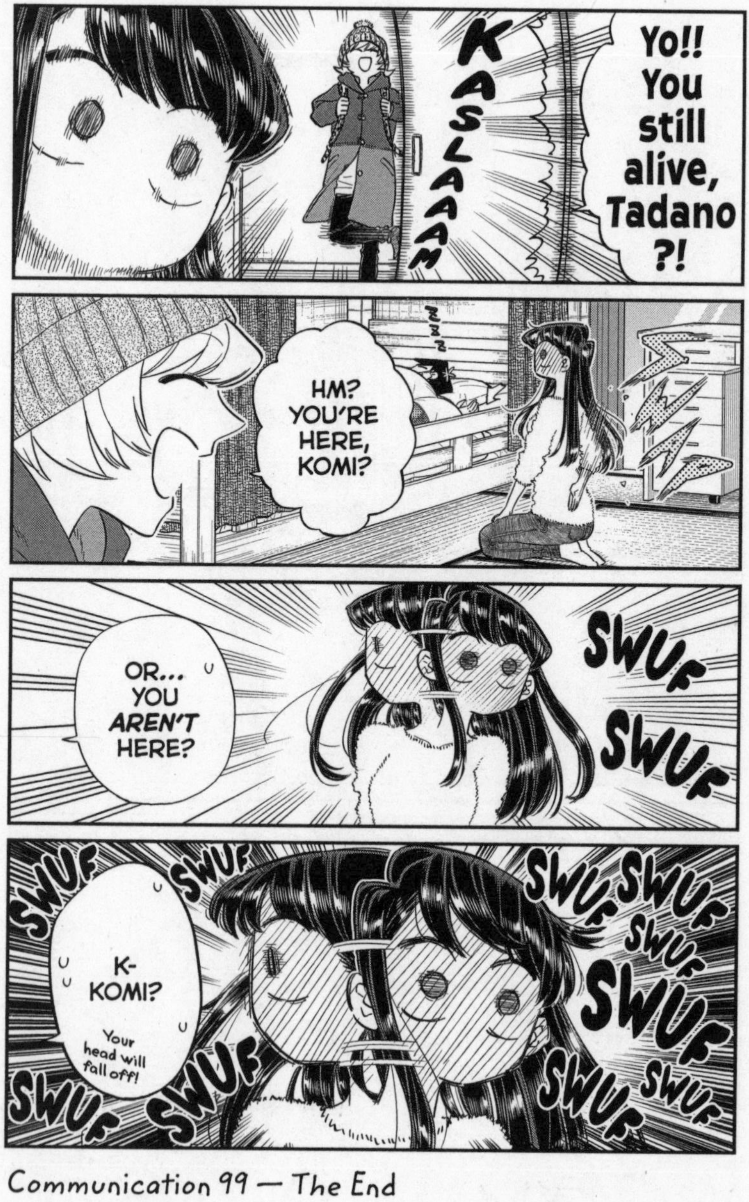
Yo!! You still alive, Tadano?!
KASLAAAAM
HM? YOU'RE HERE, KOMI?
SWUF SWUF
OR... YOU *AREN'T* HERE?
SWUF SWUF SWUF SWUF SWUF SWUF SWUF SWUF
SWUF SWUF SWUF SWUF
K-KOMI?
Your head will fall off!

Communication 99 — The End

Komi Can't
Communicate

Komi Can't Communicate Bonus

Hitomi Tadano Isn't Ordinary: She Wishes She Had Been There

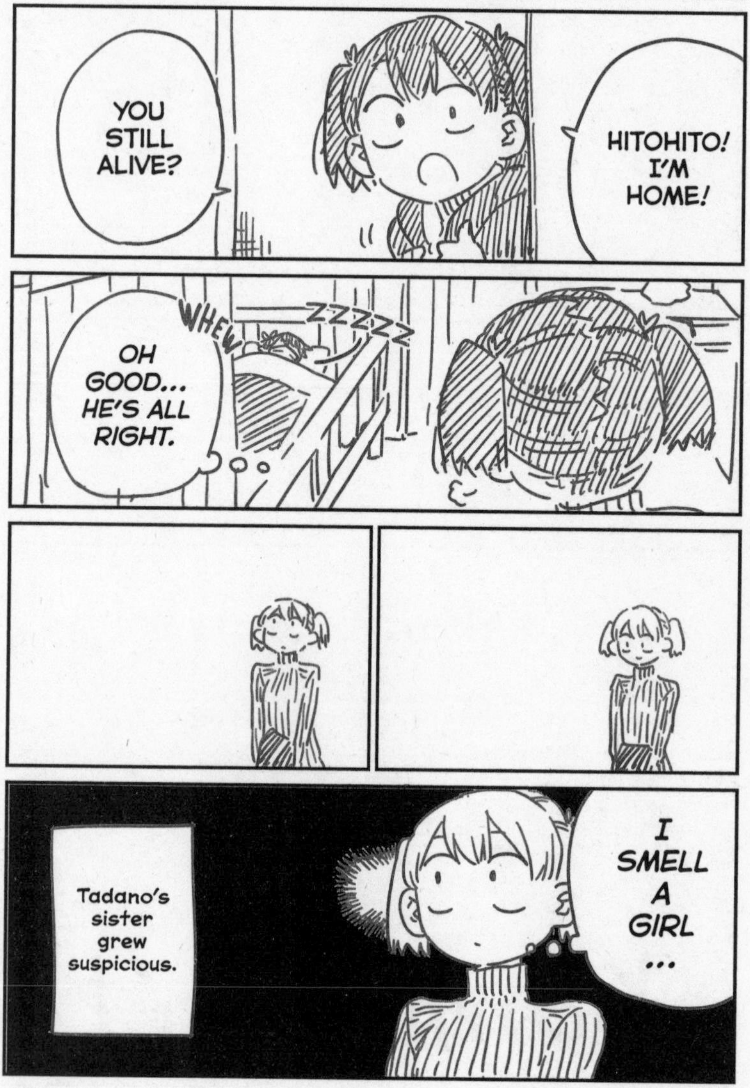
HITOHITO! I'M HOME!
YOU STILL ALIVE?
ZZZZZ
WHEW
OH GOOD... HE'S ALL RIGHT.
I SMELL A GIRL...
Tadano's sister grew suspicious.

Komi Can't Communicate Bonus

Can Komi Make 100 Friends?: Young Friends from the War

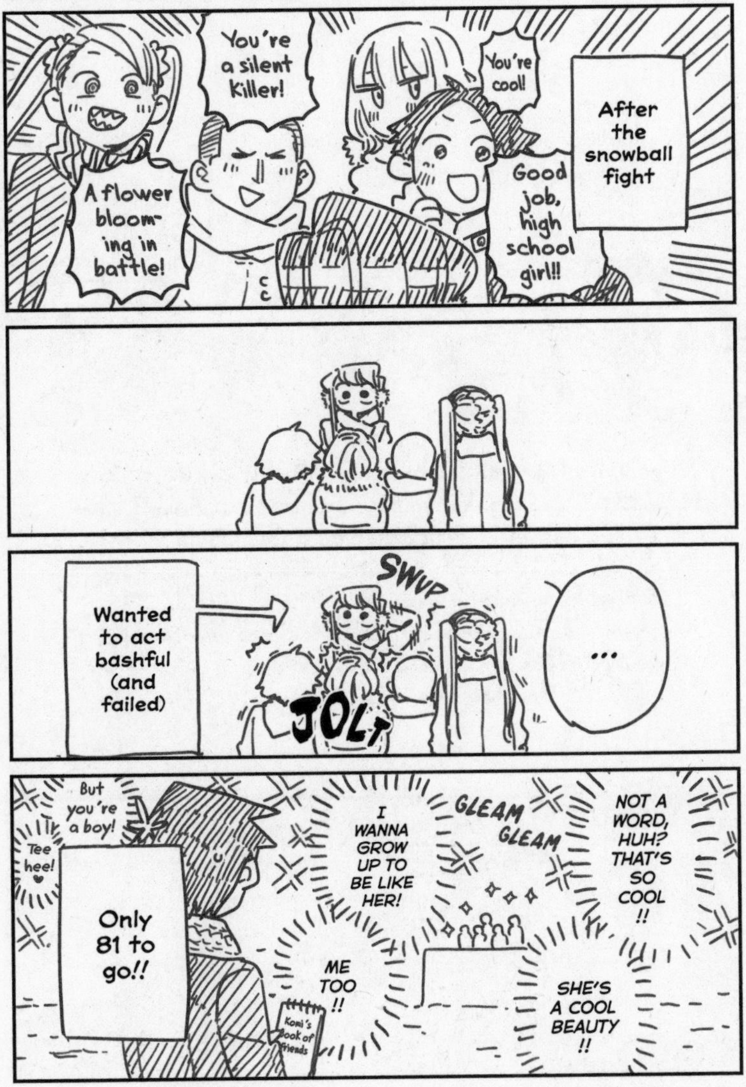
After the snowball fight
You're cool!
Good job, high school girl!!
You're a silent Killer!
A flower bloom-ing in battle!
...
SWUP
JOLT
Wanted to act bashful (and failed)
NOT A WORD, HUH? THAT'S SO COOL !!
SHE'S A COOL BEAUTY !!
GLEAM GLEAM
I WANNA GROW UP TO BE LIKE HER!
ME TOO !!
Komi's Book of Friends
Only 81 to go!!
But you're a boy!
Tee hee! ♥

Tomohito Oda won the grand prize for *World Worst One* in the 70th Shogakukan New Comic Artist Awards in 2012. Oda's series *Digicon*, about a tough high school girl who finds herself in control of an alien with plans for world domination, ran from 2014 to 2015. In 2015, *Komi Can't Communicate* debuted as a one-shot in *Weekly Shonen Sunday* and was picked up as a full series by the same magazine in 2016.

Komi Can't Communicate

VOL. 7
Shonen Sunday Edition

Story and Art by Tomohito Oda

English Translation & Adaptation/John Werry
Touch-Up Art & Lettering/Eve Grandt
Design/Julian [JR] Robinson
Editor/Pancha Diaz

COMI-SAN WA, COMYUSHO DESU. Vol. 7
by Tomohito ODA
© 2016 Tomohito ODA
All rights reserved.
Original Japanese edition published by SHOGAKUKAN.
English translation rights in the United States of America, Canada, the United
Kingdom, Ireland, Australia and New Zealand arranged with SHOGAKUKAN.

Original Cover Design/Masato ISHIZAWA + Bay Bridge Studio

Printed in the U.S.A.

Published by VIZ Media, LLC
P.O. Box 77010
San Francisco, CA 94107

10 9 8 7 6 5 4 3 2 1
First printing, June 2020

viz.com

shonensunday.com

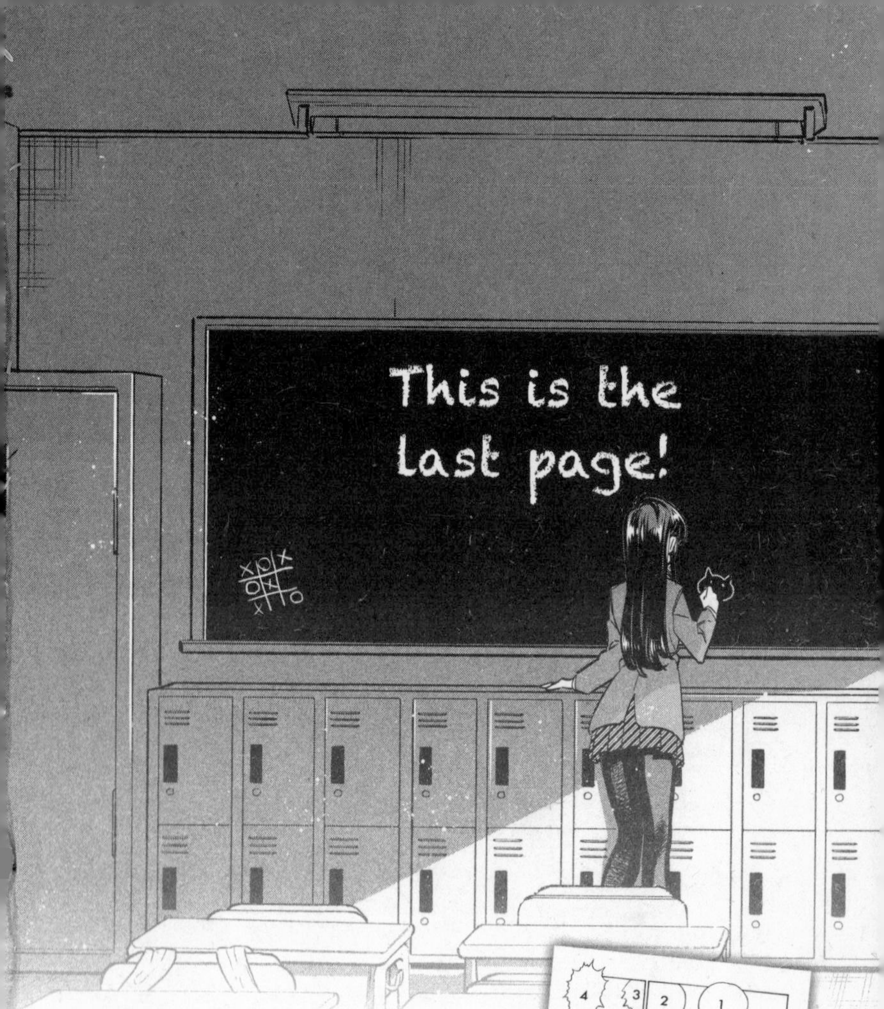
This is the last page!

Komi Can't Communicate has been printed in the original Japanese format to preserve the orientation of the artwork.

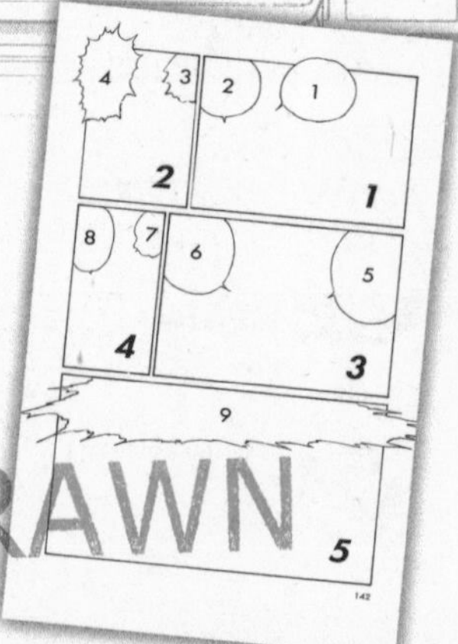

Follow the action this way.